Our Eleanor

A SCRAPBOOK LOOK AT ELEANOR ROOSEVELT'S
REMARKABLE LIFE

Our Eleanor

A SCRAPBOOK LOOK AT ELEANOR ROOSEVELT'S
REMARKABLE LIFE

CANDACE FLEMING

AN ANNE SCHWARTZ BOOK

ATHENEUM BOOKS FOR YOUNG READERS

New York   London   Toronto   Sydney

Atheneum Books for Young Readers

An imprint of Simon & Schuster Children's Publishing Division

1230 Avenue of the Americas, New York, New York 10020

Book design by Patti Ratchford

The text for this book is set in Electra.

Manufactured in the United States of America

First Edition

2 4 6 8 10 9 7 5 3 1

Library of Congress Cataloging-in-Publication Data

Fleming, Candace.

Our Eleanor : a scrapbook look at Eleanor Roosevelt's remarkable life / Candace Fleming.— 1st ed.

p. cm.

"An Anne Schwartz book."

ISBN-13: 978-0-689-86544-2

ISBN-10: 0-689-86544-9

1. Roosevelt, Eleanor, 1884–1962—Juvenile literature.

2. Presidents' spouses—United States—Biography—Juvenile literature. I. Title.

E807.1.R48F57 2005

973.917′092—dc22

2004022825

Acknowledgments

So many scholars, librarians, and friends have helped me during the writing of this book that to name some is to overlook others. Still, special thanks to:

Dr. Allida Black, director and editor of the Eleanor Roosevelt and Human Rights Project at George Washington University, who early on provided invaluable insight into the life of Eleanor Roosevelt.

Dr. Herbert Lasky, professor of history and dean of the Honors College at Eastern Illinois University, who graciously took on the monumental task of verifying the facts in this book.

Margaret Logan Marquez, who shared both her memories and her memorabilia in a way that truly made Eleanor come alive.

Mark Renovitch of the Franklin D. Roosevelt Library, who, with wonderful zeal, answered endless questions, searched for dozens of obscure documents, printed hundreds of photographs, and safely navigated me through the voluminous Eleanor Roosevelt Papers.

Marie Barbot-Cooper of the Library of Congress, who worked miracles obtaining several hard-to-find and never-before-published Roosevelt photographs.

Holly Pribble, who once again came to my aid with her prodigious artistic skills.

All those generous librarians who graciously shared their vast knowledge of informational books with me.

My writing friends—Eric Rohmann, Karen Blumenthal, and Sally Walker—who always listened, often advised, and occasionally consoled.

My family, who took on many of this project's more tedious tasks—photocopying manuscripts, downloading electronic files, photographing points of interest in Hyde Park, etc.

All those wonderful behind-the-scenes people at Simon & Schuster—Dorothy Gribbin, Ann Bobco, Patti Ratchford, Jordan Brown, Ann Kelley—who always make me look so good.

And last, but not least, the exceptionally kind, talented, and invincible Anne Schwartz. How lucky I am to work with her!

Contents

A Personal Note

When my editor suggested I write a biography of Eleanor Roosevelt, I jumped at the chance. After all, Mrs. Roosevelt was legendary, larger-than-life, a real hero! Eagerly I plunged into the research. For months I obsessively pored over photographs, read everything I could about her, took mountains of notes, and wrote a lengthy outline. Still, something wasn't quite right. Some piece of the puzzle that was Mrs. Roosevelt's life was missing. I knew I couldn't write her story without it. And so I went searching. I traveled to her hometown of Hyde Park, New York.

I adored being in that tiny Hudson River town. Just feeling the air and walking the bricked streets made me feel closer to her. That first day I wandered through the cold formality of Springwood—the Roosevelts' mansion—and understood why she never called the "big house" home. I shivered beside baby Franklin's grave in the St. James Episcopal Cemetery and wondered how she had borne such grief. I drove out to Val-Kill Cottage—her one, true home—where I climbed the narrow stairs to her sleeping porch and looked out across the sweeping grounds. I imagined her at her writing desk, chronicling her grandchildren's activities, detailing the beauty of the blossoming roses, giving impressions of the famous people who came to visit. Later I rummaged through her things at the Franklin D. Roosevelt Library, home to her personal papers. I listened to recordings of her high, fluttering voice and watched hours of film footage. But as my time in Hyde Park drew to a close I still felt I hadn't found that missing puzzle piece, until . . .

Serendipity!

On my last afternoon in the library I wandered out to the rose garden and met Margaret Logan Marquez, a lively octogenarian with twinkling blue eyes and a way with words. "I was born on the Roosevelt estate," she told me. "Eleanor and I were friends. I was friends with Franklin, too."

"Tell me about them," I begged.

So she did. For an entire evening she regaled me with quirky anecdotes and revealing stories. She told me about the time she visited the Roosevelts at the White House: "We were sipping tea in the rose garden when a sudden shower sent an entire delegation of female Democrats scrambling into the East Room." She described a dinner at Val-Kill with Marshal Tito, the portly president of Yugoslavia: "Not much came out of Tito's mouth, but plenty sure went in." And she passed on a wealth of telling details: Mrs. Roosevelt favored red nail polish; she often wore white tennis shoes to church; she made "mock mincemeat" from her green tomatoes; she had a powerful sweet tooth.

Margaret's stories delighted me. They intrigued me. And they changed everything. Before coming to Hyde Park, I had envisioned a saintly, not quite human Mrs. Roosevelt who solemnly and admirably devoted herself to the service of mankind. But now I saw Eleanor—a daring, romantic, adventurous woman who struggled as a parent, battled mood swings, and often doubted her abilities. Still, she never gave up. Instead she faced life's slings and arrows, creating an ardent, exhilarating life devoted to passion and experience, to thinking and doing and growing.

This passionate life touched men, women, and children everywhere. Why? Because in Eleanor's vision of a more generous world she included people of every race and religion, of every social and economic class. Her profound sincerity caused them to believe—with her—in the innate goodness of humanity.

A quote sprang to mind: "Eleanor Roosevelt," a close friend of hers once said, "cares first and always for people . . . her interest is human beings, her hobby is human beings, her preoccupation is human beings, her every thought is for human beings." Suddenly, right there in Margaret's living room, I found it, the final piece of the puzzle. It was Eleanor's utter devotion to the people—to all of us—that moved me. And even today, more than forty years after her death, we are still inspired by her. She is our Eleanor.

Now more than anything I wanted to bring a new perspective and fresh excitement to her life. I wanted to introduce my readers to her power, vision, and grace. I wanted them to be as delighted and intrigued by her as I was. But how?

After much thought I decided to present her life in a loose chronological fashion, dividing it into chapters with titles such as "Sad Little Nell," "A Devoted Wife and Mother," and "Self-Discovery." I describe this form as *loosely* chronological because there are places throughout where the presentation changes to a thematic approach, places where certain subjects have been lumped together. For example, in the chapter titled "A Devoted Wife and Mother" I have included all of Eleanor's personal themes as they relate to her forty-year marriage. In the chapter "Self-Discovery" I gather together all the themes dealing with Eleanor's growing sense of independence and her burgeoning political awareness. This unorthodox approach will help you look past the minutiae of dates and events to the more important tones and motifs of Eleanor's life. It will help you gain a deeper understanding of particular topics. And it will allow you to see the many roles Eleanor juggled during each stage of her life. You will discover how she learned from life's challenges, grew from hardships, and turned vulnerabilities into strengths.

Additionally, each chapter is chock-full of photographs, letters, cartoons, and more, which will bring you face-to-face with Eleanor and transport you back in time. In case you're interested in dates, I've included a time line at the front of the book. There's an index at the back if you're searching for a specific person or event. And in between you'll uncover Eleanor's thoughts on sex, see her report card, eavesdrop on a conversation between her and two garbage men, paw through her FBI file, and much, much more. Best of all, like a jigsaw puzzle, the many pieces of her life will slowly fit together to form the picture of an extraordinary woman who devoted her life to making the world a more just, more tolerant, more understanding place. In short, you will truly see our Eleanor.

—Candace Fleming

Eleanor's Days

1884   Anna Eleanor Roosevelt is born in New York City on October 11.

1892   Mother, Anna, dies and grandmother Mary Hall assumes responsibility for Eleanor's care.

1894   Eleanor's beloved father, Elliott, commits suicide.

1899   Eleanor arrives at the Allenswood School in England.

1902   Returns from England. Makes her social debut in New York's fall-winter social season. Becomes reacquainted with cousin Franklin Roosevelt.

1903   Begins teaching calisthenics and dancing at the Rivington Street Settlement House.

1905   Marries Franklin on March 17 in New York City, where the couple establish their first home.

1906   Daughter, Anna, is born on May 3.

1907   Son James is born on December 23.

1909   Son Franklin Jr. (the first) is born on March 18. He dies that same year on November 1.

1910   Son Elliott is born on September 23. Franklin is elected to the New York State Senate.

1911   Eleanor and her family move to Albany, New York.

1913   Eleanor and her family move to Washington, D.C., after Franklin is appointed assistant secretary of the navy.

1914   Son Franklin Jr. (the second) is born on August 17.

1916   Son John is born on March 17.

1917   The United States enters World War I in April. Eleanor begins her volunteer work.

1918   Eleanor becomes active with naval hospitals and the American Red Cross canteens. In September she discovers Franklin's affair with Lucy Mercer. Decides not to divorce her husband after he promises never to see Lucy again.

1920   Eleanor and her family return to New York after Franklin is defeated as the Democratic candidate for vice president of the United States. After women gain the right to vote, Eleanor joins the National League of Women Voters.

1921   Franklin is stricken with polio while vacationing at Campobello Island.

1922   Eleanor joins the Women's Trade Union League and begins work with the Women's Division of the New York State Democratic Committee.

1925   Becomes editor of *Women's Democratic News*. She and friends Nancy Cook and Marion Dickerman build Stone Cottage on the banks of Fall Kill, a stream in Hyde Park, New York.

1926   Eleanor begins teaching American history, literature, and current events at the Todhunter School in New York City after purchasing the school with Cook and Dickerman.

1927   Eleanor and friends open the Val-Kill furniture factory adjacent to Stone Cottage.

1928   Franklin is elected governor of New York. Eleanor resigns her political posts and moves her family to the governor's mansion in Albany. For the next four years she sells articles to magazines, teaches part-time at the Todhunter School, and inspects state institutions on Franklin's behalf.

1929   In October the stock market crashes, plunging America into the Great Depression.

1932   Franklin is elected president of the United States.

1933   Eleanor starts weekly press conferences for women reporters. Goes on fact-finding trips and makes appearances on Franklin's behalf. Becomes an advocate of the Arthurdale resettlement community for destitute coal miners in West Virginia. Begins writing "Mrs. Roosevelt's Page," a monthly magazine column for *Woman's Home Companion*.

1934   Begins speaking out on behalf of African Americans.

1935   Champions the National Youth Administration. Begins writing her newspaper column "My Day." Her children's book *A Trip to Washington with Bobby and Betty* is published.

1936   Eleanor begins her career on the lecture circuit. The Val-Kill furniture factory is closed. Eleanor decides to convert the building into a cottage for herself. In November, Franklin is elected to a second term as president.

1937   Eleanor publishes the first section of her autobiography, *This Is My Story.*

1938   Attends the first meeting of the Southern Conference for Human Welfare in Birmingham, Alabama, and defies segregation laws by attempting to sit with her friend Mary Bethune in the black section of the auditorium.

1939   Resigns from the Daughters of the American Revolution after the organization denies the use of Constitution Hall to Marian Anderson, an African-American singer.

1940   Addresses the Democratic National Convention in Chicago, helping unite the party behind Franklin's vice presidential choice, Henry Wallace, and becoming the first wife of a president to speak at a national political convention. In November, Franklin is elected to an unprecedented third term as president.

1941   Eleanor becomes assistant director of the Office of Civilian Defense in September. In December the Japanese bomb Pearl Harbor, thrusting the United States into World War II.

1942   Eleanor resigns her position at the Office of Civilian Defense after a firestorm of criticism. Travels to England on a goodwill tour.

1943   Visits servicemen in the South Pacific. Is instrumental in creating the first government-sponsored day care center.

1944   In November, Franklin is elected to a fourth term as president.

1945   Franklin dies on April 12. Three weeks later Germany surrenders. In June, Eleanor turns the Hyde Park estate over to the government, choosing to make her home at Val-Kill Cottage and in a New York City apartment instead. In August, Japan surrenders and World War II ends. In December, President Harry S. Truman appoints her as a U.S. delegate to the United Nations.

1946   Eleanor is appointed to Committee III of the United Nations. Wins a victory over the Soviet Union regarding the issue of refugees and gains a reputation as a skilled diplomat.

1947   Chairs the Human Rights Commission of the United Nations, which creates the Universal Declaration of Human Rights.

1948   The Universal Declaration of Human Rights is adopted by the UN General Assembly.

1949   Eleanor publishes the second volume of her autobiography, *This I Remember.*

1952   Begins her worldwide travels with trips to Israel, Pakistan, other countries in the Middle East, and India. Supports Adlai Stevenson's unsuccessful bid for the presidency.

1953   Resigns from her UN position after Dwight D. Eisenhower is elected president, but begins working as a volunteer for the American Association for the United Nations in hopes of educating citizens about the organization. Takes a five-week trip to Japan to discuss the progress of democracy in that country.

1955   Visits Bali, Thailand, and Cambodia.

1956   Supports Adlai Stevenson's second unsuccessful bid for the presidency.

1957   Travels to the Soviet Union, where she has a private interview with future premier Nikita Khrushchev.

1958   Is diagnosed with aplastic anemia, a blood disease. Publishes the third volume of her autobiography, *On My Own*.

1959   Records *Hello, World!* for RCA Victor. Begins her monthly television program, *Prospects of Mankind*.

1960   Meets with John F. Kennedy and agrees to campaign for his presidency.

1961   With Kennedy's election Eleanor is appointed chair of the President's Commission on the Status of Women. Collects the three sections of her life story into one volume, entitled *The Autobiography of Eleanor Roosevelt*.

1962   Eleanor dies of bone marrow tuberculosis on November 7.

An Abridged Roosevelt Family Tree

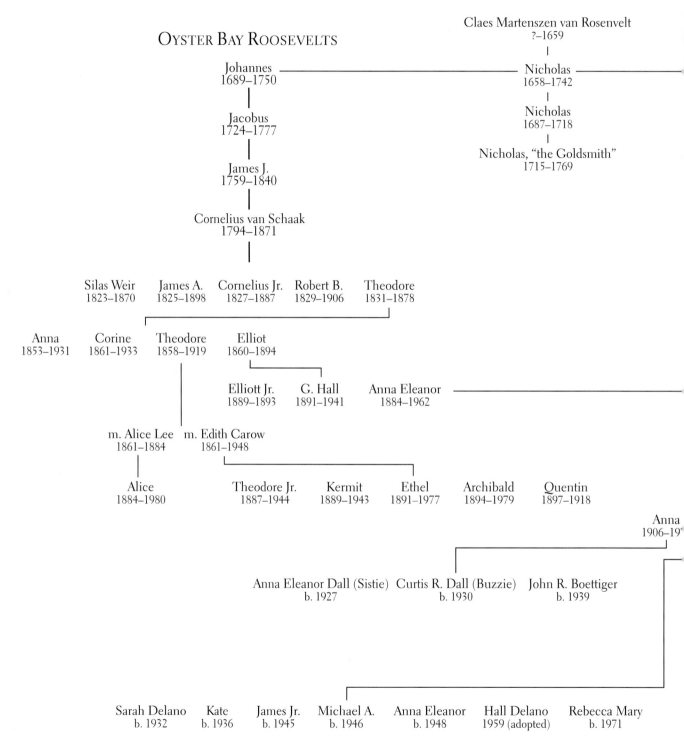

Oyster Bay Roosevelts

Claes Martenszen van Rosenvelt
?–1659

Johannes
1689–1750

Nicholas
1658–1742

Jacobus
1724–1777

Nicholas
1687–1718

James J.
1759–1840

Nicholas, "the Goldsmith"
1715–1769

Cornelius van Schaak
1794–1871

Silas Weir
1823–1870

James A.
1825–1898

Cornelius Jr.
1827–1887

Robert B.
1829–1906

Theodore
1831–1878

Anna
1853–1931

Corine
1861–1933

Theodore
1858–1919

Elliot
1860–1894

Elliott Jr.
1889–1893

G. Hall
1891–1941

Anna Eleanor
1884–1962

m. Alice Lee
1861–1884

m. Edith Carow
1861–1948

Alice
1884–1980

Theodore Jr.
1887–1944

Kermit
1889–1943

Ethel
1891–1977

Archibald
1894–1979

Quentin
1897–1918

Anna
1906–19

Anna Eleanor Dall (Sistie)
b. 1927

Curtis R. Dall (Buzzie)
b. 1930

John R. Boettiger
b. 1939

Sarah Delano
b. 1932

Kate
b. 1936

James Jr.
b. 1945

Michael A.
b. 1946

Anna Eleanor
b. 1948

Hall Delano
1959 (adopted)

Rebecca Mary
b. 1971

Because dates of death could not be verified for all of the Roosevelt grandchildren, only their dates of birth or adoption have been includ

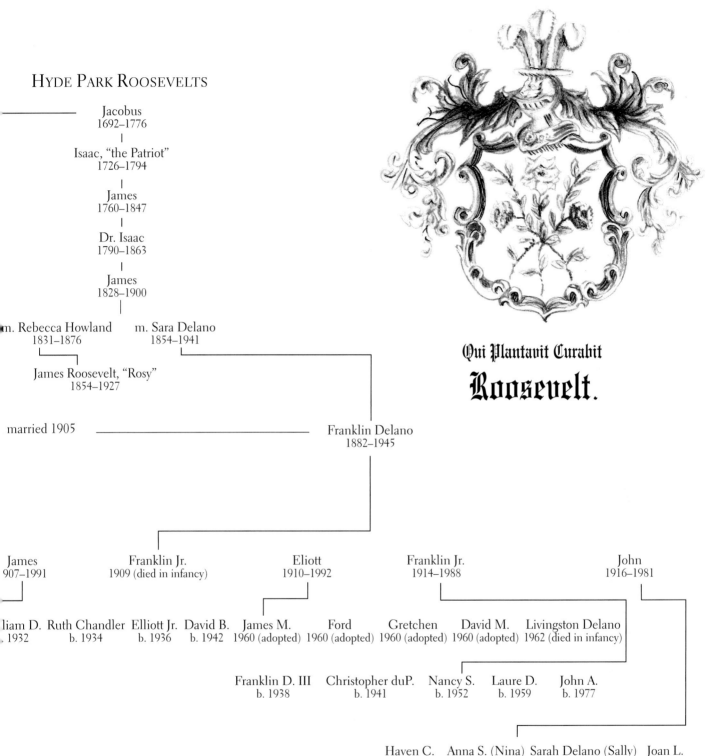

HYDE PARK ROOSEVELTS

Jacobus
1692–1776

Isaac, "the Patriot"
1726–1794

James
1760–1847

Dr. Isaac
1790–1863

James
1828–1900

m. Rebecca Howland   m. Sara Delano
1831–1876   1854–1941

James Roosevelt, "Rosy"
1854–1927

married 1905   Franklin Delano
1882–1945

James   Franklin Jr.   Eliott   Franklin Jr.   John
907–1991   1909 (died in infancy)   1910–1992   1914–1988   1916–1981

liam D.   Ruth Chandler   Elliott Jr.   David B.   James M.   Ford   Gretchen   David M.   Livingston Delano
1932   b. 1934   b. 1936   b. 1942 1960 (adopted) 1960 (adopted) 1960 (adopted) 1960 (adopted) 1962 (died in infancy)

Franklin D. III   Christopher duP.   Nancy S.   Laure D.   John A.
b. 1938   b. 1941   b. 1952   b. 1959   b. 1977

Haven C.   Anna S. (Nina)   Sarah Delano (Sally)   Joan L.
b. 1940   b. 1942   b. 1946   b. 1952

Qui Plantavit Curabit

Roosevelt.

Sad Little Nell

✿

I was not a happy child so I learned earlier than most how important the happy moments are. —Eleanor Roosevelt, *This Is My Story*

Eleanor's mother, Anna Hall Roosevelt, in 1881

ANNA HALL was acclaimed as New York society's most glamorous woman. "She is [the] loveliest, most beautiful, most graceful of America's daughters," gushed a reporter for the *New York Herald*. "Her mere presence is a blessing." So admired was her beauty that the poet Robert Browning once begged permission to "simply gaze upon [her] countenance" as she sat for a portrait.

But Anna was more than beautiful. She was also wellborn. A charter member of the "Four Hundred," New York City's exclusive social world limited to four hundred of what were deemed the very best people, her ancestors had signed the Declaration of Independence and administered the oath of office to President George Washington. No wonder her marriage on December 1, 1883, to another member of the Four Hundred—handsome, wealthy Elliott Roosevelt—was singled out as "the most brilliant social event of the season." The bride, noted the *New York Herald*, "appeared every bit a queen," while the groom "was worthy of her."

❖

ELLIOTT ROOSEVELT was charming, handsome, and rich. Heir to his family's multimillion-dollar banking and investment firm, Elliott bounced from job to job, never settling on one for long. Instead, his life revolved around polo, fox-hunting, and horse shows. A world traveler, he had lived on a frontier post in Texas and hunted tigers in India. He was one of the most dashing men in New York.

His marriage to Anna Hall did not change this easy, carefree lifestyle. He whiled away his days raising thoroughbred horses and pedigreed bull terriers. With Anna, he lunched at the club, went to late-night cotillions, danced at balls, and attended the opera. The Roosevelts became, as the newspapers dubbed them, "the Swells," part of a golden circle of privilege to which one either did, or did not, belong.

Eleanor's father, Elliott Roosevelt, in 1881

Record of Eleanor's birth

On October 11, 1884, Anna gave birth to her first child, a blue-eyed daughter who was, wrote Elliott, "more wrinkled and less attractive . . . than the average." Although both parents had fervently hoped for a "precious boy," Elliott declared himself well pleased with his daughter. "She is," he proclaimed, "a miracle from heaven." The new parents named their baby Anna Eleanor—Anna for her mother, and Eleanor for her father, whose nickname was Ellie. But no one ever called the baby Anna. All her life she would be known simply as Eleanor.

Bouncing Baby Eleanor

Eleanor at age two and a half

Eleanor was born in her parents' well-situated brownstone on New York City's fashionable Fifth Avenue. It had all the luxuries—crystal chandeliers, Oriental rugs, and a bone china dinner service imported from England. It also had a staff of well-trained servants whose job it was to see to the family's every need.

The family, however, was rarely at home. Always up for a jolly spree, they wintered with Anna's mother at her estate in Tivoli, New York, and summered with friends on Long Island or in Bar Harbor.

When Eleanor was only two and a half years old, Anna and Elliott traveled to Europe. They did not take their toddler. Instead they left her behind with James and Anna Gracie, Elliott's great-aunt and -uncle.

Feeling abandoned by her parents, little Eleanor grew fearful and anxious. "She seemed helpless and pathetic to us," Aunt Gracie wrote in a long letter to a friend. "She asked 2 or 3 times . . . where her Papa was. . . . I told her, 'They have gone to Europe.' She said, 'Where is baby's home now?' I said, 'Baby's home is with Uncle and Aunt Gracie.' This answer seemed to satisfy the sweet little darling. . . . Still, she is often worried and alarmed."

When her parents finally returned six months later, they began building a large house in Hempstead, on Long Island. Here, wrote Elliott, "Baby Eleanor is happy as the day is long, plays with her kitten, the puppy and the chickens all the time and is very dirty as a general rule."

But their idyllic family life was short lived. The Roosevelts stayed in Hempstead only two years.

Four-year-old Eleanor, looking self-conscious and solemn

"I always had the feeling from a very young age that I was ugly," Eleanor wrote. This feeling came from her mother, who often gazed at her daughter coolly, as if she couldn't imagine having such a plain-looking, solemn-faced daughter. Forced to wear a back brace to correct a curvature of the spine, Eleanor knew, "as a child senses those things," that her mother was bitterly disappointed in her physical features. "I can remember," wrote Eleanor, "standing in the door, very often with my finger in my mouth—which was, of course, forbidden—and I can see the look in her eyes and hear the tone in her voice as she said: 'Come in, Granny.' If a visitor was there, she might turn and say: 'She is such a funny child, so old-fashioned that we always call her Granny.' I wanted to sink through the floor in shame."

Eleanor tried desperately to please her mother. Small as she was, she often sat and rubbed Anna's temples for hours on end, easing her migraine headaches. "The feeling that I was useful," Eleanor later said, "was perhaps the greatest joy I experienced."

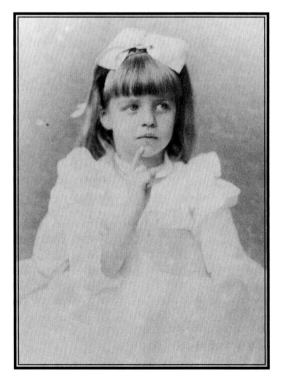

Eleanor with her brothers, Hall (seated on her knee) and Elliott Jr.

In October 1889 Anna gave birth to her second child, Elliott Jr. Although the birth of a son was the fulfillment of her parents' "heart's desire," Eleanor's father continued to dote on her. She never doubted she was "first in his heart." With her mother, however, the birth of little Ellie, and Hall a year later, *did* make a difference. "My mother made a great effort," Eleanor later admitted. "She would read to me and . . . would keep me after the boys had gone to bed." But Eleanor still felt separated. Her mother adored her sons and often compared them with her daughter. "[Elliott Jr.] is a saintlike child, simply perfect, never grumbles or complains of anything and is so loving and attractive," Anna once told a friend, "while Baby Hall is a lovely boy with a strong will." Only Eleanor was "a problem" because she was "so grave." No wonder Eleanor "felt a curious barrier between [herself] and [those] three."

Eleanor with her father, Elliott

Eleanor's father called her Little Nell because she reminded him of the gentle character in the book *The Old Curiosity Shop*, by Charles Dickens. He made her his constant companion, taking her along on errands, teaching her to ride horses, reading poetry to her, and telling her stories about his travels. In his presence Eleanor did not feel ugly. Instead she felt loved and secure. "With my father I was perfectly happy," she later wrote. "He was the center of my world."

On Thanksgiving Day, 1890, six-year-old Eleanor Roosevelt sat beside her father in their horse-drawn carriage. She was going to the Newsboys' Lodge, a place established by her grandfather for homeless boys who made their living selling newspapers on New York City's streets. At the lodge the boys received a hot meal and a bed. On this day, however, they would be receiving something else—a feast. And Eleanor would help to serve it. As soon as she arrived, she was handed a ladle. For the next hour she scooped potatoes onto plates and passed out slices of pumpkin pie. By mid afternoon she was tired but also full of good feelings for having helped those less fortunate. "Very early," Eleanor later wrote, "I became conscious of the fact that there were people around me who suffered in one way or another." And even though she went to the lodge only that one time, she never forgot it. Seeing the contrast between the boys' poverty and her "life blessed with plenty," she said, "pricked my conscience. I felt troubled. . . . Sometimes, feeling troubled is a good feeling."

Elliott's older brother, Theodore Roosevelt, who helped teach Eleanor about doing good works

Theodore Roosevelt was an energetic, reform-minded politician. Elected governor of New York when Eleanor was just fifteen, he became the twenty-sixth president of the United States three years later. He was also Eleanor's godfather. Uncle Ted always called Eleanor his favorite niece. She recalled her childhood visits to his Oyster Bay home on Long Island as terrifying. Said Eleanor, "He was horrified that I didn't know how to swim so he thought he'd teach me as he taught all his own children, and threw me in. And I sank rapidly to the bottom. He fished me out and lectured me on being frightened."

Uncle Ted lectured on lots of other subjects too. The most important was social responsibility. In New York's finer society well-brought-up girls were taught to do good works—they were expected to take part in charitable projects deemed proper for their position. As a five-year-old, Eleanor had sung carols and decorated a Christmas tree in Hell's Kitchen, one of the worst slums in New York City. And she often visited sick children in the New York Orthopaedic Hospital with her Aunt Gracie. But what Uncle Ted was suggesting was something more. Roosevelts, he declared, should use their power and position to "fight for the less fortunate." They should try to make "lasting changes in people's lives."

SO MANY FEARS

Young Eleanor was full of fears—of the dark, of mice, of dogs, snakes, and other children. But what did she claim to fear most? "I was afraid . . . of being scolded, afraid that other people would not like me."

Father's Weakness

Elliott Roosevelt could be loving and warm, generous and good-natured. But he also drank too much—and when he was drinking, everything changed. He went on binges with his friends, often disappearing for days on end, only to return home reeking of liquor. He grew violent, loudly arguing with his wife and threatening to kill himself. During one particularly drunken summer he humiliated his family by making a servant girl pregnant. The scandal wound up in the newspapers.

Anna tried to get her husband to break his addiction. "Dearest," she begged him, "throw your horrid cocktails away. . . . Remember that your little wife and children love you tenderly and will try to help you . . . conquer in this hard, hard, fight."

But it was a fight Elliott couldn't win. When, in 1890, the Roosevelts traveled to Europe, they visited health resorts in Germany, Italy, Austria, and France, searching for a cure for Elliott's "weakness." They were desperate to hold the family together, but nothing worked. By the time they reached Paris, his prolonged bouts of drunkenness were so bad that Elliott's brother, Theodore, was forced to step in and take charge of the family's affairs. Hurrying to Paris, Theodore convinced his brother to separate from his family for one year. During that time Elliott would have to "regain command of himself, stop drinking, choose an occupation and stick to it."

Although Elliott considered the whole idea "wicked and foolish," he agreed to it because "it [was] Anna's wish." He went to live in Abingdon, Virginia, where he managed his brother-in-law's mining company. "I will do anything," he wrote to his wife, "to prove the completeness of my cure and my desire to atone."

Meanwhile, an anguished Anna returned to New York City with the children. "I so long to help him, not to make him suffer more," she said. But she knew he would never be able to change. Determining to start a new life without him, she bought a house on East Sixty-first Street, widened her circle of friends, and hired a tutor for Eleanor.

For eight-year-old Eleanor life without Father was frightening and confusing. Sometimes at night she heard Anna and the other grown-ups whispering about his problems. "I acquired a strange and garbled idea of the troubles around me," she said. "Something was wrong with my father, [but] from my point of view nothing could be wrong with him." Eleanor blamed her mother for Elliott's absence and dreamed of the day when the family would be together again.

THE HABIT OF LYING

Eleanor claimed to have been a liar as a child. Why did she tell fibs? To get attention—something she desperately craved.

In the winter of 1890, when Eleanor and her family lived in Paris, Anna sent her to a convent for young girls to get her six-year-old out from underfoot. But the other girls weren't interested in the solemn, English-speaking child. They didn't invite her to play games or go on walks. No one sat with her at teatime. Years later Eleanor admitted:

"I longed to join them but was always kept on the outside. . . . Finally, I fell to . . . temptation. One of the girls swallowed a penny. Every attention was given her, she was the center of everybody's interest. I longed to be in her place. One day, I went to one of the sisters and told her I had swallowed a penny too. It must have been evident my story was not true, so they sent for my mother. She took me away in disgrace. . . . I remember the drive home as one of utter misery, still this habit of lying stayed with me for years."

ELEANOR IS TAUGHT BY HER FIRST TEACHER, PROFESSOR FREDRIC ROSER

As a child, Eleanor did not go to school. Various relatives tried to teach her reading and writing, but by the age of seven she still could do neither. So in the fall of 1892 her mother turned part of the upper floor of the house into a schoolroom, invited a few other girls Eleanor's age, and hired Fredric Roser to teach them. Roser was not one of New York's most gifted tutors, though he may have been one of its most fashionable. He wore "a Prince Albert coat," remembered one former student, "and had side whiskers. Not one grain of humor, though. There was nobody in the world as pompous as he." Specializing in the subjects of English, French, arithmetic, and writing composition, Roser claimed to "make intellects out of imbeciles."

He scared shy eight-year-old Eleanor. On her first day of lessons, Professor Roser asked her to

spell the word "horse," she remembered. Poor Eleanor! She didn't even know what letter it began with! She could only stand there "frozen by shyness." Later her mother (who had sat in during the lesson) scolded Eleanor, claiming she "could not imagine how her daughter would end up."

Eleanor continued studying with the professor for the next seven years. Sometimes these classes were at her home, other times in the homes of other wealthy girls. And despite her wobbly start, she became a good student. She learned to speak fluent French, add long columns of numbers, and write intelligent essays. Only spelling continued to elude her, as this passage written by twelve-year-old Eleanor proves: "Now I want to tell you about what I going to have next May in scholl, a written examination in History and Geographay and I am the youngast one to have it."

"Suddenly, Life Changed!"

At the end of November 1892, when Eleanor was only eight years old, her mother contracted diphtheria, a bacterial infection causing a high fever and sore throat. The disease progressed quickly, and within days Anna was dead. Writing an account of her mother's death almost forty-five years later, Eleanor did not dwell on the loss. Instead she focused on the return of her beloved father.

"I can remember standing by a window when Cousin Susie told me my mother was dead. . . . Death meant nothing to me, and one fact wiped out everything else. My father was back and I would see him very soon. [When he] came to see me . . . [he] sat in a big chair. He was dressed all in black, looking very sad. He held out his arms and gathered me to him. In a little while he began to talk, to explain to me that my mother was gone, that she had been all the world to him, and now he had only my brothers and myself, that my brothers were very young, and that he and I must keep close together. Some day I would make a home for him again; we would travel together and do many things . . . to be looked forward to in the future. . . .

"When he left I was all alone to keep our secret of mutual understanding and to adjust myself to my new existence."

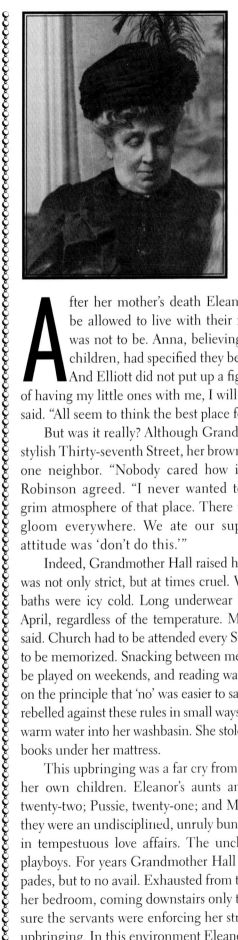

Grandmother Mary Hall, the Roosevelt children's new guardian

After her mother's death Eleanor hoped she and her brothers would be allowed to live with their father in Abingdon, Virginia. But this was not to be. Anna, believing her husband incapable of raising the children, had specified they be raised by her own mother, Mary Hall. And Elliott did not put up a fight. "As sorely as I think myself in need of having my little ones with me, I will return [to Virginia] without them," he said. "All seem to think the best place for them is with their Grandmother."

But was it really? Although Grandmother Hall lived on New York City's stylish Thirty-seventh Street, her brownstone was "grim and ill-kept," recalled one neighbor. "Nobody cared how it looked." Eleanor's cousin Corinne Robinson agreed. "I never wanted to go there," she remembered. "The grim atmosphere of that place. There was no place to play games, unbroken gloom everywhere. We ate our suppers in silence. . . . The general attitude was 'don't do this.'"

Indeed, Grandmother Hall raised her grandchildren with a set of rules that was not only strict, but at times cruel. Warm water was forbidden, so morning baths were icy cold. Long underwear had to be worn from November until April, regardless of the temperature. Morning and evening prayers had to be said. Church had to be attended every Sunday. And hymns and Bible verses had to be memorized. Snacking between meals was not permitted, games could not be played on weekends, and reading was not allowed in bed. "I was brought up on the principle that 'no' was easier to say than 'yes,'" Eleanor recalled. Still, she rebelled against these rules in small ways. When no one was looking, she poured warm water into her washbasin. She stole candies from the kitchen. And she hid books under her mattress.

This upbringing was a far cry from the way Grandmother Hall had raised her own children. Eleanor's aunts and uncles—Vallie, twenty-five; Eddie, twenty-two; Pussie, twenty-one; and Maude, sixteen—still lived at home, and they were an undisciplined, unruly bunch. The aunts were constantly involved in tempestuous love affairs. The uncles were high-spirited, heavy-drinking playboys. For years Grandmother Hall had tried to deal with their wild escapades, but to no avail. Exhausted from the effort, she spent most of her time in her bedroom, coming downstairs only to greet infrequent visitors and to make sure the servants were enforcing her strict rules regarding her grandchildren's upbringing. In this environment Eleanor remained for almost seven years.

Soon after their mother died, both Elliott Jr. and Hall came down with a highly contagious disease called scarlet fever. To keep Eleanor from catching it as well, Grandmother Hall sent her to a friend's home in the country. There she waited for news of her brothers. She soon learned that baby Hall had recovered but Ellie's condition was worsening. Once again Eleanor's father was summoned from exile. He hurried to New York, where he telegraphed a message to his daughter: "Dear little Ellie is very, very ill and may go to join dear Mother in heaven. There is just a little chance that he may not die but the doctors all fear that he will."

Three-year-old Ellie died on May 29, 1893. "Now there was just the two of us," Eleanor later wrote. But she rarely saw her baby brother, Hall, who was not quite two years old. "A half dozen servants cared for him," Eleanor later said, "while I, for the most part, was left very much alone."

A letter from Eleanor to her father

For the next two years Elliott made irregular visits to Grandmother Hall's house. Eleanor would always rush down the stairs to fling herself into his arms. The two took long walks together or carriage rides through Central Park or simply sat in the parlor chatting. But Elliott was unreliable. More than once he promised to visit, only to break Eleanor's heart when he didn't show up, and he occasionally appeared reeking of alcohol. Once, he took eight-year-old Eleanor and three of his terriers for a walk. As they passed the Knickerbocker Club, he told her to stay with the animals for a moment while he went inside for a quick drink. Holding the dogs, Eleanor waited. And waited. And waited. "When he failed to return after six hours," she wrote, "the doorman took me home." After that Grandmother Hall began limiting his visits. "He is charming," she told a friend, "but entirely unsuitable."

As their visits together grew less frequent, father and daughter began writing each other more often. Her letters were full of loneliness and longing. "I thought of you all day long, and blessed and prayed for your happiness," she

once wrote. Another time she wrote, "I wish you were here to ride [horses] with me." His letters to her were tender, playful, and full of fatherly advice. When Eleanor started being tutored, he wrote, "There are a lot of little workmen running about in your small head called 'ideas' which are carrying a lot of stones . . . called 'facts,' and these little 'ideas' are being directed by your teacher." Later, when Eleanor was having problems with math, he advised, "Devote yourself—howbeit against the grain—to the harder studies in life." Eleanor read and reread his words. And they had a profound effect on her. "I knew a child once who adored her father," she later wrote. "She was an ugly little thing . . . and her father, the only person who really cared for her, was away much of the time . . . but he wrote her letters telling her how he dreamed of her growing up and what they would do together in the future, but she must be truthful, loyal, brave and well-educated . . . [and] the child . . . made herself . . . into a good copy of the picture he had painted."

In August 1894, when Eleanor was not quite ten years old, Elliott wrote: "Darling Little Nell, what must you think of your father who has not written for so long. . . . I have after all been very busy, quite ill [from the effects of alcohol], at intervals not able to move from my bed for days. How is your pony and the dogs . . . too? . . . With tender affection, Ever devotedly, your father." Hours later a drunken Elliott jumped out his bedroom window and died. "There were," wrote Eleanor, "no more letters after this for me."

HEARTBREAK Without going into any of the details, Eleanor's aunts Maude and Pussie Hall broke the terrible news—her father was dead! Eleanor sought comfort in her imagination. She invented for herself a world where her father still lived, and created stories of a life they'd never had together.

"While I wept long and went to bed still weeping, I finally went to sleep and began living in my dreamworld as usual. . . . From that time on I knew in my mind that my father was dead, and yet I lived with him more closely [in my imagination] than I had when he was alive."

Eleanor with her bicycle, in front of the Hall estate in Tivoli, New York, 1893. Her aunt Maude is in the horse cart.

Eleanor now spent her summer months at Oak Terrace, Grandmother Hall's country estate. Her days were happier there. She took long walks, rode her horse, and went on picnics. Sometimes she broke her grandmother's rule and played games along the house's high gutters with her brother, Hall, or slid down the roof of the icehouse, getting her clothes dirty. She even practiced her high kicking, but she had to do it secretly. Remembered Eleanor, "When I expressed my admiration for ballet, Grandmother told me no lady did anything like that."

Most of all, Tivoli was for reading. During those long summer days Eleanor got into the habit of taking a book "out into the fields, or the woods," she said, "and sitting in a tree or lying under it, completely forgetting about the passage of time." On rainy days she curled up on a pile of mildewing cushions in the attic and read the hours away. What did she read? Books by Charles Dickens, Charlotte Brontë, and Nathaniel Hawthorne. "Sometimes," Eleanor later confessed, "I even managed to read a forbidden modern novel which I would steal from my young aunts purely because I heard it whispered that the contents were not for young eyes."

The year Eleanor turned fourteen she was allowed to attend a Christmas party at the home of her aunt Corinne (Elliott's sister) in New York City. Appearing in a knee-length child's party dress, she was mortified to discover the other girls wearing long, sophisticated gowns. "I was different . . . and . . . they did not hesitate to point it out," she later recalled. With "more pain than pleasure," Eleanor stood on the sidelines and watched her cousin Alice dance with another cousin, sixteen-year-old Franklin Delano Roosevelt. When the song ended, Alice whispered in his ear. He promptly crossed the floor and asked Eleanor to dance.

This was not their first meeting. Years earlier their families had met at Franklin's Hyde Park home. While the grown-ups had talked, two-year-old Eleanor had galloped around the nursery on four-year-old Franklin's back. Eleanor, of course, did not remember this incident. Still, she suddenly felt a familiar kinship when dancing with Franklin.

Eleanor's fifth cousin Franklin Delano Roosevelt at age sixteen

Her shyness slipped away, and the two talked of books and other subjects of mutual interest.

The next day, when describing the dance to his mother, Franklin said, "Cousin Eleanor has a very good mind."

Eleanor at fifteen

She was blond, blue eyed, very tall, and very slender. "Poor little soul, she is very plain," said Theodore Roosevelt's wife, Edith, about the teenager. "Her teeth and mouth seem to have no future. But the ugly duckling may turn out to be a swan."

Sent Away

Just before her fifteenth birthday Eleanor was sent to school in England. Over the years her uncles Vallie and Eddie had become dangerous and unpredictable. The summer before, the two men had stood at an upstairs window with a gun and—out of their minds with liquor—had shot at family members sitting on the lawn. Everyone scattered, taking refuge behind trees and bushes. As if that weren't enough, her tempestuous aunts Maude and Pussie began smoking cigarettes and stepping out with unsuitable men—scandalous behavior for the time! Even from her bedroom Grandmother Hall realized it was not good for Eleanor to remain with them. "Your mother wanted you to go to boarding school," she said, "and I have decided to send you." "Thus," said Eleanor, "the second period of my life began."

In the fall of 1899 Eleanor arrived at Allenswood, an exclusive girls' finishing school. Clutching her father's letters, she felt "lost and very lonely." But not for long. Thirty-five students between the ages of thirteen and nineteen were enrolled, most of them English-speaking, though French was the required language inside the classroom. This was not a hardship for Eleanor, who had learned the language as a young child. At the "first meal," a classmate recalled, "when we hardly dared open our mouths, she sat opposite [the headmistress] Mlle. Souvestre chatting away in French. . . . We admired her courage."

Eleanor's classmates would come to admire other attributes as well. Kind, helpful, and generous, Totty, as Eleanor was nicknamed (no one knows why), became very popular with the other girls. "She was 'everything' at school," recalled one friend. "She was beloved by everybody. Saturdays we were allowed a sortie [trip] into town which had stores where you could buy books, flowers. . . . You bought violets or a book and left them in the room of the girl you were idolizing. Eleanor's room every Saturday would be full of flowers because she was so admired." For the first time in her life Eleanor began to like herself. Her winning personality began to shine through, and she developed a wide circle of friends. Yes, she had arrived lost and lonely, but three years later she left as the school's "supreme favorite."

Eleanor (third from the right in the last row) with her Allenswood classmates

Rules

At school Eleanor felt she was starting a new life, free from all her "former sins." She wrote, "There was nothing to fear if I lived up to the rules." And there were plenty of those.

"On the outside of the bathroom door were pasted the bath rules and I was appalled to find that we had to fight for three baths a week and were limited to ten minutes before 'lights out' was sounded! . . . When we got out of bed [in the morning] we had to take the bedclothes off and put them on a chair to air. Our rooms were inspected after breakfast and we were marked on neatness. . . . Any girl whose bureau drawers were out of order might return to her room to find the entire contents of the drawers dumped on her bed for rearranging. . . . After breakfast we were all taken for a walk on the common—and you had to have a good excuse to escape that walk! It was cold and fairly foggy—but still we walked. . . . Classes began immediately on our return from the walks, and each of us had a schedule that ran through the whole day—classes, hours of practice, time for preparation—no idle moments were left to anyone."

An entry from fifteen-year-old Eleanor's diary, November 13, 1899

To be the thing we seem
To do the thing we deem
enjoined by duty
To walk in faith nor dream
Of questioning God's scheme
of truth & beauty.

It is very hard to do what this verse says, so hard I never succeed & I am always questioning & questioning because I cannot understand & never succeed in doing what I mean to do, never, never. I suppose I don't really try. I can feel it in me sometimes that I can do much more than I am doing & I mean to try till I *do* succeed.

Eleanor's years at Allenswood shaped her tastes in literature, music, theater, and the arts. But it was Mlle Marie Souvestre who trained her mind. "She exerted perhaps the greatest influence on my girlhood," Eleanor said. Intellectual independence, open-mindedness, and a lively sense of curiosity were the traits Mlle Souvestre tried to develop in her students. If a girl handed in an essay that simply parroted the headmistress's own ideas, she would tear it up in front of the class. As the pieces fluttered to the floor, she would cry, "Why was your mind given you, but to think things out for yourself." Eleanor found this form of teaching exhilarating: "[She] shocked me into thinking, and that . . . was very beneficial."

Eleanor soon became the teacher's pet. Mlle Souvestre realized she "could give a great deal to that really remarkable, sad young girl." She advised Eleanor on health, grooming, fashion. She broke Eleanor of her nail-biting habit and was so appalled by the girl's made-over clothes that she sent her to a Paris dressmaker. "I still remember my joy in that dark-red dress," Eleanor recalled years later. "As far as I was concerned, it might have been made by Worth [an exclusive dressmaker], for it had all the glamour of being my first French dress." During school holidays Mlle Souvestre took Eleanor to Italy and France, Austria and Germany. They stayed in modest inns, ate modest food, traveled off the beaten track, and changed plans on the spur of the moment. This style of traveling was a revelation for restrained Eleanor. "Never again would I be the rigid little person I had been before," she later wrote.

When Eleanor's time at Allenswood ended, "the thought of . . . separation seemed hard to bear." Mlle Souvestre found it hard too. "I miss you," the headmistress wrote to her student. "A thousand and a thousand tendernesses to my Totty, whom I shall always love." For the next three years they wrote each other weekly, until Mlle Souvestre's death from cancer in 1905.

Eleanor's final report card

Eleanor studied hard at Allenswood. She took French, German, *and* Italian. She studied English literature and was remembered by the teacher of that subject as "a tall, slim elegant young girl who was so much more intelligent than the others." Eleanor also took Latin, algebra, and three years of drawing, which she obviously enjoyed, since she covered her notebooks with portraits and baroque lettering. Still, she claimed she "could not draw, much less paint." She took music lessons but with indifferent results: "I struggled over the piano and was always poor." And when she enrolled in a drama class, she "envied every good actress, but could not act." Sewing and dance classes rounded out her very busy schedule. No science courses were offered, and there was little concern for history or government. There was, however, a physical education requirement, which horrified gangly Eleanor. Courageously she went out for field hockey. "I had never seen a game of hockey," Eleanor later admitted, "but I had to play something." And play she did—miserably. But she kept at it and, after many long hours of practice, made the first team. "It was," she said, "one of the proudest moments of my life."

Eleanor's teachers filled her report cards with glowing comments such as "very advanced," "very industrious," "excellent." Wrote Mlle Souvestre on her last report card, "Eleanor has had the most admirable influence on the school and gained the affection of many, the respect of all."

On a bright summer's day in 1902 seventeen-year-old Eleanor boarded a train bound for her grandmother's estate in Tivoli, New York. Having just returned from school in England, she looked forward to a quiet, uneventful summer in the country. She had just settled into her seat and opened a book when she heard someone holler hello.

Eleanor looked up and into the startling blue eyes of her cousin Franklin.

He grinned. What a coincidence, he exclaimed. He was traveling with his mother to their country estate in Hyde Park. Wouldn't Eleanor like to come and sit with them?

Eleanor preferred to stay with her book. But good manners forbade her from saying no. She agreed and spent the next hour nervously chatting with Franklin and his formidable mother, Sara.

Franklin was charmed. At seventeen Eleanor had, a friend once wrote, a "Gibson-girl figure, a pensive dignity, the charm of tenderness, and the sweetness of youth." When the social season began a few weeks later, he traveled from Harvard to attend some of the parties—something he had never done before—where he often bumped into his cousin. He began writing about Eleanor in his diary. He was, recalled one friend, "smitten to the core."

❧ A Few Words About Franklin ❧

Five-year-old Franklin with his mother, Sara . . . and his father, James

"You couldn't find . . . two such different people as Mother and Father," Eleanor and Franklin's daughter, Anna, once said.

Unlike Eleanor, Franklin had a stable, loving childhood growing up on his parents' country estate, Springwood, in Hyde Park. An only child, he was the center of his parents' universe. He was deferred to as Master Franklin by the Springwood servants, educated by nurses and private tutors, dressed and bathed by his doting mother.

His father, James—a sometime attorney, full-time country gentleman—taught him to be stoic and to avoid unpleasantness. James advised him always to help those less fortunate. And before dying of heart disease when Franklin was eighteen, James instilled in his son a belief that he could succeed at anything he set his mind to.

From his mother, Sara—overly fond, often overbearing, and frequently nosy—Franklin learned the uses of charm and misdirection, frequently telling half-truths or leaving out important details to get his way. Because his mother asked endless personal questions and regularly read his diary, Franklin also learned to keep his feelings to himself.

This last skill came in handy when fourteen-year-old Franklin was sent to boarding school. There, and later at Harvard University, he had difficulty fitting in but hid his feelings behind a very charming exterior. Classmates belittled him for being all shining surface with no seriousness and called him a hypocrite. Even his own cousin Alice (Theodore Roosevelt's daughter) once remarked, "He was the kind of boy whom you invited to the dance but not the dinner . . . a good little mother's boy whose friends were dull, who belonged to the minor clubs, and who was shallow . . . but always charming."

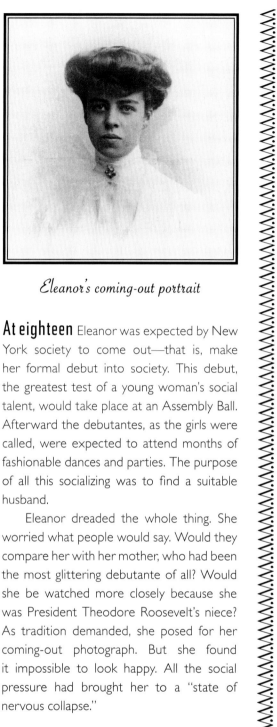

Eleanor's coming-out portrait

At eighteen Eleanor was expected by New York society to come out—that is, make her formal debut into society. This debut, the greatest test of a young woman's social talent, would take place at an Assembly Ball. Afterward the debutantes, as the girls were called, were expected to attend months of fashionable dances and parties. The purpose of all this socializing was to find a suitable husband.

Eleanor dreaded the whole thing. She worried what people would say. Would they compare her with her mother, who had been the most glittering debutante of all? Would she be watched more closely because she was President Theodore Roosevelt's niece? As tradition demanded, she posed for her coming-out photograph. But she found it impossible to look happy. All the social pressure had brought her to a "state of nervous collapse."

The big Assembly Ball took place on December 11 and was, said the *New York Times*, "*the social event of the season.*" The debutantes, wearing white gowns and long white gloves, curtsied to their hostesses. Then Eleanor entered the ballroom, where she was expected to dance with a handsome young man. But Eleanor didn't know any young men. The only man she knew was a middle-aged friend of her Aunt Bamie's (as Theodore Roosevelt's sister Anna was called). He danced with her and introduced her to others, but Eleanor later confessed the evening had been "utter agony. There was nothing about me to attract attention. I was tall, I did not dance well . . . by no stretch of the imagination was I a popular debutante! I went home early, thankful to get away. . . . I knew I was the first girl in my family who was not a belle and . . . I was deeply ashamed."

Eleanor must have made a better impression at the Assembly Ball than she thought, because afterward she was invited to dozens of receptions, cotillions, and house parties. Even Mrs. John Jacob Astor, wife of the richest man in America and the grande dame of New York society, included Eleanor on her winter ball guest list. Recalled one acquaintance, "[Eleanor] wasn't a belle. . . . But she was an interesting talker." Men and women alike found her warm manners, her lively mind, and her sympathetic ear very appealing. And while she was no beauty, one friend said, her eyes "softened the hearts of all men . . . and her face did things that were suddenly lovely."

Eleanor (middle), pictured with some of her society friends

As a debutante, Eleanor was automatically enrolled in the Junior League, an organization of wealthy young society women. The league's purpose was to assist people living in New York's slums by offering them classes and recreation. It was important work. More than five million immigrants had arrived in America since 1880. Crammed into disease-ridden tenement houses, women workers were employed in the garment industry for as little as three dollars a week. Children as young as four worked six days a week in factories, mills, and mines.

Most Junior League members, however, simply hosted fund-raising parties and other events that financed these programs. Few actually worked in the slums. But Eleanor did. With her friend Jean Reid she taught calisthenics and dancing to children in a settlement house on Rivington Street. "The dirty streets crowded with foreign-looking people filled me with terror," she admitted, "but the children interested me enormously." Eleanor enjoyed her job so much she refused to miss any of her scheduled afternoons. Once, it conflicted with a party her cousin Susie was throwing. "[Susie] says I am the most obstinate person she knows [for thinking work is more important than the party]," Eleanor said.

Other people occasionally scoffed at her do-good attitude too. But Eleanor was making a difference and it felt good: "I still remember the glow of pride that ran through me when one of the little girls said her father wanted me to come home with her, as he wanted to give me something because she enjoyed her classes so much."

Eleanor worked at the settlement house for more than a year before she was forced to resign. Her family, she explained, "worried [she] would bring home terrible diseases." Sadly, she gave up "an occupation [she] truly loved."

An early invitation to the White House

While Eleanor was away at school in England, her uncle Theodore Roosevelt had been elected vice president on a ticket headed by William McKinley. Less than a year later McKinley was killed by an assassin's bullet and Theodore became president. As his niece, Eleanor was occasionally invited to the White House. In January 1903 she arrived at the president's New Year's reception and discovered cousin Franklin had been invited too. Together they danced, dined, and watched with fascination as thousands of people crowded into the East Room to meet the president. Could they have imagined that one day they would be greeting crowds in the White House?

The President and Mrs. Roosevelt request the pleasure of the company of Miss Eleanor Roosevelt at dinner on Friday evening March 20th at 8 o'clock.

1903.

Dating in Eleanor's Day

In those formal Victorian days couples were never left alone, and it was not unusual for cousins to date. Whenever Franklin and Eleanor met for lunch, or to take walks or carriage rides, a third person—either a relative or servant—was always present. And there were other rules too, as Eleanor described in her autobiography:

"It was understood that no girl was interested in a man or showed any liking for him until he had made all the advances. You knew a man very well before you wrote or received a letter from him. . . . There were few men who would have dared to use my first name. . . . You never allowed a man to give you a present except flowers or candy or possibly a book. To receive a piece of jewelry from a man to whom you were not engaged was a sign of being a fast woman, and the idea that you would permit any man to kiss you before you were engaged to him never even crossed my mind!"

Eleanor with a playful Franklin

After the White House reception shy, serious Eleanor and jaunty, self-assured Franklin began to see each other often. He invited her to weekend parties at his Hyde Park home, where they played tennis, sang songs after dinner, and even, wrote Franklin, "walked to the river in the rain." During the summer of 1903 he asked Eleanor and a group of friends to his mother's cottage on Campobello Island, off the coast of Maine. Here the young people sailed, went on hay rides, and picnicked on the sand. Later Eleanor's friend Mrs. Hartman Kuhn told her, "That first summer at Campo I saw most clearly how much Franklin admired you." Few, however, were as perceptive as Mrs. Kuhn. No one else realized that Eleanor had a beau.

Childhood's Last Summer

THE SUMMER OF 1903 WOULD BE ELEANOR'S FIRST—AND LAST—CAREFREE ONE. SHE WAS ON THE BRINK OF A NEW LIFE.

As I try to sum up my development in . . . 1903 I think I was a curious mixture of extreme innocence and unworldliness with a great deal of knowledge of some of the less agreeable sides of life—which however, did not seem to make me any more sophisticated or less innocent.

A Devoted Wife
and Mother

❦

*I had high standards of what a wife and mother should be
and not the faintest notion of what it meant to be either a wife or a mother.*
—Eleanor Roosevelt, *This Is My Story*

*Franklin and Eleanor the year he asked
her to be his wife*

In November 1903 Eleanor accepted Franklin's invitation to the Harvard-Yale football game. She traveled to Boston with her aunt and a cousin—the inevitable chaperones—but the couple managed to slip away. Alone with her at last, Franklin asked Eleanor to be his wife. "With your help," he said, "I am sure I will amount to something some day."

"Why me?" she replied. "I am plain. I have little to bring you."

But Franklin persuaded Eleanor that he needed her. He loved Eleanor's seriousness and how she talked about life's realities. Her intelligent conversation made him think, and her opinions dazzled him with their originality. She was, he later admitted, "the most remarkable woman I've ever known, the smartest, the most intuitive, the most interesting."

Blissfully happy, Eleanor said yes. "You are never out of my thoughts dear for one moment," she wrote him days later. "Everything is changed for me now. Oh! so happy & I love you so dearly."

"I am the happiest man just now in the world," declared Franklin. "Likewise the luckiest."

Sara Delano Roosevelt standing between her son, Franklin, and Eleanor

Sara Roosevelt

was shocked when her son told her of his engagement. Strong-willed and domineering, she had devoted her life to her "darling Franklin." He was the center of her world, and she certainly was not ready to give him up. She questioned Franklin. Could he really be sure he cared *enough* for Eleanor? she asked slyly. They were so young. Shouldn't they think it over and see what the passing of time, and being away from each other, would do to their feelings? Sara pleaded with Franklin to keep the engagement a secret for one year. During that time she would take him on a Caribbean cruise. It would be, she explained, a true test of his love for Eleanor.

Grudgingly, the young couple agreed. For the next year they attended the same parties and dinners without telling anyone about their relationship. They tried to pretend they were only friends. But some people were not fooled. "I think he is very crazy for her," cousin Corinne confided in her diary. In February 1904 Sara sailed away with her son, leaving Eleanor behind. "The world [has become] such a dreadful place," Eleanor wrote him. "I wonder if you know how I hated to let you go." The next five weeks dragged. Eleanor worried. Would they survive this test of love? Would Franklin still want her?

When Franklin returned, his feelings had not changed. Joyfully they announced their engagement. "Hurrah! Hurrah! Hurrah!" wrote Corinne when she heard the news. "Everyone is thrilled." Everyone, that is, but Sara. "I am feeling blue," she wrote to Franklin. "You are gone . . . but I must try to be unselfish."

Why Franklin?

Why did Eleanor, who had never shown much interest in men, suddenly choose Franklin as her husband? One family friend explained it this way:

"[Franklin] was very attractive, very outgoing—a dashing personality, someone who laughed and was easy with people. And [Eleanor] was flattered by the attention and she fell in love with him. It wasn't hard to do."

Why Eleanor?

Why did debonair, charming, high-spirited, and social Franklin choose solemn Eleanor to be his wife? Those who knew him claimed that beneath his surface gaiety lay a seriousness about life. FDR, they said, was a man with big plans. With Eleanor at his side he believed his own dreams of greatness would stand a better chance of coming true. A close family friend once explained it this way:

"[Franklin] harbored large ambitions which required a helpmate rather than a playfellow. . . . He recognized life . . . had touched [Eleanor] and made its mark in a certain aloofness from the careless ways of youth. The world had come to her as a field of responsibility rather than a playground. . . . His choice showed remarkable clarity."

Eleanor in her wedding gown ~~~~~~~~~~~~~~~~~~~~~~~~~~~~~

Although there were still traces of snow on the street, March 17, 1905, was bright and sunny. Downstairs in the drawing room of cousin Susie Parish's New York townhouse dozens of servants rushed about lighting candles and setting out vases of flowers. Upstairs Eleanor and her six bridesmaids (cousins Alice Roosevelt, Ellen Delano, Muriel Robbins, Isabella Selmes, Corinne Robinson, and Helen Cutting) primped and curled, while in a small room off the parlor Franklin and his groomsmen paced and joked.

Finally, at 3:30, Grandmother Hall, wearing black velvet, and Sara Roosevelt, wearing white silk, were ushered to their seats in front. Aunts Pussie and Maude sniffled as the orchestra played "The Wedding March" and the bridesmaids—in cream taffeta, with three silver-tipped feathers in their hair—moved down the circular staircase and up the satin-ribboned aisle. Behind them came Eleanor on her uncle Theodore's arm. As she made her way toward the altar, many of the two hundred guests gasped; in her satin and lace gown, wearing pearls and diamonds, Eleanor looked very much like her mother.

At the altar she handed her bouquet of lilies to one of the bridesmaids, then turned to face Franklin. They smiled at each other as the rector led them through the Episcopal wedding service. Once, Franklin faltered. He could not remember the words to the service. But Eleanor helped him and he quickly recovered. Then the two exchanged vows. They kissed. They were pronounced man and wife.

~~~~~~

Eleanor's uncle, President Theodore Roosevelt, arrives at his niece's wedding.

THEODORE had been thrilled to hear about Eleanor's engagement. Not only did he agree to attend the wedding, but "on that day," wrote his wife, Edith, "he feels he stands in your father's place." Theodore promised to walk her down the aisle.

News of the president's promise traveled fast, and on the big day a large crowd gathered outside the townhouse. When Theodore's carriage finally pulled up, people clapped, screamed, and waved American and Irish flags. (Many of them had come directly from the Saint Patrick's Day parade.) Without even a friendly wave, Theodore hurried inside to escort his niece down the aisle.

"Well, Franklin," he said in his high-pitched voice when the ceremony was over, "there's nothing like keeping the name in the family." Planting a kiss on his niece's cheek, he sailed into the dining room for refreshments. Soon the room crackled with the president's jokes and stories.

Drawn to his merriment, the guests abandoned the bride and groom. They "were more concerned with greeting the President than congratulating them," Franklin's mother, Sara, recalled. "For an awful moment . . . they were entirely alone while the crowd hovered around President Roosevelt."

Bride and groom, however, didn't seem to mind. "We simply followed the crowd," Eleanor wrote, "and listened with the rest."

A (Very) Few Words About Sex

Eleanor never spoke about her sexual relationship with Franklin. But once when her son Franklin Jr. pressed, she replied:

"Well, you know, we were Victorians. I knew my obligations as a wife and did my duty."

HONEYMOONING IN ITALY, 1905

After their wedding the couple remained in New York so Franklin could complete his first year at Columbia Law School. It wasn't until June that they set sail on their honeymoon. For the next three months they toured Europe. All in all, it was a happy trip. But one event gave Eleanor pause. While visiting friends in Scotland, she was asked to explain the difference between America's state and national governments. Eleanor opened, then closed, her mouth. Her cheeks flamed red with embarrassment. She . . . she . . . couldn't! Even though her uncle Theodore was, at that time, president of the United States, Eleanor had "never realized there were any differences! I vowed that once . . . back in the safety of the United States I would find out something about my own government."

MOTHER-IN-LAW PROBLEMS

Sara gives her son's new bride some advice, 1906.

Sara Delano Roosevelt was a strong, domineering woman who was "determined to bend [her son's] marriage the way she wanted it to be," Eleanor claimed.

In the early days Sara succeeded. Longing to be loved as a daughter, Eleanor devoted herself to her mother-in-law. Deliberately self-effacing, Eleanor never expressed her own preferences. Instead she listened dutifully while Sara lectured on everything from the proper diet for Franklin to the best way to arrange furniture. She gave up her beloved social work when Sara declared it improper. And she allowed Sara to hire her servants, decide on her wardrobe, and choose her friends. "I was beginning to be an entirely dependent person," Eleanor later wrote. "For the first few years of my married life . . . my mother-in-law did everything for me."

Sara frequently made thoughtless, stinging comments that deeply hurt Eleanor. Once, in front of a dozen dinner guests, Sara turned to her daughter-in-law. "If you'd just run a comb through your hair, dear," she said, "you'd look so much better." Another time, during a luncheon party, Sara left Eleanor standing while she showed all the other guests to their seats. She was already serving the soup when she finally turned to her daughter-in-law. "Oh, yes, Eleanor," she said snidely, "you sit there."

With the births of Franklin and Eleanor's five children, Sara's interference became intolerable, causing terrible family friction. Sara spoiled them from infancy to adulthood with expensive presents—ponies, trips, cars, apartments. As one of the children put it long afterward, "Granny's ace in the hole . . . was the fact that she held the pursestrings in the family." Worse, Sara undercut Eleanor's authority and confidence by repeatedly calling the children *hers*. She once told little Jimmy, "Your mother only bore you, I am more your mother than your mother is."

This situation was made even worse by Franklin's refusal to take sides. "If something was unpleasant and he didn't want to know about it, he just ignored it," Eleanor said. "He always thought that if you ignored a thing long enough, it could settle itself."

This 1920 picture of the Roosevelts and their children shows Sara—in her favorite spot, between Franklin and Eleanor— looking directly into the camera while Eleanor looks miserable.

Franklin and Eleanor tried

to settle into marriage. But their temperaments, values, and upbringings made adjustment difficult. Eleanor had high and precise standards of how a young husband should behave, and Franklin disappointed her at every turn. He was often late—a fault that drove prompt Eleanor crazy. He forgot birthdays and anniversaries—events his wife believed were special and important. He did not share his deepest feelings—something she longed for him to do. And he was a poor letter writer, while she was a diligent correspondent. "I was horribly disappointed by your hasty little scrap of a note yesterday after not getting anything from you for two days," she wrote in the summer of 1906.

Eleanor took on the role of prodder and manager. When babies were born, she sent the congratulations and ordered the gifts. When someone was ill, she visited. When friends or relatives died, she was the one who wrote. She had an obsession about paying the bills promptly (Franklin was very casual about this) and had the habit of making long to-do lists for her husband. How did he respond? Sometimes he did as she requested, other times he completely ignored her list. "Anything left undone will be smoothed over by Eleanor," he once explained to a friend.

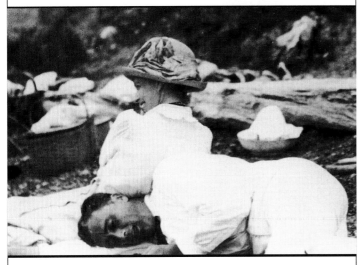

Franklin and Eleanor five years after their wedding

Eleanor in the throes of a "Griselda mood," 1911

Griselda Mood

All her life, but especially during the early years of her marriage, Eleanor went through periods of moodiness and depression. She called them her "Griselda moods," after the long-suffering character in Geoffrey Chaucer's story "The Clerk's Tale."

"I developed a bad tendency to shut up like a clam . . . not telling anyone what was the matter, and being much too obviously humble and meek, feeling like a martyr and acting like one."

Early Homes

ELEANOR AND FRANKLIN'S FIRST HOME, AT 125 EAST THIRTY-SIXTH STREET IN NEW YORK CITY

In the summer of 1905, with Franklin and Eleanor away on their honeymoon, Sara took it upon herself to rent a house for "the children," furnish it, and staff it with three servants. It was a mere three blocks from her own residence. Although Eleanor had been looking forward to house hunting when she returned from Europe, she accepted her mother-in-law's gift docilely. The couple lived there for the next two years as Franklin attended law school and Eleanor attended luncheons and teas with her mother-in-law.

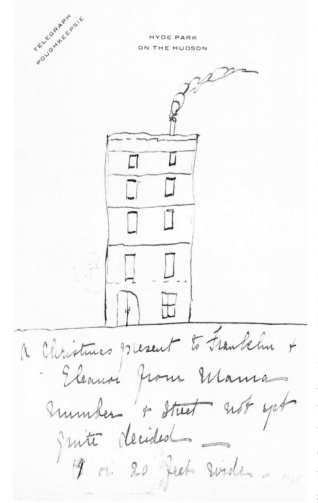

TELEGRAPH
POUGHKEEPSIE

HYDE PARK
ON THE HUDSON

A Christmas present to Franklin +
Eleanor from Mama —
number + street not yet
quite decided —
19 or 20 feet wide.

A sketch drawn by Sara Roosevelt of the house she built for Franklin and Eleanor.

On Christmas Day, 1905, Sara gave this sketch to "the children," with the announcement that her present was to build them a brand-new townhouse. The next year she bought a plot of land on Sixty-fifth Street and had plans drawn up for adjoining houses—one for the young couple, one for herself. Eleanor said nothing during the two years it took to construct the houses. They had connecting doors on three of the six levels and provided little privacy for the young couple. "You were never quite sure when she would appear night or day" through those connecting doors, Eleanor grumbled. As for the houses' furnishings and decorations, everything—even Eleanor's dressing table—was chosen by Sara. Not once did she take into consideration her daughter-in-law's tastes or desires.

The first night in their new home Franklin returned from work to find his wife in tears. This wasn't her house, she sobbed. She had not helped plan it, and it wasn't the way she wanted to live. A bewildered Franklin wanted to know why she hadn't told him this before. "Being an eminently reasonable person," Eleanor later wrote, "he thought I was quite mad . . . and left me alone until I should become calmer. I pulled myself together . . . but there was a good deal of truth in what he said, for I was not developing any individual taste or initiative. I was simply absorbing the personalities of those about me."

Special Places

While he was growing up, Campobello—an island off the coast of Maine—was Franklin's summer home. He learned to swim and sail there, and it was there that his lifelong love of the sea was born. Eleanor visited the island for the first time in 1904 as a young bride-to-be, and every summer for the next four years she and Franklin returned. Staying in Sara's cottage, they delighted in the sunny days and fresh salt air. While Franklin golfed, swam, fished, and bicycled, Eleanor preferred reading, picking berries, and taking long walks. She grew to love the place, its peaceful solitude and relaxing atmosphere. The only dark cloud at Campo was the ever imperious Sara, who took complete control of the family affairs.

But in 1909 all that changed when Mrs. Hartman Kuhn, the owner of the cottage next door, died. Mrs. Kuhn's will specified that Sara could purchase the Kuhn cottage for the bargain price of $5,000 if it was given immediately to Franklin and Eleanor. Sara bought the cottage, and Eleanor was overjoyed. The first thing she did when she moved in was "rearrange all the furniture in every room." Finally she and Franklin had a place they could be alone with their children. From 1909 to 1921 summers at Campo were a family ritual. It was the place where the Roosevelt brood (called "that bunch of wild Indians" by the other islanders) could escape the daily ritual of their lives. But not all the times were good.

The Roosevelt cottage on Campobello Island

While on the island in the summer of 1921, Franklin came down with polio—the disease that would paralyze his legs for the rest of his life. The trauma of those weeks, with Eleanor constantly nursing Franklin, added a new dimension to the meaning of Campo. "There [were] good and bad memories there," Eleanor would say, "but the bad get the better of me when I'm there alone."

Although Franklin's illness and eventual political career kept him away from Campo in later years, Eleanor continued to visit. In 1962, just months before her death, she traveled there for the last time. Although ill and in pain, she gained a sense of serenity from that trip, her friends claimed. Today her cottage remains as the centerpiece of the Roosevelt Campobello International Park.

Franklin grew up on Springwood's six hundred acres of rolling hills and thick woods set on the banks of the Hudson River. As a boy, he fished, rode, and hunted there. As a man, he occasionally lived there with his wife, mother, and children. And later, as president of the United States, he went there to unwind and to find warmth, security, and peace of mind. "All that is in me," he once said, "goes back to the Hudson."

Unlike her husband, Eleanor found little pleasure at Springwood. Although she visited often, she never felt at home because Sara reigned supreme. At the dinner table Sara sat at one end, Franklin at the other, and like a guest, Eleanor was relegated to a seat in the middle. In the library two wing chairs sat beside the fireplace—one for Sara, one for Franklin. And upstairs Eleanor occupied a tiny, almost spartan bedroom adjoining Franklin's large, sunny suite. (In those days it was common for wealthy couples to have separate bedrooms.) Said Eleanor, "For over forty years, I was only a visitor there."

When Sara died in 1941, Eleanor saw an opportunity to make Springwood her own. She asked Franklin if she could redecorate, but he refused. He didn't want a single thing changed.

Wrote Eleanor, "[It] is now to be a shrine." And yet Springwood would become the final home for *both* Franklin and Eleanor. Their graves are in the estate's rose garden.

Springwood, the Roosevelts' country estate in Hyde Park, New York

Babies, Babies, Babies

For ten years I was always getting over having a baby, or about to have one. —Eleanor Roosevelt, *The Autobiography of Eleanor Roosevelt*

Eleanor with baby Anna, 1906

It's a Girl!

IN MAY 1906 twenty-one-year-old Eleanor gave birth to "a beautiful girl . . . 10 pounds and one ounce." Eleanor remembered the first time she held Anna (named for her mother) in her arms—"just a helpless bundle . . . winding itself . . . around my heart."

Eleanor delighted in her newborn and longed to take care of the baby herself. But Sara insisted the children be raised by a series of nurses, nannies, and governesses. This, she declared, was the Roosevelt tradition. Besides, in those days ladies of wealth and social class did not care for their children—such behavior was scandalous. "What she [really] wanted," Eleanor later wrote, "was to hold onto Franklin through his children; she wanted them to grow as she wished." Unable to stand up to her mother-in-law, Eleanor reluctantly yielded.

As her diary entries prove, it didn't take long for her to lose touch with her child. "Anna is upset today so I am told though I have not seen her long enough to judge for myself," she wrote when Anna was only eight months old. "[Nurse] Nelly thinks so, however, so she has gone to bed with a dose of castor oil." Another time, when Anna was a toddler, Nurse Nelly went away for the evening. "I am to take charge of Anna and put her to bed tonight," Eleanor wrote nervously. The next day she recorded with wonder, "I never knew before how easy it is to take care of Anna!"

But when Eleanor did take care of her daughter, she often displayed a poor lack of judgment. Believing fresh air was good for a baby, she once rigged Anna into a wire contraption that she dangled from an upper-story window. Horrified neighbors reported Eleanor to the Society for the Prevention of Cruelty to Children. Another time she tied Anna's thumbs to the palms of her hands so the toddler couldn't suck them.

Not surprisingly, mother and daughter never developed a closeness. "She was very unhappy," admitted Eleanor, "though I did not realize it. . . . She tried to hide her feelings by being rather devil-may-care."

Eleanor and Franklin with Anna and baby James, 1908

It's a Boy!

ON DECEMBER 23, 1907, the second Roosevelt baby—James—arrived. "He is lovely and looks like a 3 week old child. . . . Weighs 10 lbs. 5 oz!" bragged Franklin. As for Eleanor, her "heart sang . . . with . . . relief and joy" at the birth of her son. But she soon discovered that James was a handful. He displayed a wildness that worried her. "James," she reported to Franklin in 1909, "won't sit still and Anna kicks him whenever she can." James knew how to defend himself. "He is very naughty and poor Anna's arm is all blue where he bit her yesterday."

To counteract this wildness, Eleanor "enforced a discipline which in many ways was unwise," she later admitted. Instead of letting "the chicks run wild," as Franklin recommended, she insisted they sit quietly, scolded them for being too loud, and usually said no to their requests for outings and playmates. Her expectations were "often unreasonable," she confessed. "I can remember . . . expecting my year old baby to sit on the sofa beside me while I poured tea with all kinds of good things on the tray. His manners had to be so perfect that he would never even reach or ask for these forbidden goodies."

The result of this rigid training was often noticed by outsiders. One day a family friend invited six-year-old James and eight-year-old Anna "on a hunt for wild flowers up a mountain path." The children shook their heads. Anna worried she might get dirty. James worried about the steep curves and sharp rocks. Feeling sorry for the "poor, unadventurous darlings," the friend left them behind to "primly parade on the asphalt drive."

As James grew older, Eleanor tried to be more playful. She took him fishing—"We fished off the float and caught eleven flounder!" She taught him to play croquet—"A good exercise for James' temper." She even took him on a tour of the naval academy at Annapolis and "could hardly drag him past the football field." But even as she went through the motions she was unable to relax and truly enjoy herself.

Little Angel

Eleanor holding the first Franklin Jr.

THE
Middle Child

Eleanor with Anna, James, and baby Elliott, 1911

On March 18, 1909, another baby joined the Roosevelt family. Franklin Jr. was "really lovely and very big, 11 lbs." Despite his size, baby Franklin was delicate. He often breathed rapidly, and his skin sometimes took on a blue tinge. But a series of doctors could find nothing wrong with the baby. Worried, Eleanor fussed over his food and schedule, giving the nurses and nannies lots of extra instructions. In October, while Eleanor was visiting New York City, the baby suddenly grew ill. Eleanor raced back to Hyde Park to discover that his "little heart had almost stopped." For the next four days the family watched helplessly as little Franklin fought for air. But on November 1, "the little angel ceased breathing."

Eleanor was devastated. Standing beside his tiny headstone after the funeral, she burst into tears. "How cruel it seemed to leave him out there alone in the cold," she later wrote. She reproached herself for "having done so little about the care of this baby," confessing, "I felt he had been left too much to the nurse, and I knew too little about him, and that in some way I was to blame." This guilt, as well as the grief, remained with Eleanor for the rest of her life.

On September 23, 1910, just ten months after Franklin Jr.'s death, Elliott Roosevelt (named for Eleanor's father) came into the world. He weighed a whopping eleven pounds fourteen ounces. If Eleanor worried about this baby's health, her fears were quickly put to rest. Elliott was "a loud, active, excitable boy . . . often temperamental and defiant." Once, after he bit his brother hard, Eleanor spanked him with a slipper. She expected him to cry. But Elliott refused. "He made a long upper lip," she reported to Franklin, "but insisted that 'it didn't hurt so very much, Mother!'" Another time, she claimed, Elliott became so angry "he went for me with both fists!" He bickered constantly with his older siblings, bit, and hit. When Eleanor pleaded with Franklin to help her stop his roughhousing, he replied, "Oh, let him scrap. It's good exercise for him."

Eleanor tried a number of ways to curb Elliott's wildness. She spent time with him on his lessons and read to him. She also had a French governess to help him learn French. "Elliott goes to Mlle. now for French every morning, and I think has learnt a good deal, though if you ask him to say anything he promptly refuses." Eleanor also tried a relaxation method she had learned from her former teacher Mlle Souvestre. After lunch she had Elliott and the other children lie flat on the floor. "Relax your muscles completely," she softly commanded. When they were physically as well as mentally relaxed, she read to them—poetry, stories, thought-provoking essays. She hoped this method would increase the children's powers of concentration while calming them, but she was never able to tell if it really worked.

Though Elliott's temper and focus were short, he was long on charm. Refusing to attend college, he displayed a restlessness that kept him moving in and out of houses, jobs, and marriages for the rest of his life.

THE TEAM

Of all her children, the two youngest—the second Franklin Jr. (born August 17, 1914) and John (born March 17, 1916)—were the ones Eleanor enjoyed the most. With the Team, as she and FDR called them, she was more relaxed. She could handle their outbursts of wildness more calmly, and she had more fun with them. Franklin Jr.'s pleasing personality earned him the nickname of Sunshine Boy. Wrote his older brother James, "I went out for a walk with little Franklin, and every time he saw a child he would say hallow as if he knew them." At age five Franklin Jr. had already become a notorious flirt. "I love you very much. I want to kiss you," he wrote to his grandmother Sara Roosevelt, adding, "Please give me a light like Anna's and a firecracker." He amused his mother, too. "I asked Franklin Jr. last night what I was to ask Santa Claus to bring him and without prompting he reeled off more things than you ever heard of. I gasped and he added, 'and John just the same!'"

Once, Eleanor read the boys a children's book about the life of their great-uncle Theodore Roosevelt. Afterward five-year-old Franklin Jr. toddled over to his grandmother. "Granny," he said, "I intend to run for the presidency, and am beginning my campaign at your tea."

John, however, was not interested in politics. When asked if he wanted to be president someday, he firmly replied, "I am *not* going to be president." He liked to hoard his toys (and those of his brother, too) and showed early signs of becoming a businessman, claimed Eleanor. "I feel sure he owns everything by now," she told his father.

Like their older siblings, the Team lived with what John called a "procession of English nannies." One of these nannies—nicknamed Old Battle-Ax by the children—terrorized them. She hit them, humiliated them, and locked them in closets. This did not disturb Eleanor as much as learning Old Battle-Ax was also a secret drinker. Eleanor fired her in 1916 and did not hire a replacement. After that Eleanor gained "more confidence in [her] abilities to handle the children."

Franklin and Eleanor holding the Team— Franklin Jr. (in his father's arms) and baby John (in his mother's arms)—in 1918

Sparing the Rod

Discipline was a source of conflict in the Roosevelt household. While Eleanor tended to be too severe, Franklin preferred not to discipline the children at all, as this story told by their son Elliott shows:

Father was known to sit you down and say, "Well, now I think it's time that you let out a yell, and then [your mother will] think I've hit you, and that will be enough because I don't think what you did was serious enough to be spanked." Or . . . Father would say, "All right, we'll just talk here for a while, and when you go out, look very grave. . . ." So he was not a disciplinarian—Mother was.

Memories of Mother . . .

Anna: She was "very unpredictable and inconsistent . . . inconsistent in her feelings—sweet and lovely one hour and the next very critical, very demanding, and very difficult to be with. You could never tell what she really meant."

James: "I don't think Mother shared in the day-to-day fun in life at all, in things like skating, sledding, etc. . . . She made arrangements but she did not participate."

Elliott: "My earliest memories were of a distant, sometimes forbidding woman who could seldom find the means of making us children understand that she loved us. Warmth and affection in our lives seemed to come only from Father."

Franklin Jr.: "She did her duty. Nobody in the world did her duty more than Eleanor Roosevelt. But I don't think she understood us. She didn't enjoy us."

John: "She felt tremendous duty, but our really intimate lives were run by nurses and governesses and she had no real insight into the needs of a child for primary closeness to a parent."

And of Being a Mother

Eleanor: "It did not come naturally to me to understand little children or enjoy them. Playing with children was difficult for me because play had not been an important part of my own childhood."

Eleanor with her children (from left to right)—Anna, age thirteen; James, age eleven;
Elliott, age nine; Franklin Jr., age five; and John, age three

After Eleven Years of Marriage

On a spring night in 1916 Eleanor Roosevelt stood in the corner of Washington, D.C.'s Chevy Chase Club. She watched as her charming, flirtatious husband gathered a large group of admirers around him. "Isn't it grand?" he laughed after telling yet another humorous story. "Isn't it just grand?"

No, thought thirty-one-year-old Eleanor. It wasn't. She detested social events like this one. They made her feel uncomfortable and insecure. Desperately she longed to go home. But how could she ask Franklin to leave early again? She knew she often spoiled his fun. But not this time, she decided. This time she would take a taxi home. Stay and enjoy yourself, she told her husband.

It was three o'clock in the morning before Franklin finally sauntered up his front steps. To his amazement, he found Eleanor sitting there outside their front door, looking irritated and aggrieved.

Peevishly she told him she had forgotten her key.

Franklin asked why she hadn't rung the bell.

She hadn't wanted to wake the servants, she replied.

So why hadn't she just taken a taxi back to the club and gotten his key?

Eleanor sighed and in a martyred voice explained that she hated ruining his good time. Then she rose stiffly from the top stair and followed her guilt-ridden husband into the house.

It was a pattern of behavior Eleanor repeated hundreds of times during her forty years of marriage—making herself the wronged one through her own actions. Suggested her cousin Corinne, "She sometimes acted badly out of fear. . . . She was very insecure."

It seems that fear and insecurity kept Eleanor from participating in many activities that might have given her an easy companionship with her husband. She took up golf but quit after Franklin made a teasing remark about her swing. She took driving lessons but gave them up after bumping into a gatepost. Her fear of water kept her from enjoying the swimming and sailing Franklin loved so much.

On the whole, Franklin found her insecurities bewildering. Blithely he assumed if he left her alone, everything would be all right.

But as the years wore on, the very qualities that had attracted them to each other became their biggest sources of conflict. Eleanor began to see Franklin's charm and confidence as duplicitous and shallow. Franklin began to view Eleanor's honesty and high-mindedness as rigid and inflexible. "She bothered him because she had integrity," a friend once observed. "It is very hard to live with someone who is almost a saint. He had his tricks and evasions. Sometimes he had to ridicule her in order not to be troubled by her."

Eleanor had her tricks too. She showed her displeasure by pursing her lips and snorting whenever Franklin enjoyed a cocktail. She brooded over his shortcomings. And she often interrupted him with, "I think you are wrong, dear."

The other woman ❦ Lucy Mercer

Lucy Mercer entered the Roosevelts' life while they were living in Washington, D.C., during the winter season of 1913–1914. Pregnant with her fifth child, Eleanor felt overwhelmed by the social demands placed on her: The year before she had stepped into her role as wife of the assistant secretary of the navy and had many social obligations to fulfill. She hired the twenty-two-year-old Mercer to help her. Blue-eyed Lucy was "gay . . . smiling and relaxed . . . with a rich contralto voice," remembered son Elliott, "femininely gentle where Mother had something of a schoolmarm's air about her."

Lucy claimed she and Franklin were instantly drawn to each other, and over the next eighteen months their relationship slid from friendship to love affair. The two began taking long rides together in the country and meeting *by accident* at parties. Franklin believed no one noticed them. But sharp-eyed cousin Alice, Theodore Roosevelt's daughter, did. "I saw you twenty miles out in the country," she teased Franklin. "You didn't see me. Your hands were on the wheel, but your eyes were on that perfectly lovely lady."

"Isn't she perfectly lovely?" he boldly replied.

His boldness increased in the summer of 1916. With Eleanor and the children away at Campobello, Franklin and Lucy went on picnics, sailed on the Potomac River, and dined with a circle of Washington friends who understood their relationship.

When Eleanor returned in the fall, the two acted as if nothing had happened. Lucy resumed her secretarial work and even filled in when Eleanor needed an extra woman for a luncheon or dinner party.

But Eleanor was growing suspicious. In the summer of 1917 she accused Franklin of being anxious to see her leave. Franklin denied it. "You were being a goosy girl," he smoothly lied in a letter, "to think or even pretend to think that I don't want you here [in Washington, D.C.] *all* summer, because you know I do!" His words did not completely convince her. Still, she and the children went to Campobello as planned. They expected Franklin to join them soon. But Franklin claimed he had too much work. "I do miss you so very much," he wrote a few weeks later, "but I am getting busier and busier and fear my hoped-for dash to Campo . . . will not materialize." He and Lucy spent the weekend together on a friend's yacht.

The affair continued for another year. Then in the fall of 1918 Franklin returned from a trip to Europe with double pneumonia. Unpacking her sick husband's trunk, Eleanor found a packet of letters tied with a velvet ribbon. They were love letters from Lucy.

"The bottom dropped out of my own particular world," she told a friend. After thirteen years of marriage and six children, Franklin had discarded her for a younger, gayer woman. Eleanor felt destroyed, but outwardly she remained calm. She confronted her still-feverish husband and offered him his freedom. Franklin could have a divorce if he wanted.

Divorce! In 1918 even the idea of divorce was scandalous. Fuming, Franklin's mother threatened to cut him off without a cent if he abandoned his family. Louis Howe, his closest political adviser, warned that a divorce would end his political career.

Franklin made his choice. Although he loved Lucy and wanted to marry her, he agreed never to see her again.

As for Eleanor, while she claimed she could forgive, she said, "I cannot forget."

Obviously she never did. Among the belongings on her bedside table when she died forty-four years later was a faded newspaper clipping of the poem "Psyche," by Virginia Moore.

> The soul that has believed
> And is deceived
> Thinks nothing for a while.
> All thoughts are vile.
>
> And then because the sun
> Is mute persuasion,
> And hope in Spring and Fall
> Most natural,
>
> The soul grows calm and mild,
> A little child,
> Finding the pull of breath
> Better than death, . . .
>
> The soul that had believed
> And was deceived
> Ends by believing more
> Than ever before.

Across the top of the clipping, in her cramped handwriting, Eleanor had scrawled, "1918."

FRANKLIN'S AFFAIR, Eleanor later recalled, forced her to face "myself, my surroundings, my world honestly for the first time. . . . I really grew up that year." She also grew away from Franklin. While they remained a family, their relationship entirely changed. They became partners, with mutual interests, a shared past, and common goals. But the intimacy of marriage was over. "There is no longer any fundamental love to draw on," Eleanor once told her friend Esther Lape, "just respect and affection."

This picture of Franklin and Eleanor,
taken after the affair, shows them looking very much
like the partners they had become.

"1/2 a Loaf of Love"

In later years Eleanor obviously had regrets about some of the choices she had made in her marriage, as this advice given to a young friend proves:

Of one thing I am sure . . . don't accept a compromise. . . . Someday I'll tell you why I'm sure that is so but just now . . . all the contribution I can think of is to beg you not to accept 1/2 a loaf of love.

Self-Discovery

❧

I was thinking things out for myself, and becoming an individual.
—Eleanor Roosevelt, *This Is My Story*

A QUICK PEEK AT

FRANKLIN'S CAREER

◇

When the Democratic district attorney of Dutchess County, New York, dropped by the Roosevelt estate to discuss the possibility of twenty-eight-year-old Franklin running for the state legislature, Eleanor encouraged her husband to listen. She knew he could never be happy as a lawyer. "He needs a career in which his charm will be an important asset," she once told a friend, "a career full of excitement, variety . . . one in which he is able to have broad, human contact." Politics seemed the perfect answer, and if that required her to make some changes, so be it. "I willingly made adjustments," she said.

Her first adjustment was switching political parties. "Many of the Roosevelts had been Democrats until the Civil War," Eleanor once explained, "but they became Abraham Lincoln Republicans. Later some of them returned to their Democratic allegiance, but some remained Republicans." Franklin's side of the family was staunchly Democratic, a political party favoring free trade and attracting farmers and immigrants. But Eleanor's side (including her uncle, President Theodore Roosevelt) was Republican, a political party favoring business interests, and emphasizing national unity. What to do? Although Eleanor adored her uncle Theodore and had been raised in a household where Republicanism and respectability went hand in hand, she followed her husband's political allegiance. "It hardly mattered at the time," she later admitted, "because I did not envisage a political role for myself."

{36}

Below is a brief time line of Franklin's momentous political career.

1910 Is elected to New York State Senate

1912 Is reelected to New York State Senate

1913 Resigns position to join President Woodrow Wilson's administration in Washington, D.C., as assistant secretary of the navy, a post he held until 1920

1920 Runs for vice president of the United States on a Democratic ticket headed by James Cox but loses

1928 Is elected governor of New York

1932 Is elected to first term as president of the United States

1936 Is elected to second term as president of the United States

1940 Is elected to third term as president of the United States

1944 Is elected to fourth term as president of the United States

State senator Franklin Delano Roosevelt

Franklin eagerly agreed to run for the New York State Senate in 1910. He ran an active campaign, visiting every general store, speaking in every village, shaking hands everywhere he went. And where was Eleanor during all this? Pregnant again, she stayed at home with her two small children. Naively she believed her husband's entrance into politics wouldn't greatly affect her day-to-day life. "I listened to all his plans with a great deal of interest," she said. "It never occurred to me that I had any part to play."

Eleanor soon learned differently. On her very first day as a state senator's wife she met hundreds of people and had to cope with all kinds of new situations. "We held a reception in our Albany house for as many of Franklin's constituents as wished to come," Eleanor wrote. "People wandered in from the three counties for three solid hours while our servants, nurses, caterers and children were still trying to settle in. . . . It was uncomfortable . . . but I faced this chaos with a certain fearlessness." To her delight, she discovered that not only could she manage, but she liked it. She held receptions and teas and made it a point to meet people from all walks of life, not just society folks. "My shyness," she later admitted, "was wearing off."

AS THE WIFE OF THE ASSISTANT SECRETARY OF THE NAVY, ELEANOR (LEFT) MASTERED NAVY PROTOCOL AND OTHER POLITICAL RITUALS.

Franklin worked hard for Woodrow Wilson's presidential campaign. When Wilson was elected, the new president returned the favor by making Franklin the assistant secretary of the navy in 1913. That year the Roosevelts moved to Washington, D.C., and while Franklin learned the ropes of his new position, twenty-eight-year-old Eleanor learned the ropes of hers. She considered it her duty to learn navy protocol and ceremony, to keep her poise during a seventeen-gun salute, and to ignore the seasickness she always experienced when sailing.

Eleanor also considered it her duty to master Washington, D.C.'s ritual of calls. Every day she nervously set out on her appointed rounds: Mondays she visited the supreme court justices' wives; Tuesdays, congressional wives; Thursdays, wives of the president's cabinet; Fridays, diplomats. Wednesday was her day to receive visitors in her home. "I've paid 60 calls this week," she wrote her aunt Maude. "It is almost an impossible struggle." Eleanor managed this arduous routine by keeping to a strict schedule of six minutes a call, and while she found the whole business "nerve-wracking and exhausting," she persevered because it was in Franklin's best interests. With her systematic approach to Washington's social system, marveled a friend, she was playing the "political game far better than anyone else." She was making friends in some very high places—friends who would be helpful in later years.

The Roosevelts' first Washington, D.C., home

In 1913 the Roosevelt family moved to Washington, D.C., and settled into a house at 1733 N Street—a comfortable, cluttered old-fashioned home. With three small children underfoot, Eleanor was thankful for the garden in the backyard. She was also thankful to be away from her mother-in-law's influence. Still, Sara's domineering personality persisted. After visiting the family for the first time, Sara wrote in her diary, "Dined at 1733 N. Street. Moved chairs and tables and began to feel at home." The Roosevelts spent the next four years on N Street. But with the birth of their fifth and sixth children, the place became too small. Eleanor packed up again, this time landing the family at 2131 R Street. There they remained until 1920.

The house on N Street

WORLD WAR I

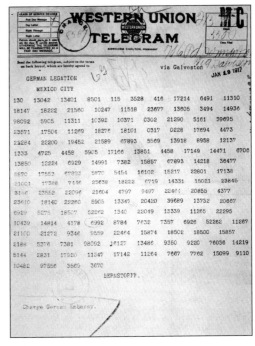

The Zimmerman telegram
propels America into war.

IN 1914 WAR BROKE OUT IN EUROPE, pitting Germany and Austria-Hungary against Russia, France, and Britain. President Wilson quickly proclaimed America's neutrality. But in early 1917 Germany announced it would attack, without warning, all enemy and neutral ships found near British waters. At the same time the British passed along an intercepted telegram from the German foreign minister, Arthur Zimmerman, to the Mexican foreign office. Written in a numeric code, it proposed a German-Mexican alliance against the United States. What would Mexico's reward be for such an alliance? The return of territory it had lost in Texas, New Mexico, and Arizona. Wilson could no longer remain neutral. On April 2, 1917, he asked Congress for a declaration of war. "I listened breathlessly," recalled Eleanor, who went with Franklin to the Capitol Building to hear the president's address, "and I returned home still half-dazed by the sense of impending change."

N ow that America was at war, some sacrifices needed to be made. One of these was food conservation. The head of the Food Administration, a government agency overseeing U.S. food supplies during World War I, urged housewives to observe "meatless Mondays" and "wheatless Wednesdays" in an effort to feed the thousands of American soldiers fighting in Europe.

Like most women, Eleanor responded to this call enthusiastically. Embarking on a rationing crusade, she reduced the amount of coffee Franklin could drink at breakfast from four cups to two. She eliminated bacon from her grocery list and served corn bread instead of wheat bread. She even left an empty place at the dinner table—complete with silver, china, and a napkin tucked into a ring—to remind her family that while they were making small sacrifices by eating meat only once a day and giving up teatime, thousands of hungry soldiers were fighting for democracy. "It doesn't seem much to do," she once explained to her complaining children, "considering what the soldiers must do."

When the Food Administration heard of Eleanor's rationing plan, they chose it as a national model for other large households. But after the *New York Times* ran this article about it, she became the laughingstock of Washington, D.C.:

Mrs. Roosevelt does the shopping, the cooks see that there is no food wasted, the laundress is sparing with her soap, each servant has an eye for evidence of shortcomings on the part of the others; and all are encouraged to make helpful suggestions. Added Mrs. Roosevelt, "Making the servants help me do my saving had not only been possible, but highly profitable."

Joked Franklin after reading the piece, "I am proud to be the husband of the Originator, Discoverer and Inventor of the New Household Economy for Millionaires."

Eleanor moaned, "I'd like to crawl away in shame."

BLOOD or BREAD
Others are giving their blood
You will shorten the war—
save life if you eat only what
you need and waste nothing.
UNITED STATES FOOD ADMINISTRATION

An emotionally charged poster extolling all Americans—including Eleanor—to save food

A World War I Red Cross canteen similar to the one in which Eleanor worked

———— •:• ————

Washington, D.C., was a major railroad junction, and some days as many as ten trains filled with troops passed through the yards. That meant three or four thousand soldiers a day who needed food, drink, and a place to rest. In response the Red Cross—a charitable organization providing relief to the needy—set up a canteen for the soldiers. It consisted of a small army kitchen in a tin shack where the women volunteers, including Eleanor Roosevelt, brewed great cauldrons of coffee and put together hundreds upon hundreds of jam sandwiches. In a small room off the kitchen they set up a shop where they sold cigarettes, candy, and postcards at a reduced price. "The shop," recalled one canteen worker, "was where Mrs. Roosevelt shone. . . . She never made a mistake giving change, no matter how long the line, or how impatient the men who had only minutes before the train whistle blew."

Eleanor was superb at other canteen jobs too. She cheerfully scoured pots, mopped floors, supervised other volunteers, and organized committees. She was also one of the few volunteers who had tamed the bread-cutting machine. But one busy morning, while running loaves through the steel demon, she sliced her finger to the bone. "Mrs. Roosevelt! Your hand!" cried one of the ladies. "There was no time to stop," recalled Eleanor, "so I wrapped something tightly around it and proceeded during the day to wrap more and more handkerchiefs around it, until it finally stopped bleeding." She didn't see a doctor until that evening, and she bore the scar the rest of her life.

Though Eleanor had volunteered out of a sense of duty, she discovered that helping the soldiers brought her a deep sense of satisfaction. Other volunteers simply handed them refreshments; Eleanor took the time to ask where they were from and where they were going, and she worried whether they had gotten enough to eat. So involved was she in canteening, that she worked almost nonstop. "It was not unusual for me to work from nine in the morning until one or two the next morning, and be back again by ten." Was she exhausted? Hardly. Eleanor found the experience exhilarating. "I was learning to have a certain confidence in myself and in my ability to meet emergencies and deal with them," she wrote.

The Red Cross had confidence in Eleanor, too. They wanted to send her to England to help set up canteens for the American servicemen there. "It is a fearful temptation," she wrote to Sara Roosevelt, "because I feel I have the strength and probably the capability for some kind of work and one can't help wanting to do the real thing instead of playing at it over here." Why didn't she go? Because, she later wrote, she didn't feel independent enough. Besides, she said, in "my heart of hearts I felt I needed to stay home with my children."

WOUNDED SOLDIERS RELAX AND RECOVER.

At war's end Eleanor's focus shifted from the canteen to the thousands of wounded American soldiers returning home. She made it a point to visit the naval hospital in Washington, D.C., once a week, taking flowers and chocolates, and saying a word of cheer. In the wards she saw many tragedies. "There was a woman who sat for days by the bed of her son who had been gassed," recalled Eleanor. "There was a chance he might be saved if he could get to the dry air out west. She could not afford to go with him, but we finally obtained permission to send a nurse." Besides visiting the hospital wards, she also invited recovering soldiers to her home. Noted Sara Roosevelt in the winter of 1918, "Eleanor had a Christmas tree and twelve soldiers from Mrs. Lane's Convalescent Home and twelve sailors from the Naval Hospital." This contact with the soldiers, Eleanor later claimed, taught her an important lesson: "I was beginning to feel pity for the human condition. I was beginning to ask what I could do."

ST. ELIZABETH'S HOSPITAL FOR THE INSANE, WHERE ELEANOR VISITED BOYS DIAGNOSED WITH SHELL SHOCK

Washington's military hospitals filled so quickly with wounded soldiers that those who were psychologically damaged were treated at St. Elizabeth's, a federally run hospital for the insane. Eleanor visited its naval unit and was appalled by what she saw. While the soldiers received excellent treatment—going outside every day, playing games, getting rest and exercise—there was not enough money, nurses, or equipment for the other patients. "I drove through the grounds," she recalled, "and was horrified to see poor demented creatures with apparently little attention being paid them, gazing from behind bars or walking up and down on enclosed porches." Eleanor felt she had to do something. As wife of the assistant secretary of the navy, she knew many influential people in Washington, D.C. One of them was Franklin Lane, secretary of the interior and overseer of the hospital. She asked him why the government could not improve conditions, and insisted

he see for himself. Lane declined her invitation but did appoint an investigating committee, whose report ultimately resulted in more funding for the hospital. With that money doctors were able to transform the place "into a model of its kind"—a source of pride for Eleanor.

"Out of these contacts with human beings during the war," she wrote, "I became a more tolerant person, far less sure of my own beliefs and methods of action, but more determined to try for certain ultimate objectives. I had gained some assurances about my ability to run things and the knowledge that there is joy in accomplishing a good job. I knew more about the human heart."

A Defining Moment

IN AUGUST 1919 thirty-four-year-old Eleanor traveled to Tivoli, New York, for her grandmother Mary Hall's funeral. As the coffin was lowered into the ground, she began to wonder about her grandmother's life. "If she had had some kind of life of her own, what would have been the result?" Eleanor asked herself. "When she was young, she painted rather well. Could she have developed that talent . . . had friends of her own . . . been her own woman? Would she have been happier?" Standing there, Eleanor suddenly realized that being only a wife and mother, like Mary Hall, was not enough. One should strive to do more—much more. "Life," she determined, "was meant to be lived. One must never turn his back on life."

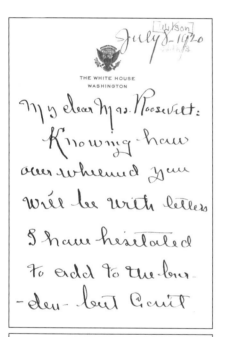

A letter from former first lady Edith Wilson wishing Eleanor success in Franklin's bid to become vice president of the United States

In 1920 the Democratic presidential candidate, James Cox, asked Franklin to run as his vice president. Franklin seized the opportunity. The election, of course, would thrust him—and Eleanor—onto the national stage. This was the first year in which women could vote in a national election, and a candidate's wife could have a huge effect on these brand-new voters. Her job? To stand at her husband's side with a rapt look as he made the same speech over and over again.

But as their campaign train traveled from New York to Colorado and back again, Eleanor grew frustrated. Her only use, she wrote to her mother-in-law, involved "yanking [Franklin's] coat tails" when his speeches went on too long. Still, her warmth and courtesy drew people to her. Franklin's campaign adviser, Louis Howe, soon saw that Eleanor could be a real asset. He brought drafts of speeches to discuss with her and was surprised by her intelligent, reasoned responses. He explained the politics of each town they traveled through, and encouraged her to relax around the press. By the end of the trip she had learned "volumes about national policy, political maneuvering, and speaking to the people." She was also amused when reporters made funny faces at her. "They tried, and occasionally succeeded, at breaking the look of total absorption I adopted for my husband's speeches." Though she still lacked self-confidence, she was growing aware of her abilities—her good judgment, her remarkable energy, her gift for organization. Others noticed these abilities too. Noted one voter to Franklin after he and Cox lost the election, "Eleanor is your real running mate."

Although Eleanor came to symbolize the independent and politically active woman of the twentieth century, her views early in life reflected those of most women of her time and class. In 1910, when Franklin was elected to the state senate, Eleanor "took it for granted that men were superior creatures and knew more about politics than women did." She said, "While I realized that if my husband was a suffragist [a supporter of women's right to vote] I probably must be, too, I cannot claim to have been a feminist in those early days." But as Franklin's political career expanded she learned how important it was for women to have a political voice. When women finally gained the right to vote, Eleanor admittted to having become a much more ardent citizen and feminist than anyone would have dreamed possible. "I had learned that if you want to institute any kind of reform you could get far more attention if you had a vote than if you lacked one."

Eleanor exercising her right to vote

The "Intensive Education of Eleanor Roosevelt"

After Franklin's loss in the election, Eleanor returned to New York City. But her experiences with the Red Cross, and her time in Washington, D.C., and on the campaign trail, made it impossible for her to return to the conventional pattern of life. Instead she made some drastic changes, searching for an expanded life.

> I did not look forward to a winter . . . in New York with nothing but teas and luncheons and dinners to take up my time . . . that seemed an impossible mode of living . . . so I mapped out a schedule for myself. I decided I would learn to cook and I found an ex-cook. . . . I went twice a week and cooked an entire meal which I left with her for her family to criticize. I also attended a business school, and took a course in typewriting and shorthand. . . . I joined organizations . . . made lasting friendships . . . and discovered standards of work and interests which played a great part in what might be called the "intensive education of Eleanor Roosevelt" during the next few years. . . . I had begun to realize that in my development I was drifting far afield from the old influences.

A National League of Women Voters poster urges women to use their political voice.

As part of her effort toward independence, Eleanor joined the National League of Women Voters. This organization—founded by veterans of the long battle for woman suffrage—educated women about voting and promoted women's active participation in politics. Eleanor first served on the league's legislative board in 1920, reporting to members on proposed new laws. Said Eleanor, "I doubted my ability . . . I felt humble and inadequate." Still, she tackled the project head-on, spending hundreds of hours studying the *Congressional Record*, investigating pending bills, and preparing reports. Her hard work paid off. Organization leaders soon recognized Eleanor's quick mind, dedication, and passion. One of these leaders, the famous suffragist Carrie Chapman Catt, became a lifelong friend. "I recognized in [Eleanor] a fellow crusader," Catt said.

When the league asked her to attend the 1921 annual convention as the delegate from New York, Eleanor hesitated, then agreed. "It was a

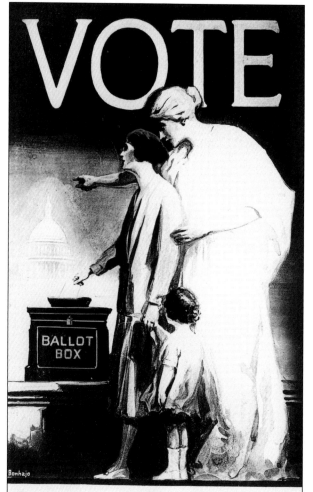

League of Women Voters

fine opportunity," she later admitted. "I gained immensely in self-confidence." In January 1922 she was elected to its board of directors and was asked to chair the committee to revise the organization's constitution. Again she hesitantly agreed, and again her self-confidence grew as a result of her successful work. By 1923 she felt comfortable enough to accept the position of vice president of the league's New York State chapter.

Through this work Eleanor met women who emotionally supported and educated her. She learned about the intricacies of public policy, advocacy, and politics. And she developed leadership abilities and important organizational skills—skills she relied on for the rest of her life. Although she resigned from her league office in 1924, she remained active in the organization all her life, speaking at events, publicizing league accomplishments, and championing it as the most important and reliable source of information on political issues.

Independence-seeking Eleanor took up driving—an uncommon activity for women of her social class, who usually took taxis or rode in chauffeur-driven cars—in 1920. She had tried to learn years earlier, but an incident involving a car bumper and a gatepost had put her off. Now, however, she longed to experience the freedom of driving. There were mishaps. "Your running into the ditch was all right," Sara wrote her in 1922, "so long as you were not hurt." Still, Eleanor drove herself to church, to luncheons, to speaking events. Once, to her family's dismay, she even drove herself on a camping trip to Canada and reported only three minor accidents. Admitted her son James, "Mother's driving was worse than anyone's." She scraped, bumped, and banged her way down the road until 1946, the year she fell asleep behind the wheel. Her car veered across the highway, slammed into another vehicle head-on, then sideswiped one more. The accident cost Eleanor her two front teeth.

MRS. ROOSEVELT'S CAR AFTER COLLISION

A close-up of the front of wrecked automobile of the widow of the late President after the three-car crash on the Sawmill River Parkway at Lockwood avenue, Yonkers. Mrs. Roosevelt was only slightly injured.

❧ Polio ❧

The waves were white capped and the sun was warm as Franklin's sailboat, the *Vireo*, skimmed across the water in August 1921. Onboard, the whole family—all five children and Eleanor—laughed when salt water sprayed over them, and Franklin laughed too. After his long, exhausting campaign for the vice presidency it was good to be at Campobello. He hoped the fresh air and exercise would make him feel better. For days he had complained of feeling logy and tired. Now, thinking it would do him good, he took a dip in the bay's icy water. But he did not get the glow he expected. By the time they arrived home, Franklin was too tired to change his clothes. Instead he sat around in his wet bathing suit, looking through his mail and feeling chilled. "It was getting near supper time," Eleanor recalled, "when Franklin started to go upstairs and said his back ached, and he didn't feel very well. And by the next morning he could hardly stand, and by the next day he could not stand at all."

Eleanor sent for the island doctor, who diagnosed Franklin's illness as a cold. But as he grew more ill and his temperature spiked higher, Eleanor became worried. Finally a friend suggested they canvass the nearby resorts in search of medical help. They found Dr. Keen, a famous diagnostician from Philadelphia. After examining Franklin, Dr. Keen determined that a blood clot had settled in his spine, and recommended daily massages. For the next two weeks Eleanor cared

for her husband day and night. She moved a cot into his room, bathed him, and massaged his legs. But nothing worked. Although Franklin's temperature had returned to normal, he could not move his legs. Fearing the worst, Eleanor called in yet another doctor, this time an orthopedic specialist from New York. His diagnosis? Polio, a contagious viral disease that is transmitted from person to person, affecting the nervous system and often resulting in paralysis. At the time there was no vaccine for polio and no effective cure. Franklin, the doctor said, would never walk again.

Franklin was moved to a hospital in New York—a painful trip from Campobello by boat, train, and ambulance. At the hospital he faced weeks of torturous therapy as doctors put his legs in casts and stretched his muscles, hoping to get him to walk. But his legs remained paralyzed. Eventually he returned to the Roosevelts' New York townhouse, bearing both the pain and his sense of helplessness "without discouragement or bitterness," recalled Eleanor.

Franklin's mother, however, dealt with Franklin's illness differently. "She had made up her mind that Franklin was going to be an invalid for the rest of his life," wrote Eleanor. She insisted "he retire to Hyde Park and live there."

But how could Eleanor possibly return to Hyde Park to live in Sara's shadow now that she was coming

Franklin, pictured with Eleanor on the beach at Campobello in 1921, before polio struck

into her own? No, if she wanted to live an independent life, Franklin would have to live one too.

The winter of 1921–22 became a contest of wills. For the first time thirty-seven-year-old Eleanor argued bitterly with her mother-in-law. She refused to listen when Sara insisted her mother's heart knew what was best for Franklin. Furious, Sara retaliated by dismissing Eleanor's opinions and trying to enlist the children to side with her. Eleanor became so angry that once she blocked the sliding doors connecting the twin townhouses with all the large pieces of furniture she could find. "In many ways this was the most trying winter of my life," she later wrote.

One afternoon while she was reading to Franklin Jr. and John, she suddenly burst into tears. "I could not think why I was sobbing, nor could I stop. Elliott came in from school, dashed in to look at me, and fled. Mr. Howe came in and tried to find out what the matter was, but he gave it up as a bad job. The two little boys went off to bed and I sat on the sofa in the sitting room and sobbed and sobbed. . . . Finally . . . I locked the door and poured cold water on a towel and mopped my face. Eventually I pulled myself together."

But this breakdown did not weaken her resolve. Deciding to free herself from her mother-in-law's domination once and for all, Eleanor called in Dr. George Draper, a polio specialist. All three Roosevelts—Franklin, Eleanor, and Sara—agreed they would abide by the doctor's decision.

Sara addressed the doctor the moment he arrived. "Dr. Draper, I'm sure you will agree with me that Franklin is an invalid. He should therefore be retired to a wheelchair."

Eleanor bit back her anger. "I know my husband well enough to feel that this would be the worst thing you could do to him. He is not an invalid. . . . Association with friends . . . and activity . . . will be the best thing in the world for him."

"I ought to know what is best for my son," snapped Sara.

"We must do what you think best, Dr. Draper," said Eleanor, "but . . . if he fights, he may overcome his handicap."

Dr. Draper considered both women's positions for a moment. Then he said to Eleanor, "You are right. He is not an invalid and there is no reason why he should be treated as one."

It was a glorious moment. The struggle with her mother-in-law was finally over—Eleanor had won. "She dominated me for years," Eleanor later wrote. But Franklin's illness had led to freedom from Sara's influence and, Eleanor said, "made me stand on my own two feet in regard to my husband's life, my own life, and my children's training." She believed that if she had given in to Sara, she would have become "a completely colorless echo of my husband and my mother-in-law and torn between them. I might have stayed a weak character forever."

ANGUISHED, ELEANOR WROTE THIS LETTER TO A RELATIVE AFTER THE DIAGNOSIS OF POLIO HAD BEEN MADE:

"I dread the time when I have to tell Franklin and it wrings my heart for it is all so much worse to a man than to a woman but the three doctors agree he will be eventually well if nothing unfavorable happens in the next ten days or so & at present all signs are favorable so we should be very thankful. Much love, Eleanor."

ELEANOR ON THE DOCK AT CAMPOBELLO WITH FRANKLIN JR. AND JOHN

After being stricken with polio, Franklin was frequently away seeking a cure for his paralyzed legs. His absence forced Eleanor to become both mother and father to the children. This was not so difficult to do with James and Elliott, who were already teenagers and away at boarding school. But Franklin Jr. was only seven, and John five. "They had to learn to do the things boys must do—swim, ride and camp," Eleanor wrote. "It began to dawn on me that if these two youngest boys were going to have a normal existence . . . I would have to become a good deal more companionable, and more of an all-round person than I had ever been before."

Eleanor enrolled in swimming lessons at the YWCA pool in New York so she could teach the boys to swim. She took them on camping trips. And in 1929, when Franklin Jr. was fifteen and John was thirteen, the three of them sailed off to Europe—no nanny, no husband, no mother-in-law. Eleanor soon discovered, however, that the boys were a handful. In France they became so quarrelsome she left them in the hotel while she toured a nearby church. On her return she heard screams and saw crowds in the street. "You will never believe it," she wrote their father. Franklin Jr. had pushed John out the window and was "holding him head down dangling by the heels."

The already troubled relationship between Eleanor and her teen-aged daughter was made worse by Franklin's illness. When the family returned from Campobello Island, Eleanor insisted Anna give up her room so Louis Howe, a political associate, could stay close to the ailing Franklin. "Granny [Sara Roosevelt] . . . started telling me that it was inexcusable that I, the only daughter of the family, should now have a tiny bedroom in the back," Anna later said. "I went to Mother . . . she was anything but sympathetic . . . in fact she was very stern." Anna stopped talking to her mother. And while Eleanor knew her attitude toward her daughter had been wrong, she didn't know how to apologize. The strain of the situation, recalled Eleanor, "got on my nerves . . . and I suddenly found myself sobbing . . . nor could I stop." When Anna saw her mother crying, her anger softened. Sitting beside her mother, Anna "poured out some of her troubles," said Eleanor, "and from that day on our mutual understanding improved."

But still there were problems. In 1924 Anna rebelled against making her debut in society. Although Eleanor

Eleanor wrestling with her daughter, Anna, in 1925

remembered vividly the nightmare of her own debut twenty-two years earlier, she insisted her daughter participate. It was a Roosevelt tradition she felt should not be broken. Anna submitted to the humiliation but refused to let her mother attend, so deep was her resentment.

A year later Anna told her parents that she had decided against attending college. While Franklin accepted the news calmly, Eleanor was aghast. No college? What would Anna do with her future? How would she ever find personal fulfillment? Without asking her daughter's permission, Eleanor enrolled her full-time in the school of agriculture at Cornell University. Maybe, thought Eleanor, she'd like to manage the family estate in Hyde Park someday. When Eleanor drove her to college, the furious Anna refused to say a word. She would not kiss her mother good-bye, and she didn't write home for the entire first semester. Months later she stunned both parents when she quit school altogether to marry Curtis Dall, a stockbroker ten years her senior. Explained Anna, "I got married when I did because I wanted to get out."

LOUIS HOWE

Eleanor's tutor in the art of politics

Louis Howe always claimed his face was "one of the four ugliest in the state." But ugly or not, he had possibly the shrewdest political mind in America. And he used it to catapult Franklin into the White House. Louis first met the Roosevelts in 1911, when Franklin was a state senator and Louis a newspaper reporter. The two men hit it off, and when Franklin became assistant secretary to the navy, he asked Louis to become his personal assistant. To Eleanor's dismay, Louis agreed. She could barely stand being in the same room as that "odd, disheveled, chain-smoking gnome." How would she tolerate his daily presence? But over the next ten years Eleanor began to recognize Louis's "extraordinary eyes and . . . fine mind." In 1921, after Franklin's polio attack, "Louis was . . . convinced that Franklin's political career must be continued," recalled Eleanor, "and he decided I should work with the Democratic Party as a whole and keep contacts alive for Franklin."

Nervously Eleanor agreed, and the two became partners in Franklin's career. Acting as her adviser, Louis encouraged her to join the National League of Women Voters and other political organizations. He convinced her to write and edit political tracts that put forth Franklin's views on government policy. And he directed her to invite important people in state politics to the house so Franklin could meet them.

In 1921 the still-shy Eleanor gave her first speech at a Democratic fund-raiser. Terrified, she couldn't control her high voice, which fluttered up and down. She giggled nervously at the wrong times, making an unattractive and disconcerting snorting sound. And she kept wandering from the main point of the speech. Louis, who had stationed himself in the back of the room, pointed out these mistakes afterward. "Why do you laugh when you're making a serious speech?" he asked. "Have something to say, say it, and sit down."

Louis came to admire Eleanor's convictions. He encouraged her to believe in her own ideas and to work for social advocacy. When Franklin was elected president in 1932, Louis moved to the White House with him. Taking up residence in the Lincoln Bedroom, he inspired Eleanor to take an active role as first lady, suggesting she hold her own press conferences and "create [her own] persona." He became so convinced of her political abilities that one day he stepped into her White House sitting room, propped himself cross-legged on her daybed, and said, "Eleanor, if you want to be president in 1940, tell me now so I can start getting things ready." Eleanor's reply? "One politician in the family is enough."

When Louis died in April 1936, both Roosevelts lost more than a friend. Said Eleanor's son Elliott, "[Louis] gave Mother not only a tremendous amount of practical advice, but also the courage and the confidence to become an influential person in her own right." Eleanor named Louis Howe—along with her mother and father; Marie Souvestre, the headmistress of the boarding school she attended; her aunt Pussie Hall; Sara Roosevelt; and Franklin—as one of the seven individuals who had "most influenced [her] life."

Out of the Kitchen and into Politics

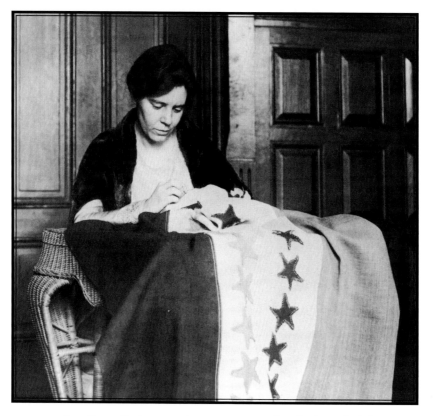

Alice Paul sewing a star on her flag. Each star represents a state that had ratified the Nineteenth Amendment.

When Eleanor entered politics, it was a man's game. Having won the right to vote, "women," declared Eleanor, "have the power, but they don't know what to do with it."

The solution?

A woman needed to learn the machinery of politics, said Eleanor. Then she would know how "to checkmate her masculine opponent. Or it may be that with time she will learn to make an ally of her opponent, which is even better politics."

This was women's political goal throughout the 1920s—to be taken seriously by men, to share in the selection of candidates, and to have an equal say in the shaping of national policies. "We want," wrote Eleanor, "to gain for ourselves a place of real equality, and the respect of men. . . . This means *with* the men, not for them."

To this end, women all over the country began organizing. They were, for the most part, a circle of reform-minded, politically savvy women—teachers, lawyers, union organizers, social activists—who held strong convictions and progressive goals. They lobbied for a fair minimum wage, funds for women's and children's health clinics, the end to child labor, and the right of women to form trade unions, among other things. And they believed they brought a special, social conscience to the smoke-filled world of male politics. Among the numerous groups they founded were:

The National Woman's Party

Founded in 1916 by Alice Paul, it called for a federal amendment to the Constitution that would give women the right to vote. When that vote was won in 1920, Paul reorganized the NWP. Three years later the group proposed an Equal Rights Amendment to the U.S. Constitution. Known as the ERA, this piece of legislation would, claimed Paul, ensure equal rights for women in all aspects of their lives—socially, politically, economically. Paul's group—the most militant of the women's organizations—often picketed the White House, held sit-ins, and waged hunger strikes. Although the NWP had fewer than ten thousand members, its energy and persistence kept the issue of an Equal Rights Amendment alive for decades. Not until 1982—fifty-nine years after it was first proposed—did the ERA finally go down in defeat after the required thirty-eight states failed to ratify it. As for the National Woman's Party, it was disbanded in 1976, just one year before Alice Paul's death.

The National League of Women Voters

Started in 1920 by Carrie Chapman Catt, one of the leaders in the campaign for the recently ratified Nineteenth Amendment (which gave women the right to vote), the group sought to educate women about the political process. It sponsored lectures explaining the importance and purpose of elections and handed out literature describing candidates' stands on issues, hoping women's votes would become an important force in national politics. The league is still active today.

Carrie Chapman Catt

The Women's Division of the Democratic National Committee

Within the Democratic Party itself, women were fighting for a political voice. Under the leadership of Molly Dewson, this group was formed in 1923. Its purpose? To establish women's importance within the Democratic Party and to press for issues important to Democratic women—a forty-hour workweek for women, the end to child labor, the right of women to organize trade unions. Toward this end they organized a powerful network of woman voters across the country. Candidates soon began courting these votes by promoting women's issues and appointing women to major policy-making positions.

The Women's Bureau

Formed in 1920 as part of the U.S. Department of Labor, it was led by Mary Anderson, who believed women's votes could bring about important social changes. In an effort to keep women informed, the bureau issued bulletins publicizing the conditions faced by female factory workers. It also recommended safety standards and advocated better wages, hours, and working conditions. Anderson's emphasis on women's work issues resulted in important changes. In 1938 women were included in the Fair Labor Standards Act, which set minimum wages and working hours—the first time in American history that women were covered under a federal labor law.

The efforts of these groups and others resulted in huge strides toward political equality. In just ten years every state had a women's legislative council that monitored the progress of woman-supported bills under consideration by state legislatures, and at the federal level women's groups lobbied Congress. With this new political clout came new opportunities, and suddenly women found themselves being elected to courts and legislatures. They were appointed to head government agencies and political committees. In short, wrote Eleanor, "the ladies have become a force to reckon with."

New Friends

Eleanor's work at the National League of Women Voters brought her in contact with women whose values and behavior were different from anything she had ever known—accomplished women who did things outside the home, independent women who lived together and were well satisfied with their lives. Two were Elizabeth Read, a lawyer, and Esther Lape, a college professor and writer. The first time Eleanor met them, she "felt humble and inadequate." Still, she said, "I liked [them] at once and . . . our relationship became lasting and warm."

Although her close friendship with this same-sex couple inevitably led to gossip—her cousin Alice Roosevelt once remarked loudly in a fashionable Washington restaurant, "I don't care *what* you say, I simply cannot believe Eleanor Roosevelt is a lesbian"—Eleanor didn't care. She was entranced by the stimulating lives her new friends led. In their book-lined house they discussed politics and public policy with Eleanor during candlelit dinners and read French poetry after dessert. And Eleanor found the strength and encouragement to do things on her own and explore her own talents. "They played a substantial role in my education,"

she later admitted. With their support she began speaking out on behalf of political reform, workers' rights, and children's issues.

How did Franklin feel about his wife's relationship with this lesbian couple? While he joked about her "squaws" and "she-men," he realized that under Esther and Elizabeth's influence Eleanor was becoming an excellent politician—good for his own career.

Eleanor's relationship with the two women also opened her up emotionally. Over the years the women developed a warm and playful intimacy. They kissed and hugged one another when they met. They had pillow fights on the nights Eleanor stayed over at their home. And they wrote one another long, loving letters when apart. (Sadly, none of these letters still exist. One evening after Eleanor's death Esther sat beside her fireplace and burned all their correspondence.) In later years Eleanor even kept an apartment in Elizabeth and Esther's home, using it as an escape from her hectic life at the White House. After Elizabeth's death in 1943 Eleanor planted tulip bulbs on her grave for the following spring and made it a point to visit Esther often. The two remained close until Eleanor's death.

Esther Lape (left) and Elizabeth Read (right),
two women who played an important role in Eleanor's political awakening

Eleanor with her two close friends Marion Dickerman (far left) and Nancy Cook (second from right). They are shown with Marion's sister Peggy Levenson.

Eleanor met vivacious Nancy Cook in 1922 after speaking at a fund-raising luncheon for the New York State Democratic Committee. Nancy, who was director of the organization, was so impressed by Eleanor's talk she asked her to chair the division's finance committee. Eleanor agreed, and the two quickly became close friends.

Soon Nancy introduced Eleanor to her longtime partner, Marion Dickerman, a teacher at the Todhunter School, an exclusive girls' school in Manhattan. What resulted was an extraordinary triple friendship that thrived throughout the 1920s and well into the 1930s. The three women did everything together, from attending political meetings to going on camping trips. It was, said Marion, "a warm, wonderful relationship."

Problem was, whenever Eleanor invited these friends to Hyde Park, Sara Roosevelt seethed. She refused to be polite to this same-sex couple, considering their relationship unnatural and immoral. Her open hostility made Nancy and Marion uncomfortable. It infuriated Eleanor.

Franklin, on the other hand, liked the women, and because they were so deeply involved in state politics and held so much sway with woman voters, he always listened closely to their ideas. "They are," he once told his political adviser, Louis Howe, "the sort of persons a politician should know."

One weekend in 1924 Franklin, Eleanor, Nancy, and Marion were picnicking on the grassy bank of the Fall Kill, the Creek near their Hyde Park estate, when Franklin said, "Why don't you girls build a cottage for yourselves? . . . If you mark out the land, I will give you a life interest."

The three women eagerly agreed. They chose a favorite family picnic spot on the bank of the Fall Kill for the house site and allowed Franklin to design a beautiful fieldstone cottage inspired by his love of Dutch architecture. Construction moved quickly, and by New Year's Day, 1926, the three ate their first meal in Stone Cottage, sitting on nail kegs and using a crate as a table.

"The peace of it is divine," Eleanor told Franklin the following summer. From then on, though she stayed at the big house whenever Franklin and the children were in Hyde Park, Stone Cottage became Eleanor's true home. "Can't you tell me why Eleanor wants to go to [that] cottage to sleep every night?" Sara asked Franklin. "Can't she sleep here? This is her home. This is where she belongs."

But Eleanor knew she belonged with Nancy and Marion. Calling their place their "honeymoon cottage" or "the love nest," the women shared everything—bathing suits, lipstick, closet space. They even had their joint initials—EMN—stitched on all the towels and bed linens.

The three friends shared other interests too. In 1925 they founded the newsletter *Women's Democratic News*. In 1926 they bought the Todhunter School together and began teaching there. And in 1927 they opened a furniture factory at Val-Kill a short distance from Stone Cottage. But for all their mutual interests, their intense friendship did not last. During an all-night conversation in 1938 Eleanor and Nancy had an argument. (Marion was in Europe at the time.) Both became emotional and said "things that should not have been said," Nancy later admitted. What did the women say? Only they know. But the conversation hurt Eleanor so profoundly she never again visited Stone Cottage. The three women's friendship was over.

IN 1922 Eleanor joined the WTUL, a radical group whose purpose was to bring the working women of New York's factories together in hopes of gaining an eight-hour workday, increasing wages, and ending child labor. She threw herself into trade union work. Believing working-class women needed "roses as well as bread," she gave weekly readings from American literature at the league's headquarters on Lexington Avenue. She taught a current-events class every Saturday morning. And from 1925 to 1946 she hosted a Christmas party for members' children. Since most league members were working women with little money, this party was especially welcome. Eleanor bought all the gifts—roller skates, dolls, clothing—handed out cake and ice cream, and led the children in singing Christmas carols. She threw parties for the children's mothers, too. In 1929 two hundred women members sailed up the Hudson River from New York City to spend the day at Hyde Park with Franklin (then governor of New York) and Eleanor. "Never before," noted the *New York Times*, "had a governor feted members of a labor organization in such a setting." Seven years later (when Franklin was president) Eleanor invited delegates to the WTUL convention in Washington, D.C., to stay at the White House. Some league members called Eleanor their "fairy godmember." Others were amazed by her continued support of "the regular gals." But Eleanor believed her ties to the league had a "symbolic, even democratic meaning." After all, if the wife of the governor of New York, and later of the president of the United States, thought the plight of working women was important, shouldn't everybody? Eleanor stayed close to the organization until it disbanded in 1955.

Eleanor's Top Ten Ways to Become a Political Figure

By the time Franklin returned to politics in 1924, the name Roosevelt was recognized all across New York. But which Roosevelt? Eleanor's honesty, vigor, and sincerity had made her as much of a political figure as her husband. How did she do it? Below is just a fraction of the jobs Eleanor tackled on behalf of Franklin, and ultimately herself.

1. Edited *Women's Democratic News*, a political newsletter for women.

2. Worked long hours at the New York State Democratic headquarters doing whatever needed to be done, from licking stamps to raising funds.

3. Visited every county in New York (114 in all!), organizing women's groups and campaigning for women's opportunities in the Democratic Party.

4. Devised a campaign car, complete with a red-white-and-blue banner and a megaphone, for John W. Davis, the 1924 Democratic presidential candidate, then drove it across New York.

5. Drove voters to and from the polls in the family Buick during the 1924 and 1928 elections.

6. Spoke at hundreds of luncheons, picnics, teas, and dinners.

7. Wrote dozens of magazine articles and newspaper editorials.

8. Handed out campaign literature.

9. Raised more than $50,000 (the equivalent of $500,000 in 2003) throughout the 1920s for the Women's Division of the New York State Democratic Committee by soliciting contributions from prominent Democrats and speaking at fund-raising events. The money went toward getting out the women's vote.

10. Brought hundreds of people to meet Franklin—key party officials and public personalities, as well as lesser-known folks whose points of view should have interested him.

Franklin during a deep-sea fishing trip aboard his houseboat, the LAROOCO, *in 1923*

Between 1922 and 1924 Franklin spent most of his time fishing, relaxing, and recuperating in the warm waters off the coast of Florida. Believing exercise combined with fun would improve his condition, he bought a houseboat, invited dozens of guests on board, and set sail for good times. It was, he wrote his mother in March 1923, "a somewhat negligee existence. All wander around in pajamas, nighties and bathing suits!"

It was exactly the kind of environment Eleanor detested—rife with dirty jokes, half-naked guests, free-flowing cocktails. She didn't even like the climate. When they were anchored on the boat at night, she felt unprotected: "It all seemed eerie and menacing to me." Worse, her claustrophobia made it impossible for her to sleep belowdecks. Instead she slept up top, where, she said, "Florida's mosquitoes all converged on me. . . . I always wound up with enough bites to look like an advanced case of smallpox."

For these reasons Eleanor rarely joined Franklin in Florida. While he sailed through tropical breezes, she remained in New York, giving speeches, writing articles, reading at the Women's Trade Union League in the evenings, and gaining a political name for both herself and her husband.

Soothing a Husband's Ego

Although Franklin valued his wife's budding political abilities, he never happily surrendered the limelight. "Eleanor has been leading an even more hectic life than usual," he wrote a friend. "Bok Peace Award, investigation by the Senate, Democratic females, in Philadelphia, etc. etc. Perhaps I should go on vacation. Then she will be more quiet, as she will have to stay home with the children more!" Recognizing her husband's discomfort, Eleanor wrote him this reassuring letter on February 6, 1924:

"I'm only active till you can be again—it isn't such a great desire on my part to serve the world and I'll fall back into habits of sloth quite easily! Hurry up for as you know my ever present sense of uselessness of all things will overwhelm me sooner or later."

The New York State Democratic Committee began publishing a monthly newsletter in 1925. As a member, Eleanor took an active part in all phases of the newsletter's operation. She sold advertising and wrote editorials. She learned the tricks of layout and headline writing. And she brimmed with ideas for enlightening articles, informative features, and creative columns. The sixteen-page monthly included lengthy explanations of political issues and serious profiles on prominent women in government. In order to make the high-minded publication more palatable to its readers, Eleanor suggested adding drama and movie reviews. She also urged inclusion of a tongue-in-cheek feature called "Not in the Headlines," which told stories of male bias against women in politics.

For the next three years Eleanor worked at making the newsletter a wellspring of political education for women. But after Franklin was elected governor of New York in 1928, she resigned "because I promised long ago to quit opining on any subject bordering on politics" if Franklin returned to office. Still, she continued to write and edit articles anonymously, and after moving to the White House in 1933, she began producing a monthly column. Written in the form of a personal letter, "Passing Thoughts of Mrs. Franklin D. Roosevelt" appeared in *Women's Democratic News* until the paper ceased publication in 1935.

---

6   **WOMEN'S DEMOCRATIC NEWS**

NEW YORK STATE

Women's Democratic News, Inc.

15 East 40th St., New York City
Tel. Murray Hill 3655

PUBLISHERS

Mrs. Daniel O'Day, *President*
Mrs. Henry Morganthau, Jr., *Vice-Pres.*
Miss Nancy Cook, *Business Manager*
Mrs. Franklin D. Roosevelt, *Editor and Treasurer*
Miss Marion Dickerman, *Secretary*

Vol. 3 Old Style.   Vol. 1 New Style.

DECEMBER, 1925.   No. 8

"PEACE ON EARTH, GOOD WILL TO MEN"

Nearly two thousand years ago that message was rung out at midnight to a hushed and sleeping world, a world of war and strife, then as now.

Was that message lost to mankind? Has it been forgotten?

Perhaps the darkest days the world has ever known were those of the great war when to many it seemed not only that our civilization was on trial, but that Christianity itself was being tried.

At this Christmas tide, we find the hearts of men and of nations charged with the deathless teachings of the Nazarene and in the place of hatred and war, there is the Will to Peace.

The treaties of Locarno prove that this Will to Peace is not merely a hope born of the despair of prostate, war-torn countries but is a vital surging force so strong that it can not be gainsaid. After four years of bitter struggle and seven years of agonized adjustments, we find Europe setting his house in order and the warring nations holding out to each other friendly hands in the realization that there is a long period of rebuilding before the war-weary world; and that only by the will to concede, to conciliate and to understand, can the right sort of rebuilding be achieved. This spirit, it was, that inspired the Conference held in the little Swiss village, and at that Conference was born the blessed promise of Peace that glows through the world today.

In the world's rebuilding, Labor will have a great part, and here too, in spite of temporary conflicts there is the Will to Peace.

Labor finds itself emerging triumphantly from its old struggle for recognition and is demanding its share in the control of industry. By many signs we read that this is coming about through peaceful methods of conference between employer and employees, between Capital and Labor, two forces that together can make this world what they will.

In the League of Nations, the signers of the Locarno Pact find the machinery through which their high resolve can be accomplished. There is the Council of the League, and the Permanent Court of International Justice, both successfully functioning, and to these the nations can appeal for a settlement of questions that effect the peace of the world.

A conference on disarmament is to be called by the League. We, alas, together with Turkey, Russia and Mexico, will stand apart but sooner or later we must make the decision as to whether or not we will march with the fifty-five nations of the world that have already set out on the long road toward a lasting peace.

Clearer and clearer becomes the vision that was vouchsafed to Woodrow Wilson at a time when the nations of the world were blinded by hatred and fear. The eyes of the world are now unsealed and we are ready to follow the call of that leader of Democracy who first felt within his great heart the Will to Peace that prevails over all the earth this Christmas tide.

More and more it strikes us that we, in this country, who believe so firmly in education for our young people to fit them for every conceivable walk in life, are strangely inconsistent in not believing in the same methods to fit them for citizenship and bring them into the political parties. Mr. Davis in an article said, "One of the greatest dangers to this country is the fact that the passenger list is overloaded. There are too many on board who do not try to pull their own weight in the boat. Not all, of course, can wear officers' stripes, but it must be a dull conscience that can be content without making some effort to do one's share of the common work. Much of the work of political organization, like work in other lines, is drudgery, but is none the less useful and important because of that fact. And, of course, with the realization of personal responsibility there comes a desire for personal information and an eagerness to assist in the education of others." Now in other things young people are constitutionally opposed to being passengers. Why this apathy about their Government. To us the answer is that they have never been educated to feel their individual responsibility. It is the duty of the Democratic Party to actively try to instruct the young people before they are of age to vote. In this way they will at least know why they are Democrats!

Election day is past. We Democrats have cause to be proud. The Governor made a wonderful campaign for the passage of the Constitutional Amendments and against heavy odds he again indicated his faith in Democracy and in the ability of the people to do the right thing when it is clearly put before them. Every amendment carried and it now remains for the Legislature this coming winter to pass laws which will put into effect the will of the people of the State. In New York City, the Hon. James J. Walker and the entire Democratic ticket had an overwhelming victory. A few Assemblymen were gained but the Assembly is still controlled by the Republicans. In a future number we will give in detail the vote on the amendments, Assemblymen, Mayors and County Supervisors throughout the State but from the figures we have been able to obtain it would seem safe to say that the party was gaining slowly but surely even in the great Republican strongholds up State.

In this issue we announce the winner in our Bermuda Club contest. The editors wish to congratulate her on her energy and enthusiasm and hope that she will have a most delightful trip to Bermuda. To those who were not this time successful, however, we wish to say that we are grateful to them for the help which they have given us in building up the work of organizing our women throughout the State. A new contest starts NOW to end July 1st, 1926, and may one of the present losers be a future victor!

Mrs. Marion Wime, of Bernard's Bay, Oswego Dist. No. 3, sent in her name too late to appear in last month's "Roll of Honor," but she volunteered to give "all the time I can" and we hope she was able to give much.

The Women's Democratic Club of the City of New York, Mrs. John Enos Quinn, President, held an extremely interesting "School of Political Education" recently at the Hotel Commodore. We wish that their example might be followed in many other places, for so much enthusiasm and interest can and does grow from such schools.

Give Yourself A Christmas Present of A Year's Subscription to the News.

In 1928 Franklin won the election for governor of New York. When asked by a reporter if she was excited by the outcome, forty-four-year-old Eleanor replied almost ungraciously, "No, I am not excited about my husband's election. I don't care. What difference can it make to me?" Years later Eleanor wondered if she had "really wanted Franklin to run," saying, "I imagine I accepted his . . . election as I had accepted most things that had happened in life thus far; one did whatever seemed necessary and adjusted one's personal life to the developments in other people's lives." Her first adjustment was to withdraw from political life. She understood that the voters expected her to assume the traditional role of governor's wife—hosting teas, lending her name to charities, standing quietly at her husband's side. Sadly she resigned from her political posts in the Democratic Party. She stopped making speeches and refused to accept any invitations that "savored of politics."

On the surface it looked as if Eleanor had retreated into the shadows while her husband ran the state without her. But politics was in her blood. It had become a source of personal accomplishment and satisfaction. So Eleanor found less-public ways of being active. She continued writing political articles and editorials, but now she wrote them anonymously. And she stayed in touch with other political women across the state.

Franklin soon encouraged Eleanor to begin attending political meetings again: "Sending Eleanor," he confessed to a staff member, "is almost as good as going myself." Eleanor was acting as his stand-in yet again, but she didn't mind. She faced the tediousness of these events good-naturedly and with a sense of humor. "Arrived at 12:30, stood and shook hands till 1:30, ate till 3:30, talked till 5:20; home here at 6:40 nearly dead!" she wrote Franklin.

"I TEACH BECAUSE I LOVE IT," Eleanor said shortly after her husband, Franklin, was elected governor. "I cannot give it up." At Todhunter, the school she partially owned, Eleanor taught courses in drama, literature, and American history. In her history class she emphasized "the connection between things of the past and things of today" and used the "project method" in homework assignments. Once while teaching the Declaration of Independence, she told the girls, "Read any life [of a signer] you like. Get any pictures you can. Visit the museum . . . write about their present day descendants . . . make a book with pictures." Later she taught a unique current-events class called "Happenings," in which she took her students (most of them from wealthy, socially prominent families) to courts, police lineups, markets, and tenement houses. She wanted the girls to see firsthand how the city was run. "It was an exciting class," declared one student, "and Mrs. Roosevelt was an exciting teacher."

Once Franklin was governor, Eleanor taught only three days a week instead of five, commuting by train from the state capital of Albany to New York City every Sunday evening and returning on Wednesday afternoon to resume her duties as the governor's wife. On the train she diligently graded papers and wrote lesson plans. She liked teaching, she said, "better than anything else I do." But in 1933 Eleanor resigned her teaching position after Franklin was elected president. "One cannot be both a teacher and the first lady," she observed. Still, as part owner, she remained close to the school, attending graduation ceremonies, speaking during its special lecture series, and hosting an annual weekend of senior students to the White House until the school's merger with the Dalton School in New York City in 1939.

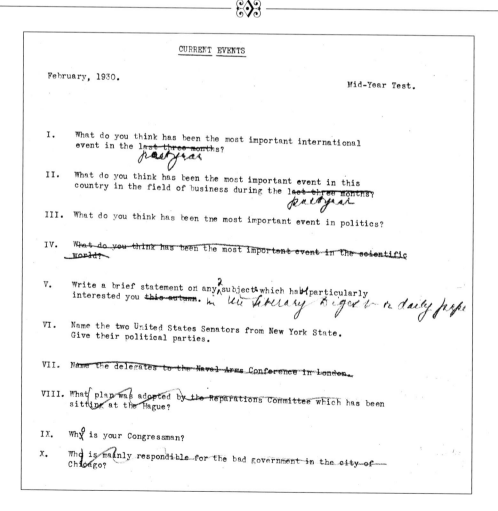

A first draft of a test prepared by Eleanor for her current-events class at the Todhunter School

Eleanor with her friend and bodyguard, Earl Miller, in 1929

A Real Romance?

He was a former stuntman, circus acrobat, amateur boxing champion, and New York state trooper. But it wasn't until 1928 that Earl Miller got the job of his life—bodyguard to the governor's wife, Eleanor Roosevelt. His fellow troopers teased him. "Imagine," they laughed, "being assigned to that old crab." But Eleanor's warmth soon won Earl over.

When he noticed her shyness around cameras, he tried to help her overcome it by standing behind the photographer and making silly faces until she relaxed and laughed. He helped her perfect her dive, taught her to play pool, and showed her how to shoot a gun. He even monitored her checkbook in an attempt to protect her from con men and cheats. She "was never one to check the truth of those begging for her help," Earl once lamented.

Even after Eleanor left the governor's mansion, Earl continued to be her champion and defender. They agreed on most political issues and shared many interests. They took long walks in the snow-covered woods together and read poetry aloud to each other. She fussed over his house and adored buying him gifts. In 1940, while Eleanor was first lady, the two vacationed in Florida together. And after Franklin's death in 1945 they saw each other often. Their time together was tranquil and satisfying. And Eleanor obviously looked forward to it. One evening in 1952 a friend arrived at Eleanor's apartment unannounced. She rang the bell and heard Eleanor hurry to the door. Dressed beautifully, Eleanor flung open the door with excitement. But her big, warm smile quickly vanished. "Oh," she said. "I was expecting Earl, but do come in."

All this togetherness caused tongues to wag. But the gossip didn't bother Eleanor. When rumors of an affair were published in a nationally syndicated newspaper column, Earl got "into a real lather," remembered Eleanor's secretary, "but it didn't bother [Mrs. Roosevelt]." People, however, continued to speculate about the true nature of their relationship. Even the oldest Roosevelt son, James, believed Earl was his mother's "one real romance." Earl and Eleanor remained close until her death in 1962.

Restlessness...
Hopelessness...
Despair

During Franklin's first term as governor, the United States economy went from boom to bust almost overnight. In October 1929 the stock market crashed, plunging the entire nation into an economic tailspin. Although only a small percentage of Americans had invested in the stock market, the impact of plummeting stock prices was quickly felt across the country. Many banks—hard-hit when stock investors were unable to pay back their loans—closed their doors. The life savings of millions of Americans were wiped out. Businesses began failing at an alarming rate—more than fifty thousand between 1929 and 1932. And as businesses failed, people lost their jobs. Nearly one quarter of all Americans suddenly found themselves unemployed. Stores closed; factories and mines stood idle; railroad cars sat silent and empty; and millions of workers roamed the cities looking for jobs. In Chicago approximately half of the city's workforce was unemployed, while 80 percent of the workers in Toledo, Ohio, were searching for jobs. Observed the poet Langston Hughes, "Everybody in America was looking for work."

Without jobs, people struggled to provide for themselves and their families. Unable to pay for food, hungry Americans stood in long lines at charity soup kitchens and foraged in garbage cans. Unable to pay for housing, some homeless Americans built makeshift shelters out of scrap iron, packing boxes, and other thrown-away items. Others piled their belongings into their car and headed west, searching for a better life. They didn't find it. Everyone everywhere was suffering. Despair had crept over the country. Said one unemployed schoolteacher, "If, with the advantages

THE FACE OF AN AMERICAN FAMILY
STRICKEN BY THE DEPRESSION

I've had, I can't make a living, I'm just no good, I guess. I've given up ever amounting to anything. It's just no use."

While other governors in other states still clung to the belief that private charities could meet relief needs, New York's Governor Roosevelt created the Temporary Emergency Relief Administration. It provided state-funded jobs for the unemployed, granted loans to faltering businesses, and gave pensions to the elderly. "The country needs, and unless I am mistaken, the country demands bold, persistent experimentation," declared

Franklin. "If it fails, admit it frankly and try another. But above all, try something."

Eleanor, too, believed in a caring government that acted to help the needy and unemployed. "Our desire," she later wrote, "was to achieve through political action real gains for the people. The citizens, we believed, were depending on us."

Because of his bold, progressive policies Franklin was reelected governor in 1930 by the biggest margin ever recorded in New York. His smashing victory thrust him into the national spotlight. "Almost overnight," wrote the historian Fillmore H. Sandford, "millions of desperate Americans saw FDR as the one great hope in the midst of their despair. They perceived him as a warm and understanding man, a man with great power and status, a man with competence who was, above all, a champion of the little man."

Franklin and his political supporters were elated by all the attention. "I do not see how Mr. Roosevelt can escape becoming the next presidential nominee of [the Democratic] party," said Franklin's campaign manager just a few days after the gubernatorial election. "And once his nomination has been secured, the [Depression] is sure to carry him straight into the White House."

UNABLE TO AFFORD FOOD, THOUSANDS OF PEOPLE LINED UP DAILY IN NEW YORK CITY AND WAITED TO BE FED. BREADLINES LIKE THIS ONE BECAME A COMMON SIGHT IN TOWNS AND CITIES ALL ACROSS THE COUNTRY.

IN THE FALL OF 1930 MORE THAN SIX THOUSAND UNEMPLOYED WORKERS SOLD APPLES FOR FIVE CENTS APIECE TO EARN MONEY TO LIVE.

POLICY MAKER

Under Eleanor's tutelage Franklin had become more enlightened about women's rights, but Eleanor knew he basically considered politics a man's business. Still, she managed to shape the character of Franklin's administration without ruffling any male feathers, as the following letter written to Franklin in 1929 shows. Franklin, by the way, took her advice.

"I hope you will consider making Frances Perkins Labor Commissioner. She'd do well, and you could fill her place as Chairman of the Industrial Commission by one of the men now on the Commission and put Nell Schwartz (now Bureau of Women in Industry) on the commission so there would be one woman on it. These are, of course, suggestions which I'm passing on, not my opinions for I don't mean to butt in."

The Importance of Eleanor

After Franklin was reelected governor in 1930, Democrats all over the country began considering him as their next presidential candidate. Franklin "had it all," said Jim Farley, chairman of the New York State Democratic Party. "He was handsome, charismatic and had the ability to get his message across to the average American. . . . Most of all, however, he had Mrs. Roosevelt." How important was Eleanor to Franklin's presidential aspirations? Farley explained it this way:

She was prepared to put her full strength—which was considerable—into the battle for his presidential nomination. . . . Everyone [in state politics] recognized her as a strong and influential public figure in her own right. We also knew women figured importantly in our campaign plans, and according to our calculations, in counties where the women Mrs. Roosevelt had organized were at work, the total party vote picked up 20 to 30 percent. . . . We felt the same type of job could be done on a national scale. . . . If so, that made Mrs. Roosevelt the governor's most important political asset.

Franklin did not tell me when he decided to run for the Presidency," wrote Eleanor. Instead she learned of his decision from his campaign manager, Louis Howe. He explained to her that it was a good time to run because the Depression was growing worse by the day and most voters blamed President Herbert Hoover, a Republican. Feeling was running so high against Republicanism in 1932 that Franklin felt almost any Democrat could win the presidential election. FDR liked those odds.

Franklin also liked the idea of helping the nation. His sense of stewardship, his democratic feelings, and his personal experience with suffering had given him great empathy for the American people. He sincerely wanted, wrote Eleanor, "to help make life better for the average man, woman and child."

But while Eleanor understood Franklin's desire to make life happier for people, she was not pleased with his decision. "I did not want my husband to be president," she wrote, "but I never mentioned my feelings to him." Instead she was quietly and "deeply troubled." She said, "As I saw it, this meant the end of any personal life of my own. I knew what traditionally should lie before me. I had watched [my aunt] Mrs. Theodore Roosevelt and had seen what it meant to be the wife of a president, and I cannot say that I was pleased at the prospect. . . . The turmoil in my heart and mind was rather great . . . and the next few months were not to make any clearer what the road ahead would be."

Eleanor (in print dress) on the presidential campaign trail with (in front row, from left to right) daughter, Anna; Jim Farley; Franklin; and son James

The front page of the *New York Times*, November 9, 1932, proclaims the news—

FRANKLIN IS ELECTED PRESIDENT OF THE UNITED STATES.

Forty-eight-year-old Eleanor should have been exuberant. For months she had deeply involved herself in Franklin's campaign. She had written newspaper and magazine articles, spoken to women's groups across the country, and traveled with Franklin on his campaign train. Now all her hard work had paid off. Franklin had become the thirty-second president of the United States. But his victory plunged Eleanor into a deep depression. "I never wanted it," she admitted to her friend Lorena Hickok. "I never wanted to be a President's wife, and I don't want it now." She was sure she was going to be a prisoner in the White House with nothing to do except stand in the line and receive visitors and preside over official dinners. Horrified by this thought, she offered to answer Franklin's mail, handle his calendar, and travel the country on his behalf. He looked at her "quizzically," then turned her down. He already had a secretary, he explained. "I knew he was right, and that it would not work," Eleanor wrote, "but it was a last effort to keep in close touch and to feel that I had a real job to do." Now, she realized, she would "have to work out [her] own salvation."

A First Lady
Like No Other

❦

There isn't going to be any First Lady. There is just going to be plain, ordinary Mrs. Roosevelt. —Eleanor Roosevelt to reporters, 1932

═══ It Happened on the Way to the Capitol ═══

Eleanor rode with the former first lady, Lou Hoover, to Franklin's inauguration on Capitol Hill. What would Mrs. Hoover miss, Eleanor asked. Not being taken care of, Mrs. Hoover replied, not having train reservations made for her, not having her wishes anticipated and attended to. Her answer made Eleanor think. Right there, right on Pennsylvania Avenue, she made this decision:

I silently vowed never to permit myself to become so dependent.

Franklin takes the oath of office as Eleanor (far left) watches.

March 4, 1933—inauguration day—dawned damp and dreary. On the dais in front of the Capitol Building a cold wind blew and Eleanor shivered. Her velvet gown and coat of "Eleanor blue," which had taken her less than thirty minutes to select, were not warm enough. But she quickly forgot about the weather as she watched Franklin—supported by their oldest son, James—make his way down the red-carpeted ramp. Among the spectators she sensed a mood of helpless despair. The three-year Depression had left many Americans hungry and hopeless. Now they looked to her husband for leadership. "It was," Eleanor later wrote, "a little terrifying." Then she heard her husband's voice—clear, resonant, and buoyant. "Let me assert my firm belief," he declared, "that the only thing we have to fear is fear itself." With these words the tension in the crowd seemed to ease. It was as if, said one spectator, the new president had "passed along some sorely needed courage."

"We are in a tremendous stream and none of us knows where we are going to land," Eleanor told a friend later that day. But what was important, she now understood, was the "willingness to accept and share with others whatever may come and to meet the future courageously with a cheerful spirit."

Though tradition demanded that a first lady's role be limited to safe events—presiding at formal dinners, posing with prominent guests, attending tree planting ceremonies, greeting the Girl Scouts, staying in the background, staying at home, staying silent—from her first day Eleanor broke with these traditions. On the Monday after inauguration day she "went poking around [the White House] from basement to attic." At her side was chief usher Ike Hoover, whose job for the past forty years had been to oversee the day-to-day running of the executive mansion. To Mr. Hoover's dismay, the new first lady was soon pushing furniture around and making plans to hang her husband's sailboat prints. He gently reproved her. "That is not done, Mrs. Roosevelt." Eleanor smiled. "Oh, but it is, Mr. Hoover." Scandalized, Mr. Hoover could only watch as she walked instead of riding in the presidential limousine, operated the White House elevator by herself, scrambled and served eggs for her friends and family, answered the front door instead of the butler, and filled four long legal sheets with a new, highly organized outline of household schedules. But others were enchanted. "Washington has never seen the like," ended one exultant newspaper story; "a social transformation has taken place."

The White House as it looked when Eleanor and Franklin moved in

The Roosevelts lived in the White House for twelve years, from 1933 to 1945. In all that time Eleanor took little interest in the mansion's interior decor. To Eleanor, wrote one of their guests, "a chair was something to sit down on . . . a table was something to put things on and a wall was something to be covered . . . with pictures of sentimental value." Their private rooms re-created rooms at Hyde Park (though the housekeeper said the rug in Mrs. Roosevelt's room was so historic you caught your heels in it); other upstairs bedrooms were hopelessly Victorian—"old fashioned and indiscriminate in furnishing," said one visitor, "cluttered in decor, ugly and comfortable." Although she had a $50,000 congressional allocation for upkeep and repair, Eleanor was too busy lecturing and traveling to spend even a dime. By the time she left the White House, wallpaper was streaked and faded, furniture needed reupholstering, rugs were threadbare, and drapes hung rotting from the windows. "The White House upstairs is a mess," declared Mrs. Truman when she entered the place as first lady. The mansion's usher agreed. It "has the appearance of an abandoned hotel," he said. But no one blamed Eleanor. Explained the butler, "Mrs. Roosevelt was more concerned about people being swept under the national rug due to injustice than she was about finding dirt under the White House rug."

Eleanor consults with White House chief usher Ike Hoover.

Another woman who played an important role in Eleanor's life, Lorena Hickok

Eleanor first met Lorena Hickok—or "Hick," as she was called—in September 1928. At that time thirty-five-year-old Hick was the most famous woman reporter in the country. She was respected for her political savvy, her passionate convictions, and her fine writing style. With a cigar hanging from her mouth, and her flannel shirts and trousers loosely covering her two-hundred-pound frame, her male colleagues treated her "like one of the boys." Hick preferred it that way—"they took me seriously."

Lorena became acquainted with Eleanor in 1932 when Franklin ran for president. Part of Lorena's job was to report on the Roosevelt campaign strategy, and that meant talking to Eleanor, because the candidate's wife was also one of his most trusted political advisers. The first time the hard-boiled reporter interviewed Eleanor, she was "bedazzled." She said, "The candidate's wife, I discovered, was a woman of infinite compassion and sensitivity."

Now the more time the women spent together, the more they were drawn to each other. Eleanor recognized Hick's vulnerability. And Hick uncovered Eleanor's fear and reluctance about becoming first lady. More politically and professionally sophisticated, Hick helped Eleanor figure out how to make the job she feared into a job she wanted. Hick suggested Eleanor hold her own press conferences and publish a running account of her daily experiences in the form of a newspaper column. In the process Hick fell passionately in love with Eleanor. She even gave her a sapphire ring, which Eleanor wore to Franklin's inauguration in 1933. "Hick darling," Eleanor wrote after the event, "I want to put my arms around you . . . to hold you close. Your ring is a great comfort. I look at it and I think she does love me, or I wouldn't be wearing it."

What Franklin thought of his wife's wearing Lorena's ring is not known. He did, however, have the highest respect for Lorena's judgment. He also saw the political benefits of having a respected journalist in their camp. Lorena, he told his wife, was a journalist worth paying attention to. "Franklin used to tease me about you," Eleanor told Lorena. "He'd say, 'You'd better stick close to that Hickok woman. She's smart. . . .' He likes you a great deal."

The two women continued to enjoy a very close relationship during Eleanor's years as first lady. Not wanting to be separated from her friend, Hick gave up her work as an AP reporter and took a government job in Washington, D.C. Often she accompanied Eleanor on trips to Puerto Rico, Canada, New England, and Yosemite National Park, in California. When apart, they wrote loving letters to each other. "The nicest time of the day is when I write to you," Eleanor wrote. Promising to kiss Hick's photograph every night, she added, "Remember one thing always, no one is just what you are to me." Hick, meanwhile, counted the days until they would be together again. "Funny how even the dearest face will fade away in time," she wrote. "I remember your eyes, with a kind of teasing smile in them, and the feeling of that soft spot just northeast of the corner of your mouth against my lips."

Hick's love came at a crucial time for Eleanor. She needed Hick's loyalty, confidence, and courage as she struggled to define her new place in the world. In later years Eleanor told Hick, "You taught me more than you know and brought me happiness. . . . You made me so much more of a person just to be worthy of you."

But helping Eleanor find her wings changed their relationship. Observed one Roosevelt relative, "Once Eleanor began to fly she didn't need Hick the same way." As Eleanor grew into her role as first lady, she spent less and less time with Hick. And Hick grew sullen, moody, and demanding—behavior Eleanor found exasperating. "I know you have a feeling for me which for one reason or another I may not return in kind," Eleanor wrote in 1937, "but I love you just the same."

By the time Hick moved into a suite at the White House in 1941, their passion had cooled. The reporter soon fell in love with another woman, and Eleanor felt both relieved and apologetic. "Of course you will forget all about the sad time at the end," she wrote to Hick, "and eventually think only of the pleasant memories. Life is like that, with ends that have to be forgotten." Still, a strong friendship remained between the women—a friendship that lasted until Eleanor's death more than twenty years later.

Was She or Wasn't She? Ever since the staff at the Franklin D. Roosevelt Library in Hyde Park opened eighteen cardboard boxes containing the correspondence between Eleanor Roosevelt and Lorena Hickok in 1978, people have speculated about the first lady's sexuality. Some historians believe the intimate nature of the letters simply reflects Eleanor's Victorian upbringing, in which women tended to write romantically to one another. Other historians believe Eleanor and Lorena engaged in a fervent love affair. What is known for sure is that Eleanor did not consider lesbians—or women living in Boston marriages, as they were called—repugnant. Instead they were her closest friends, her most admired role models, and her greatest helpmates. A professed believer in sexual freedom, she wrote this sentence in her diary in 1925:

No form of love is to be despised.

THE FIRST-EVER PRESS CONFERENCE FOR WOMEN REPORTERS, HELD ON MARCH 6, 1933, JUST TWO DAYS AFTER FRANKLIN'S INAUGURATION

Eleanor stepped into the White House's Red Room, where thirty-five women reporters waited. They had been called to a press conference— all female, Eleanor explained, to encourage newspapers to hire more women. Smiling, she passed around a box of candied fruit she had brought along with her—to hide her nervousness, she later claimed. Never before had a first lady given a press conference. What were the rules? What kind of questions would the reporters ask?

That first meeting produced little news. And took lots of ribbing. Male reporters scoffed at the idea of women's press conferences and predicted they wouldn't last. But last they did, for a total of 348 conferences in all. And when Eleanor began using them occasionally to test out Franklin's ideas—voicing his opinions on everything from New Deal programs to serving beer in the White House—the "newspaper girls," as Eleanor called them, even got a few good scoops. Soon their male colleagues were begging to be part of the events too, but Eleanor stood firm. "Women only," she said. "That's the rule."

Of course, not every bit of news from the conferences was hard hitting. Over the years it was reported that Eleanor knitted to rest her eyes, was up for breakfast at eight thirty no matter what time she had gone to bed, always read herself to sleep, never suffered from insomnia, and had her hair done once a week but never had a facial because she didn't have the time—"although she would have loved one!" Eleanor's press conferences not only opened doors for female journalists (she was called by one reporter "God's gift to newspaper women"), but provided lots of favorable publicity for the first lady, too. Through these press reports she captured the public's imagination. Soon she came to personify the Roosevelt era as much as her husband did.

FROM AN AIRPLANE WINDOW AMELIA EARHART POINTS OUT THE WHITE HOUSE TO ELEANOR.

On April 20, 1933, the world-famous aviator Amelia Earhart attended a dinner at the White House. Afterward she invited Eleanor along on an airplane flight from Washington, D.C., to Baltimore and back—the first lady's first night trip. Eager to show the public how easy and safe air travel was, Eleanor quickly agreed. Afterward reporters asked how it felt to be piloted by a woman. Eleanor replied, "I'd give a lot to do it myself!" She did consider getting her own pilot's license, but Franklin vetoed the idea. "I know how Eleanor drives a car," he is reported to have said. "Imagine her flying an airplane!" Franklin's refusal did not stop his wife from enthusiastically supporting the still-new airline industry. She flew so often that as early as 1933 *Good Housekeeping* dubbed her "our flying First Lady." As for Amelia Earhart, she and Eleanor became good friends. Earhart stayed at the White House whenever she was in Washington, and she publicly supported Franklin during the 1936 election. Sadly, their friendship would be short lived. In 1937 Earhart attempted to fly around the world at the equator. But on the dangerous leg from New Guinea to Howland Island she disappeared. She was never heard from again. Eleanor, who had considered the aviator a kindred spirit, grew teary-eyed at the news. At her next press conference she told reporters that she was sure her friend's last words were "I have no regrets."

Eleanor in one of many endless White House receiving lines

Eleanor soon learned one of her most important duties as first lady was meeting and greeting people—lots of people. At first she thought it a "useless burden to receive anywhere from five hundred to a thousand people . . . shake hands with them, and then have them pass into the dining room for a cup of tea." She soon came to realize, however, that the White House had a special significance for Americans, and she said, "While shaking hands for an hour or so, two or three times a week, is not an inspiring occupation . . . I did it regularly." How did she manage to hold up? With a few trade tricks: "Don't let the [receiving] line stop, keep it moving along; grasp the fingers of the handshaker firmly, never permitting him to get a firm grip on your hand, gently draw him past as you say, 'How do you do? I'm glad to see you'; stop about every thousand handshakes to get a drink of water; bend your knees just a little, and frequently nobody will notice your discomfort."

A fashionable Eleanor poses in her inaugural gown.

A reporter one day asked Eleanor if it was true she had once bought four hats in two minutes. No, she said, smiling, that was an exaggeration; actually, it took about six minutes. Another reporter then asked what she planned to wear to an upcoming diplomatic reception. "I haven't the slightest idea," she replied, "but I might as well decide right now. That cream satin. You remember it." While never a fashion trendsetter, Eleanor did love clothes, especially hats. Her physique (she stood five feet eleven inches tall and weighed 160 pounds in 1940) did "marvelous things for clothing," claimed one fashion designer. He eagerly looked forward to receiving her orders. This she did by mail, stating her clothing needs. Often she included swatches of fabric along with lengthy descriptions of color preferences, sizes, style, and the type of needed undergarments. Although she did not make a point of dwelling on her appearance, she did pose for fashion layouts, and her wardrobe choices for holidays, inaugurations, and state dinners appeared in women's magazines and society pages all over the country. In 1934 she headed the U.S. fashion industry's list of the ten best-dressed women of the year, but she refused to dwell on the honor at her next news conference. Instead, wrote one reporter present, she cut the discussion "off with a vague sentence . . . or two." Perhaps she felt it was inappropriate to emphasize fashion when the nation was in the grip of the Depression, because without a doubt the honor pleased her. Twenty years later she wrote that to have "that title" was one of the "grandest" things to have ever happened to her.

Like handshaking, christening ships was another duty the first lady was obliged to perform. And it, too, required a special technique—"a twist of the wrist," said Eleanor, "a certain amount of aim, a strong arm." In her first year at the White House she set a christening record, breaking bottles of champagne over everything from ocean liners and airplanes to a little boy's rowboat at Campobello.

ELEANOR PACKS A PISTOL.

The first lady refused to be accompanied by the Secret Service. While this decision enhanced her public image of a woman unafraid, seeking to be herself, it was a sore spot with Franklin. When he insisted on assigning an agent to her, she snapped, "Don't you dare do such a thing. If any Secret Service man shows up . . . and starts following me around, I'll send him straight back where he came from!" So Franklin and the Secret Service compromised. They bought the first lady a gun and sent her to the FBI firing range to learn how to use it. Afterward, according to her son James, FBI director J. Edgar Hoover wrote Franklin this note: "Mr. President, if there is one person in the U.S. who should not carry a gun, it is your good wife. She cannot hit a barn door."

Eleanor with a few young guests at the White House Easter egg roll

ONE DUTY ELEANOR ADORED was hosting the traditional Easter egg roll. Since 1878 and the time of President Rutherford B. Hayes, the White House lawn had been opened to the public every Monday after Easter. On that day thousands of citizens came to roll painted eggs across the grass, search for jelly beans, and gobble chocolate bunnies. When Eleanor became first lady, she not only planned the event, but made it a point to walk among the crowd, playing games with the children and posing for photographs. Were her egg rolls a success? Even Eleanor wasn't entirely sure, as this journal entry about the 1939 event shows: "The average attendance . . . was 53,108. The records show that 180 were lost and found; two people were sent to the emergency hospital; six people fainted and twenty two had to be treated for small abrasions." Mr. Hoover assured her this was a successful event.

THE FIRST LADY TRAVELS AGAIN

"Just for one day, God, PLEASE make her tired." This was the highly publicized prayer of the weary newspaper reporters who trailed after the first lady on her many travels—some forty thousand miles her first year in the White House. Eleanor crisscrossed the country, giving speeches, meeting people, and seeing firsthand the devastation of the Depression, while still managing to fulfill her other obligations. She never seemed to tire. How did she do it? Catnaps, claimed Franklin's cousin Margaret Suckley. She recalled traveling with Eleanor once on the New York–Washington train, and this is what she observed: "She was working away the whole time with Malvina [Eleanor's secretary], and I was sitting there like a dumbbell looking out the window, and suddenly Mrs. Roosevelt said, 'Now I'm going to sleep for fifteen minutes,' and she put her head back on the seat. I looked at my watch, and just as it hit fifteen minutes, she woke up and said, 'Now . . . let's go on.' It was amazing. I was stunned." Eleanor's incredible energy level continued to stun people for years to come. Even in her seventies, said her son Elliott, she could "outwalk, outwork, outwit a person half her age."

In 1933 Eleanor invited her friend the novelist Fannie Hurst to spend the weekend at the White House. Fannie later wrote about her stay in her memoir, *Anatomy of Me*, providing a fascinating glimpse of the first lady.

Fannie arrived on a Saturday morning and barely had time to settle into the Lincoln Bedroom before she was whisked off to breakfast. The morning meal was served buffet style in a screen-partitioned hallway outside of Mrs. Roosevelt's sitting room. "The First Lady," recalled Fannie, "was deep in a stack of mail and was frequently interrupted by phone calls, secretaries and ushers. A seating chart for a state dinner the following week had to be inspected, a miniature church made out of toothpicks arrived from an admirer in South Carolina, the housekeeper appeared for a conference." During all this Eleanor still managed to ask about Fannie, her writing, and her family. Afterward there was a committee meeting, then Eleanor took Fannie to the Library of Congress so she could "gaze at a shelf of my own novels."

At lunch Fannie sat down with only the president, his mother, twenty-seven-year-old daughter Anna, and Louis Howe. When Mrs. Roosevelt came hurrying into the room, Anna adjusted her mother's blouse. "There is sometimes a hopeless discrepancy between my mother and her clothes," she said with a smile. The president seemed relaxed and ate with gusto. Between courses he smoked cigarettes in his long holder and talked with Howe about the living conditions in Russia. When a particularly gruesome detail was introduced, Franklin's mother put down her fork. "I warned you," she said sternly to her son.

A Typical Day at the White House

"You should never have recognized the Soviet Union as a nation!"

After lunch the day began in earnest for Eleanor. Fannie accompanied her to the hospital where one of the Roosevelt sons was recovering from an appendectomy. After that there was an opening of a Picasso exhibit, where Eleanor gave a speech, and then back to the White House just in time to receive a delegation of about forty educators from the Philippines, and finally a conference with a black Baptist minister from Atlanta. There were only a few minutes to change clothes before heading out again for dinner with a close friend of the Roosevelts'. At eleven o'clock Fannie and Eleanor returned to the White House to see the "first showing of a talking picture from a projector which the Metro-Goldwyn-Mayer corporation had just installed for the President's use." It was long past midnight when Fannie finally dragged herself back to the Lincoln Bedroom. She had just sunk onto the bed, "deciding for once to retire without even removing my makeup," when someone knocked on her door. "Come in," said Fannie weakly.

It was Eleanor. Clad in a black bathing suit, with a towel over her arm and a notepad and pencil in her hand, the first lady entered briskly. "What do you want for breakfast tomorrow, Fannie?" she asked.

After carefully writing down the answer on the notepad, Eleanor spread the towel on the floor. "Remember when I promised . . . to show you my yoga exercises?" she asked. And the next moment, recalled the astonished novelist, the first lady "stood on her head, straight as a column, feet up in the air."

The *Literary* First Lady

In 1933 Eleanor signed a contract with *Woman's Home Companion*, then the top-selling women's magazine, to write a monthly column. Called "Mrs. Roosevelt's Page," it first appeared in August of that year. "I want you to write to me," Eleanor told readers in her debut column. "I want you to tell me about the particular problems which puzzle or sadden you, but I also want you to write me about what has brought joy into your life." The public responded. It seems that many of the approximately 300,000 letters Eleanor received in 1933 were from her *Companion* readers. In her column Eleanor commented on a handful of these letters, along with an occasional discussion of social issues—outlawing child labor, improving factory conditions, explaining various New Deal policies. Mostly, however, she wrote about noncontroversial subjects—vacations, gardening, national holidays. Although it was popular, the column was short lived. In July 1935 the *Companion* ended publication of "Mrs. Roosevelt's Page" because it didn't want to appear too close to the Roosevelt administration in the months leading up to the 1936 election.

The debut of "Mrs. Roosevelt's Page," a monthly column published in

WOMAN'S HOME COMPANION

One of Eleanor's lifelong interests was children's books. For many years she served on the editorial board of the Junior Literary Guild—a book club for young readers—reviewing manuscripts and helping to choose selections for teenage girls. In her magazine articles she advocated reading aloud to children and believed even babies and toddlers should be immersed in the world of literature. And in 1935 she entered the world of children's literature herself with the publication of *A Trip to Washington with Bobby and Betty*—an imaginary tale of a brother and sister's trip that ends with a fantastical lunch at the White House. Well received by critics, the book was the first of only two pieces of fiction Eleanor published during her lifetime. Her second fictional tale, *Christmas: A Story*, was also for children and also well received. Published in 1940, the story takes place in the Netherlands and tells of a young girl's refusal to allow Nazism's evil to influence her.

The first edition of "My Day," a newspaper column that appeared for the next twenty-seven years

In November 1935 United Feature Syndicate—an agency providing articles and columns to newspapers across the country—asked Eleanor to write a daily four-hundred-word column. "When do I start?" Eleanor quickly replied. And just as quickly she began writing. On December 30 the first of her "My Day" columns appeared. In it she described Christmas at the White House and reported that her husband was in bed with a cold. She wrote, "So I said a polite good night to everyone at seven-thirty, closed my door, lit my fire, and settled down to a nice long evening by myself." The tone of her columns was chatty, unpretentious, and simplistic—and readers loved it! Ninety newspapers, reaching more than four million readers, carried "My Day" six days a week. At first Eleanor steered clear of political or controversial topics. Instead she wrote a diary-type chronicle based on her daily activities—family happenings, housekeeping at the White House, social events, the weather, and books, plays, and movies. "I simply tell small human happenings which may interest or amuse the average reader," she once explained.

But not everyone was amused. "Of all the nonsen-

sical and demented nonsense," complained one reader, "it takes the bun." Others called the column "artless," "rambling," and "a puffed up piece of poppycock!" While "My Day" showed Eleanor was not a great writer, it did prove once again that she had the ability to communicate with the average American. "She talked to [her readers] rather than wrote for them," noted one newspaper editor, "and that made all the difference."

No matter where she went, Eleanor wrote her column, often dashing it off (usually in half an hour) in trains, planes, cars, and ships, on picnics and in hotel rooms. On one occasion she dictated it to her secretary, who was balancing the typewriter on her knees while Eleanor drove them from Denton, Texas, to Fort Worth. Another time Eleanor became so ill Franklin offered to write the column for her. Eleanor refused. Instead she feverishly hammered out four hundred less-than-shining words because, as she said, "if it once became the President's column we would lose our readers." Eleanor had only one interruption—when Franklin died in April 1945. Even then she missed only four days.

Magazines

Many Americans met Eleanor Roosevelt in the pages of America's magazines. Some of them were serious journals—the *Atlantic Monthly*, the *New Republic*, even *Harvard Law Review*. Most, however, were popular magazines: *Collier's*, *Good Housekeeping*, *Redbook*, and *Cosmopolitan*. Eleanor liked writing for popular magazines because they helped her reach the average American. Unlike many public figures today, she did all her writing herself—no ghostwriters.

And she was prolific. During Franklin's presidency she averaged thirty to thirty-five articles a year, and she kept it up after his death. What did she write about? Politics, of course, as well as civil rights, labor legislation, peace, and foreign policy. She also wrote a good deal about women's problems as wives and mothers. Below is just a tiny sampling of her articles. Their titles tell their stories.

"Women Must Learn to Play the Game As Men Do" (*Redbook*, April 1928)

"What I Want Most out of Life: A Prominent Society Woman Reveals Her Purpose" (*Success Magazine*, May 1927)

"Mrs. Roosevelt Believes in Paroles and Providing Jobs for Released Men" (*Periscope*, October 1935)

"Stella Dallas Inspires a Discussion of a Mother's Vital Problem" (*Saturday Evening Post*, August 7, 1937)

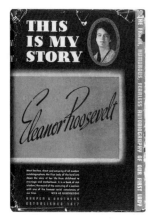

In the summer of 1936 Eleanor's literary agent, George Bye, urged her to begin writing her autobiography. By late fall the book's first chapters were written. Bye showed them to Bruce and Beatrice Gould, publishers of *Ladies' Home Journal*, who promptly bought the serial rights to the book for an astounding $75,000—equal to Franklin's salary as president! "We are thrilled with your fine, clear prose," the Goulds told Eleanor, and could not wait to publish the book in installments—two chapters each month. Eleanor was thrilled too. "I can't tell you what it means . . . to have this wonderful recognition for something I have done myself not on account of Franklin's position."

But as Eleanor continued writing, the Goulds' euphoria faded. Early chapters had been a vivid picture of a painful, insecure childhood, written with "startling honesty and courage." Then suddenly, the Goulds claimed, the book stopped being "the story of a human being and had become a mere chronicle of events." When Eleanor went to the magazine's office to work on revisions, Bruce Gould cried, "But this chapter has nothing to say—in fact—it's terrible!" Eleanor vowed to make the book better. "I did not waste my time bewailing my failures and frustrations. Instead I wrote it all down and then went back . . . for polishing." She also asked Franklin to go over the manuscript. He did and discovered much he didn't like. "This is . . . unfair to me," he wrote on the section describing his battle with polio. On another section, about infidelity, he made a large X. Eleanor softened these offending passages and rewrote others. Slowly the book began to take shape. And the Goulds began to purr. She had "picked up the dramatic thread again," they claimed, making the book "illuminating."

It was called *This Is My Story*, and its serialization was a smash success, making *Ladies' Home Journal* the most widely read magazine in the country. Harper and Brothers published it in book form to wide acclaim—the *New York Times* proclaimed it "required reading"; United Press International declared it "the greatest human document in modern times." The autobiography, however, was incomplete, taking readers only up to 1924. The public clamored for more but had to wait. Other duties demanded the first lady's attention.

SPEAKING TO THE AMERICAN PEOPLE OVER THE CBS RADIO NETWORK

Eleanor's radio career began in the 1920s, when she occasionally spoke on New York's stations about women's clubs and voting rights, but it really took off once Franklin became president. Women, particularly, liked listening to her views. And speaking to them gave Eleanor a real sense of fulfillment. "She tried consciously to envision the women who were listening," wrote her friend Joe Lash. "On lonely ranches, in mountain cabins, in tenements, and to remember that they were weighing her words against their own experience."

In 1934 Eleanor turned to commercial broadcasting. Her first sponsor, Simmons Mattress Company, asked her to do five commentaries on the weekly news. And they paid her handsomely—$500 a minute! (At this time the average salary for an American worker was $20 a week.)

Immediately the nation's other mattress makers complained to the president. "It does not seem fair that the First Lady should use her prestige to assist some single manufacturer," they grumbled. Wanting the money for charity, Eleanor responded that she would "take both the money and the gaff."

Her broadcasts for Simmons were so popular they led to another series as soon as the Simmons one ended. In 1935 Selby Shoes paid her $72,000 for sixteen fifteen-minute talks, placing her in the same class as the highest-paid radio stars of the day. *Radio Guide* praised her as a performer. Coached by technicians, she began to learn everything about radio delivery—timing, spacing, voice modulation. By 1939 the National Broadcasting Company (NBC) dubbed her the "First Lady of Radio" and claimed: "Her microphone manners are exemplary. . . . She is not averse to a little showmanship here and there, but eschews tricks. Her voice is well-pitched and she speaks softly. . . . It is not an accident that Mrs. Roosevelt's voice is studied by students of speech."

Eleanor Takes a Stand

Franklin encouraged his wife's outspokenness. "You go right ahead and stand for whatever you feel is right," he once told her. "If folks don't like it, I can always say that I can't do a thing with you." The president's hands-off policy toward his wife's views worked for both of them. It meant Eleanor could say what she wished. But it also meant her opinions could serve as trial balloons. "If some idea I expressed strongly and with which [Franklin] might agree caused a violent [public] reaction, he could honestly say he had no responsibility in the matter and that the thoughts were mine," Eleanor later explained. If, on the other hand, the idea garnered public support, Franklin would often endorse it. That, wrote Eleanor, "was a political reality." Below are some of Eleanor's more strongly expressed thoughts.

ON RACISM: *"One of the main destroyers of freedom is our attitude toward the colored race. . . . We must face this problem and change our actions, or democracy will fade."*

ON EDUCATION: *"Wherever the standard of education is low, the standard of living is low. Government must take the lead in providing all Americans with a sound and basic education."*

ON PUBLIC HOUSING: *"Decent housing is a basic human right that society is morally and politically obligated to provide all of its citizens."*

ON JOBS FOR WOMEN: *"A woman can do any job a man can . . . and she deserves to be paid equally for doing it."*

ON ECONOMIC POLICY: *"An economic policy which does not consider the well-being of all will not serve the purposes of peace and the growth of well-being among the people of all nations."*

ON DEMOCRACY: *"The function of democratic living is not to lower standards, but to raise those that have been too low."*

ON WELFARE: *"How can a few dollars a month given to needy Americans for food, shelter, and clothing be the wrong choice for a moral nation?"*

The *Secret* Politician

Publicly Eleanor denied ever wanting or having real political power. She acknowledged she worked for issues she believed in, but she never once admitted that politics, as historian Blanche Wiesen Cook wrote, "satisfied her own interests, served her own needs, or that she delighted in the rough-and-tumble of its deals and battles."

Yet Eleanor was indeed a consummate politician. Tough minded and direct, she was a leader of the Democratic Party for more than forty years—from the 1920s until her death in 1962. Articles about her and her political work appeared almost daily in the *New York Times*, and because she spoke so candidly, her major statements were often quoted in full. She never walked away from a political battle. She made hard decisions, and she followed her principles wherever they led. "She was as much a political genius as her husband," a close friend once said, "but her style was much more gracious." Some people mistakenly took this graciousness for political naïveté. When a Washington lobbyist called her a "dim bulb" in 1938, Franklin snorted with laughter. "That's grand. Really grand," he said. "Let him continue to harbor that illusion. . . . He'll soon fall victim to Eleanor's hard political heart."

But curiously, the more Eleanor achieved, the more she trivialized her success. "I am," she often said, "merely a politician's wife pushed into politics reluctantly"—and solely in support of her husband. She refused to admit her genuine pleasure in her own work, understanding that to maintain credibility as a woman in public life, she had to behave in a manner acceptable to Americans of the 1930s. What was acceptable? Being a good wife and mother. Nowhere was this double standard more clearly revealed than in a *New York Times Magazine* article titled "A Woman Speaks Her Political Mind." While the author of the article credited Eleanor with a "wider experience and richer political background than most," he praised her for never allowing her political activities to "interfere with her devotion to her home."

Still a Wife . . .

President Roosevelt gives his first lady a kiss.

She called him Franklin. He called her Babs. And while they had separate bedrooms, separate friends, and often pursued separate interests, they made, said their son Elliott, "an extraordinary team." Eleanor once described her marriage this way: "Men and women who live together through long years get to know one another's failings. But they also come to know what is worthy of respect and admiration in those they live with and in themselves. . . . He might have been happier with a wife who was completely uncritical. . . . Nevertheless, I think I sometimes acted as a spur, even though the spur was not always welcome. I was one of those who served his purpose."

But as the historian Lois Scharf noted, "He also served hers. He furnished the stage upon which her incomparable abilities and human qualities [eventually] gained the widest audience and respect."

And even though certain parts of their marriage were unfulfilling, an unshakable tenderness existed between them. In late 1944, just months before his death, Franklin gazed up at a portrait of Eleanor hanging on his study wall. "You know," he said to his secretary of labor, Frances Perkins, "I've always liked that portrait. It's a beautiful portrait, don't you think? . . . You know the hair's just right, isn't it? Eleanor has lovely hair, don't you think?" As he spoke, Perkins was struck by the "light in his eyes . . . the light of affection."

Eleanor, too, displayed affection. She was "constantly talking about what Franklin did or what Franklin said or . . . how Franklin thought about this or that," reported her secretary, Maureen Corr. "And every time she mentioned his name you could hear the emotion in her voice and see the glow in her eyes."

NAGGING ELEANOR

Franklin established one hard-and-fast routine in the White House—cocktail hour, during which nothing was supposed to be said about politics. Instead, family members and close friends swapped stories, told jokes, laughed, and gossiped. "It was," recalled political adviser Harry Hopkins, "the only time FDR could shake off the burdens of his presidency and find complete relaxation." But Eleanor was unable to stop. Her sense of urgency, her need to get things done, drove her to keep after her husband—as this story told by their daughter, Anna, shows:

"I remember one day when we were having cocktails. . . . A fair number of people were in the room, an informal group, . . . I was mixing the cocktails. Mother always came in at the end so she would only have to have one cocktail— that was her concession. She would wolf it—she never took it slowly. She came in and sat across the desk from Father. And she had a sheaf of papers this high and she said, 'Now, Franklin, I want to talk to you about this.' I have permanently blocked out what it was she wanted to bring up. I just remember, like lightning, that I thought, 'Oh God, he's going to blow.' And sure enough he blew his top. He took every single speck of that whole pile of papers, threw them

across the desk at me and said, 'Sis, you handle these tomorrow morning.' I almost went through the floor. She got up. She was the most controlled person in the world. And she took her glass and left the room. Intuitively I understood that here was a man plagued with God knows how many problems—a man who . . . needed a bit of relaxation—and right now he had twenty minutes to have two cocktails—in very small glasses— and he wanted to tell stories and relax and enjoy himself—period. I don't think Mother had the slightest realization. She just pushed him terrifically. . . . She was always giving him indigestion."

a Mother, and . . .

Even though the children were grown by now, the Roosevelt White House was "a rambunctious place full of tribal affection and high jinks," said chief usher Ike Hoover. At one family Christmas party Franklin Jr. and John crept up behind their father's chair and tickled him. The president reached his long arms behind him and pinioned the boys until they yelled uncle. Another time, according to Harold Ickes, secretary of the interior, Eleanor raised some social question at the dinner table, and "her three sons began to wave their arms in the air and take issue with her. . . . The President joined in at intervals, but he wasn't the President of the United States on that occasion—he was merely the father of three sons who had opinions of their own. They interrupted . . . and all talked at him at the same time. It was really most amusing."

As children of public figures, the Roosevelt brood found it difficult to lead private lives, and their mistakes often made front-page news. Americans read about Anna's divorce, James's tax problems, and Elliott's inability to hold a job. They knew Franklin Jr. was a speed demon who prided himself on holding the "unofficial Harvard to New York driving record." Often pulled over by police, he bitterly complained every time he saw his name in print. John, meanwhile, made international headlines after emptying an entire

Christmas morning with the family at the White House, 1939. Seated, left to right: Eleanor; Franklin's mother, Sara; Mrs. Franklin D. Roosevelt Jr., holding her son Franklin III; Franklin; daughter Anna, holding her son John; Mrs. J. R. Roosevelt, Franklin's cousin; and Mrs. John Roosevelt. Standing: son Franklin Jr.; son John; and John Boettiger, Anna's husband. Seated on the floor: granddaughter Anna Eleanor "Sistie" Dall; Diana Hopkins, daughter of political adviser Harry Hopkins; and grandson Curtis "Buzzie" Dall.

Eleanor's grandchildren, Sistie (Anna Eleanor) and Buzzie (Curtis) Dall play on a slide installed at their grandmother's request on the White House lawn.

bottle of champagne into a top hat belonging to the mayor of Cannes, France.

"One of the worst things in the world," FDR exclaimed one day, "is being the child of the President. It's a terrible life they lead!"

And what did the first lady think of her children's antics?

"There's a bond between us," Eleanor replied, "and right or wrong, that bond can never be broken. . . . They are always my children, with a right to call on me in case of need . . . or when the hard times of life come upon them, even when I know that they have brought those hard times on themselves. . . . No one ever lives up to the best in themselves all the time, and nearly all of us love people because of their weaknesses rather than because of their strengths. . . . Their father and I could not ask that they give us peace and quiet."

By the time she moved to the White House, Eleanor had four grandchildren—Anna's children Sistie and Buzzie, James's daughter Sarah, and Elliot's infant son William. Hoping to make the Executive Mansion a more pleasant place for the children, Eleanor had a nursery installed on the third floor, and a sandbox and slide placed on the south lawn. She also planned on having a tree swing, but horrified park officials refused to allow ropes to be tied to the big oak tree. The bark might become gouged and grooved, they argued. The tree could die. Eleanor waved away their concerns. "I have lived all my life where there are swings on old trees," she replied, "and I have never seen one harmed." Telephoning the secretary of the interior, she received special permission to build a swing. No wonder her grandchildren had "the constant feeling that no matter what . . . [we] always came first."

THE *OTHER* FIRST LADY

"Marguerite 'Missy' LeHand is the President's Super-Secretary," *Newsweek* announced in a glowing article written five months after Franklin became president. Her genius was not just in skillfully doing everything he asked, but in anticipating his wants and needs before he even knew them himself. Missy was known to break into the most statesmanlike conferences with the announcement that it was time for Franklin to take his cough medicine. She reminded him to wear his boots. And she rubbed his sore neck muscles when he had sat too long at his desk. Missy, who had her own room on the second floor, began every day in her housecoat in Franklin's bedroom. She ended every day in the inner sanctum of his private office for cocktails. In the car she always got the preferred

Missy LeHand seated between Franklin and a downcast Eleanor

seat next to Franklin. And whenever Eleanor was away, she presided at dinner as the president's hostess. It was, admitted one friend of the Roosevelts', a "tangled relationship."

But over the years Eleanor grew used to it. She knew that without Missy's attending to Franklin's personal needs, the independent life she had worked so hard to create would be impossible to keep. "Missy alleviated Mother's guilt," her son Elliott once said. Still, there was annoyance and resentment. Said daughter Anna, "While Mother was always high-minded and serious, Missy was easy to relax with, full of smiles and clever jokes. These were things Mother couldn't give Father. She knew that, but she was a human being and never could quite accept it."

In June 1941 Missy suffered a massive stroke. An invalid until she died three years later, she left the White House to live with her sister. Franklin paid for all her medical bills but rarely visited her. Instead it was Eleanor who sent gifts and cards and tried to keep up Missy's spirits. Many years later Eleanor alluded to Missy and Franklin's special relationship. In one of her last books she advised readers that if they were not able to fulfill the need of a loved one, they "must learn to allow someone else to meet the need, without bitterness and envy and accept it."

Eleanor converts the empty furniture factory at Val-Kill into a home all her own.

Eleanor soon discovered she needed a place where she could escape the pressures of being first lady. So in 1936, she moved out of the small stone cottage she still shared with Nancy Cook and Marion Dickerman and into the furniture factory the three women had built. Eleanor loved having her own place and delighted in remodeling it. She covered the paneled walls with photographs, filled shelves with books, and supervised the spring planting. Her garden, she insisted, had to have "some old fashioned yellow rose bushes, a bed of lilies of the valley . . . and sweet peas and pansies to grow more abundant the more you pick them." Her cheerful yellow bedroom overlooked the pond, in which sunrises and sunsets were reflected, but she preferred to sleep on the sleeping porch surrounded by trees. "In the morning," she wrote, "there is the chirping of birds to awaken me, and at night a chorus of frogs." On her bedside table rested her father's copy of the New Testament and a photograph of the first Franklin Jr., the child who had died in infancy. And although she managed only an occasional weekend visit there during her White House years, she looked forward to the peacefulness of the place.

Eleanor Roosevelt, 1933

The Eleanor Effect

Bess Truman, 1946

Mamie Eisenhower, 1952

Jacqueline Kennedy, 1961

Eleanor set new standards for first-lady leadership—standards that affected all future first ladies.

Bess Truman, wife of President Harry S. Truman, stubbornly refused to emulate her predecessor, even after Eleanor begged her to continue holding press conferences. "I couldn't possibly be anything like [Eleanor]," said Mrs. Truman. "I wasn't going down in any coal mines." To Eleanor's dismay, Mrs. Truman avoided making any public remarks or participating in any political activities.

Mamie Eisenhower, wife of President Dwight D. Eisenhower, wasn't much of a political activist either. When friends suggested she follow in Eleanor's footsteps by writing a newspaper column of her own, Mrs. Eisenhower shuddered. "It sounds a terrible chore and smacks of [the] 'My Day' column of which I have a perfect horror." Mrs. Eisenhower made a conscious decision to distance herself from Eleanor by refusing to invite the former first lady to any White House events during the Eisenhower administration.

Jacqueline Kennedy, wife of John F. Kennedy, had a brief correspondence with Eleanor about raising children in the White House. Like Bess Truman and Mamie Eisenhower, however, she avoided public discussion of her political opinions. When she refused to lobby on behalf of her pet project—government support of the arts—a newspaper article unflatteringly compared her with Eleanor. Mrs. Kennedy responded peevishly, "I am not Mrs. Roosevelt."

First ladies after Jacqueline Kennedy emulated Eleanor more directly. Lady Bird Johnson, wife of President Lyndon B. Johnson, not only shared the same political views as Eleanor (both women were liberal Democrats), but worked for issues Eleanor would surely have endorsed—equal rights for women, civil rights for minorities, and programs for disadvantaged children.

Lady Bird Johnson, 1962

Pat Nixon, 1969

Betty Ford, 1974

Rosalynn Carter, 1977

Even Pat Nixon, wife of Republican president Richard Nixon, told a reporter that she greatly admired Eleanor's active role as first lady. Mrs. Nixon followed Eleanor's lead by asking Americans to volunteer their skills and time to remedy social ills—something no first lady had done since the Roosevelt administration.

First lady Betty Ford always claimed Eleanor had been one of her childhood role models. Mrs. Ford's willingness to speak out on controversial issues such as abortion, breast cancer, mental illness, and the Equal Rights Amendment raised many eyebrows. And when she publicly disagreed with husband President Gerald Ford's economic policy, it rekindled the debate about the proper role of a first lady.

Rosalynn Carter, wife of President Jimmy Carter, once told a reporter that when she was a schoolgirl growing up in the 1930s, her idea of the role of first lady had been changed by Eleanor's behavior. When Mrs. Carter entered the White House forty years later, she followed Eleanor's example by making numerous fact-finding trips on her husband's behalf and speaking out on welfare, health, and energy programs. She even followed in Eleanor's footsteps by becoming only the second first lady to testify before Congress.

The next two first ladies, Nancy Reagan and Barbara Bush, chose more traditional White House roles. Mrs. Reagan did, however, like to quote one of Eleanor's lines in her speeches: "A woman is like a teabag. You never know how strong it is until it's in hot water." And Mrs. Bush often told the story of how her own mother—formerly a critic of Eleanor's—became an enthusiastic supporter after a visit to the Roosevelt White House.

No first lady, however, has more directly studied, appreciated, and emulated Eleanor than Hillary Rodham Clinton. Mrs. Clinton's political activism on dozens of issues (health care, welfare reform, adoption, historic preservation, education, women's rights) was the most public and controversial since the Roosevelt administration. Mrs. Clinton admitted Eleanor was her personal heroine and role model. And she confessed to often asking herself, What would Eleanor do? when faced with a difficult situation. In a December 1998 speech given at Georgetown University, she spoke about Eleanor's vision for human rights around the world and how she was trying to continue this work into the twenty-first century. Also, like her role model, Mrs. Clinton continued to live a public life after leaving the White House. In 2000 she was elected to the United States Senate, an accomplishment Eleanor would surely have applauded.

First lady Laura Bush, wife of President George W. Bush, continued Eleanor's literary tradition. Concerned about the education of American children, she focused her energies on a national initiative called Ready to Read, Ready to Learn, which stressed the importance of books and reading.

It remains to be seen what effect Eleanor will have on future first ladies, but one thing is clear: Eleanor Roosevelt so thoroughly redefined the role of first lady that her influence cannot be ignored even today.

Nancy Reagan, 1981

Barbara Bush, 1989

Hillary Rodham Clinton, 1992

Laura Bush, 2001

Friend of the People

❧

I listened to the people, and everywhere I went I asked:
"Tell me, what do you need? What do you want?"

—Eleanor Roosevelt, "My Day," October 12, 1944

Eleanor checks up on the children at the Colored Orphan Asylum, 1943.

"You know," Franklin once said to one of his advisers, "one of the greatest things about Eleanor is . . . that she goes wherever she wants to, and talks to everybody, and boy does she learn something!"

Eleanor makes friends with the Bonus Marchers.

*E*leanor had been in the White House only a few months when thousands of needy World War I veterans, seeking early payment of a government pension not due for another twelve years, crowded into the nation's capital. A year earlier, with President Hoover in office, the so-called Bonus Marchers had also converged on Washington. But the gathering turned violent when Hoover ordered the army to disperse the jobless veterans by burning tents and throwing tear gas. In the chaos hundreds were injured and three were killed, including an eleven-week-old baby. Hoping to prevent a similar tragedy, the new president opened an old army camp to the veterans and provided them with food and medical care. Even so, many Americans feared violence would erupt again—especially Franklin's adviser Louis Howe.

Louis had a plan. One afternoon he asked Eleanor to drive him out to the veterans' encampment in her new roadster. When they arrived, he announced he was going to sit in the car while she went up and down the rows of tents seeing how things were.

"Hesitatingly," Eleanor recalled, "I got out and walked over to where I saw a lineup of men waiting for food. They looked at me curiously and one of them asked my name and what I wanted. When I said I just wanted to see how they were getting on, they asked me to join them." For the next hour she chatted, had a bite to eat, and even joined in singing "The Long, Long Trail." "Then," said Eleanor, "I got into my car and drove away. Everyone waved as I called 'Good luck!' and they answered, 'Good-bye and good luck to you!'"

Although she didn't offer the pension checks they wanted, Eleanor did bring a spirit of friendship while quieting a potential storm. At her next press conference she described the camp as "remarkably clean" and the veterans as "grand looking boys." Her report not only quelled Americans' fears about the Bonus Marchers, but showed her as a woman in touch with ordinary people. The event also taught Eleanor an important lesson—that a personal appearance by a first lady can have a powerful impact on public opinion. Recalled one of the veterans, "Hoover sent the army. Roosevelt sent his wife."

Because of his disability Franklin found it difficult to travel. And yet, as president, he desperately needed to see the living conditions of his fellow citizens. What to do? Why, send Eleanor, of course! She quickly became his "eyes and ears." But it wasn't an easy task. "At first, my reports were highly unsatisfactory to [Franklin]," Eleanor later wrote. "I would tell him what was on the [prison's] menu for the day, and he would ask: 'Did you look to see if the inmates were actually getting that food?' I learned to look into the cooking pots on the stove to find out if the contents corresponded with the menu. I learned to notice whether the beds were too close together, and . . . to watch the patient's attitude toward the staff." Later, she said, he "taught me how to watch the [train] tracks and see their condition, and how to look at the countryside and note whether there was soil erosion and what condition the forest and fields were in, and as we went through the outskirts of a town or village, I soon learned to look at the clothes on a wash line and at the cars and to notice whether houses needed painting." Before long the first lady was flying all over the country, dropping in on coal miners, sharecroppers, and slum dwellers. Her travels not only created a feeling among Americans that someone high up in government truly cared about their problems, but they earned her a nickname, too—"Everywhere Eleanor."

Eleanor, wearing a miner's cap, takes a two-and-a-half-mile trip underground deep into an Ohio coal mine on May 21, 1933.

She wanted to see for herself the conditions of coal miners—"dark, dank and utterly terrifying."

Eleanor inspects a federal prison in Baltimore, 1935.

Franklin asked her to do it, but it was "a painful chore," she said, "because I could hardly bear to see people shut up." Leaving the White House early, she did not have a chance to remind him where she was going. Later in the day he asked her secretary where Eleanor was. "In prison," the secretary drily told him. "I'm not surprised," quipped the president. "But what for?"

Eleanor visits a Puerto Rican slum.

In 1934, at Franklin's request, she traveled to Puerto Rico, where she was shocked by the conditions—children near starvation, city slums filled with shacks, men working from sunrise to sunset for pennies a day. On her return she begged Franklin to send labor experts and industrialists to find ways to remedy the "pitiful situation." He did, and Puerto Ricans named their first housing project Eleanor Roosevelt.

Eleanor inspects a work program site in Oregon, 1934.

She liked just to drop in on federal relief projects, "often managing to arrive without notice so that they could not be polished up for [her] inspections."

Americans found Eleanor's travels admirable and amusing. Some publications even made up jingles about her many trips. One of them went:

Hi diddle diddle, the cat and the fiddle,
The cow jumped over the moon,
The moon laughed and laughed, and said,
"You're too late,
Eleanor passed here at noon."

A New Deal *for All Americans*

As president, Franklin responded to the nation's economic depression with reassurance, confidence, and a New Deal for the American people—a series of twenty-seven controversial, sometimes experimental government relief and recovery programs instituted between 1933 and 1940.

Eleanor exerted considerable influence on the creation of these programs by bringing to Franklin's attention many issues he didn't see, or chose to ignore. Her favorite approach was her Sunday egg scrambles. Every Sunday evening Eleanor scrambled up a few dozen eggs and invited people to a relaxed family dinner. Senators, plumbers, factory owners, homeless widows, and heads of government agencies—all came to talk informally with the president about what mattered to them. In this way Franklin was able to form New Deal policies based on the living realities of Americans. "I'm the agitator; he's the politician," the first lady once admitted. But others believed she was more than an agitator. She became, said FDR's speechwriter, "the keeper and constant spokesman for her husband's conscience."

Although Eleanor never wrote any New Deal legislation or lobbied on Capitol Hill for passage of any program, her enthusiastic support of the following measures helped bring them into existence:

Agricultural Adjustment Act (AAA)—paid farmers to reduce crops

Civilian Conservation Corps (CCC)—employed young men on public works projects

Civil Works Administration (CWA)—employed jobless people to work on federal, state, and local projects

Federal Emergency Relief Administration (FERA)—provided relief to needy people

Tennessee Valley Authority (TVA)—built dams and power plants to improve economic and social welfare in southern states

National Youth Administration (NYA)—provided job training and work to people aged sixteen to twenty-five, and part-time jobs to students

Social Security Act—provided unemployment benefits, pensions for the elderly, and survivor's insurance

Works Progress Administration (WPA)—employed people to do artistic, public works, and research projects

Fair Labor Standards Act (or the Federal Wage and Hour Law)—established a minimum wage of twenty-five cents an hour (to be raised to forty cents by 1945) and a maximum workweek of forty hours

America's First Liberal

Franklin's New Deal programs were the first of their kind—the first time the federal government had ever tried to help directly citizens who had suffered economic hardship through no fault of their own. Many critics claimed such massive government involvement was corrupt, wasteful, or socialistic. But Eleanor welcomed this new direction. Earlier Franklin had seized on the word *liberal* to explain his social and economic reform. "Liberalism," he said, "is plain English for a changed concept of duty and responsibility of government toward economic life." Eleanor, who believed that an enlightened government could bring about a just and humane society, summed up liberalism this way: "The biggest achievement of the past . . . years is the thinking of the country. Imperceptibly, we have come to recognize that government has a responsibility to defend the weak."

This 1934 cartoon pokes fun at the alphabetical names of the New Deal programs—PWA, NRA, CCC, TVA, AAA, and RFC.

But while many Americans laughed at the New Deal's silly names and initials, they applauded the Democrats (represented by the donkey) for their complex program of dealing with the Depression. In contrast, as this cartoon shows, many people believed the Republicans (represented by the elephant) knew only one set of initials—SOS, the international sign for signaling "Help!"

Newspapers called her the copresident. Politicians sought her patronage. Americans wrote to her with their requests and concerns. Why? Because everyone knew the most influential person in the president's life was his wife—Eleanor. According to economist Rexford Tugwell, Eleanor in action was a sight to behold:

> No one who ever saw Eleanor Roosevelt sit down facing her husband, and, holding his eye firmly, say to him, "Franklin, I think you should . . ." or, "Franklin, surely you will not . . ." will ever forget the experience. . . . And even after many years he obviously disliked to face that devastatingly simple honest look that Eleanor fixed him with when she was aware of an injustice amenable to Presidential action or a good deed that he could do. . . . It would be impossible to say how often and to what extent American governmental processes have been turned in new directions because of *her* determination that people should be hurt as little as possible and that as much should be done for them as could be managed; the whole, if it could be totaled, would be formidable.

Poster for Eleanor's pet program the National Youth Administration (NYA)

In May 1934 Eleanor confessed to experiencing "real moments of terror" when she thought about America's youth. Hit hard by the Depression, they were denied jobs and unable to finish their education. "We have to bring the young people into the active life of the community," she said, "and make them feel they are necessary." She took her concerns to Franklin, who agreed that something needed to be done—and by 1935 the NYA had been created. A New Deal program, the NYA had a twofold task. First, it helped high school students stay in school by giving them grants in exchange for work in libraries, in factories, and on farms. Secondly, it provided unemployed young people with job training, then helped them find work.

Eleanor became so involved in the NYA that Franklin referred to it as "the missus' organization." She dropped in at NYA sites all over the country, where young men and women were learning how to type, weld, put in plumbing, bathe babies. From program directors she demanded updates on progress and gave plenty of unsolicited advice. She often asked for a needs list, and if the government refused to pay for the necessary items, she did. "In short," said one young participant, "the NYA had no better friend than the first lady."

The "missus' organization" proved to be one of the New Deal's greatest successes, touching five million young lives before World War II ended the program in 1943. "What would we have done without Mrs. Roosevelt?" wondered one young man helped by the NYA.

ILLINIOS
NATIONAL YOUTH ADMINISTRATION

GIRLS – ARE YOU INTERESTED IN A JOB?

FIND OUT WHAT AN OCCUPATION HAS TO OFFER YOU IN
PAY - EMPLOYMENT - SECURITY AND PROMOTION
FREE CLASSES
IN OCCUPATIONS

ON   AT

THE SUBJECT WILL BE

WM. J. CAMPBELL, STATE DIRECTOR

Eleanor's Baby

During the Depression living conditions were abysmal in the Appalachian area of West Virginia. One day a journalist named Frank Kingdon entered a miner's shack and was astounded to find Eleanor Roosevelt sitting on a stained, bare mattress. She was holding a thin, naked baby on her lap while the mother stirred a pot of watery soup on the stove. "The two women were discussing their household problems as though that Appalachian hut was no different from a Washington drawing room," the journalist remembered.

That night Eleanor returned to the White House and told her dinner guests about the mining family she had visited. The father, she said, had shown her his weekly pay slips. Money had been deducted to pay for his bills at the company store, as well as his rent and oil for his lamp, leaving him with less than one dollar a week to support his wife and six children. On the table of this miner's house sat a bowl filled with scraps, Eleanor went on, "the kind most people feed their dogs," and at noon the children ran in, grabbed a handful of the scraps, ate, and ran out. As she got ready to leave, two of the children gathered enough courage to speak to her—a boy holding a white rabbit in his arms, and his older sister. The girl turned to Eleanor. "He thinks we're not going to eat his rabbit," she whispered. "But we are."

"That little boy must have heard her," Eleanor said as she finished the story, "because he clutched his rabbit closer and fled down the hill."

The next morning she received a check from one of her dinner guests. The accompanying note read, "I hope this money will keep the rabbit alive."

It was a generous gesture, but Eleanor wanted to do more for those families—much more. When charity workers from the area suggested moving the

Arthurdale as it looked in 1934

miners to a nearby farm, Eleanor seized on the idea. They could grow their own food, she thought. Start simple industries like furniture making. Regain their economic footing.

Enthusiastically she presented the idea to Franklin. He, in turn, presented it to Congress, which quickly allocated $25 million for Arthurdale, as the project was named (after a nearby town). By the end of 1933 twelve hundred acres of farmland had been purchased by the government and houses for two hundred families were being built.

But Eleanor's insistence on refrigerators, electricity, and indoor plumbing—luxuries most rural homes in the area did not have—pushed the cost of construction from $1,000 per house to almost $10,000. She clung to the idea of making Arthurdale, which became known as her "baby," a model project. She believed it could lead to a national policy of decent, affordable housing for all Americans. To this end she persuaded friends to contribute money for a small hospital, a handicraft and music program that would preserve Appalachian folk culture, and an advanced education system. She even made donations herself.

As the community took shape, it drew fire from critics. Some people complained government was giving away middle-class affluence to those who didn't work and didn't deserve it. Others claimed the project was a "design for permanent poverty, for if one expects to be given a living, one will never learn to earn one." Even members of the president's cabinet criticized Arthurdale. "We are spending money down here like a drunken sailor," complained secretary of the interior Harold Ickes. "If Mrs. Roosevelt has her way, how will we be able to tell the rich from the poor?"

"Well," replied Eleanor, "in a matter of such

The inside of an Arthurdale house

simple dignity and decency, we should not be able to tell the rich from the poor."

In June 1934 the first families moved to Arthurdale. "That day changed our life completely," said one miner's daughter. "There was our little white house set against this backdrop of green trees and green grass. And everything was nice and white and clean, and there was a bathroom! And it was ours!"

Eleanor used her connections to bring industry—a vacuum cleaner assembly plant and a furniture factory—to the area. She knew the homesteaders needed jobs if the community was ever to become self-sustaining. Disappointingly, these businesses failed to take root in Arthurdale, and many of the homesteaders remained dependent on the government. Too dependent, conceded Eleanor. "They seemed to feel government should solve all their problems, and were often unwilling to shoulder their share of the responsibility."

By 1941 the federal government no longer wanted to shoulder it either. It sold off its holdings to local residents and entrepreneurs, considering the project a failure. Still, Eleanor felt proud of her role in creating a community that had made a difference. Arthurdale's residents were certainly better off now than they had been as miners. The homes she helped build had given them a dignity they'd never known before, a chance to raise their children under a decent roof, and the ability to envision a better life. Admitted Eleanor, "Much money was spent, some of it unwisely," but "I have always felt that many human beings who might have cost us thousands of dollars in tuberculosis sanitariums, insane asylums, and jails were restored to usefulness and given confidence in themselves."

THE SOCIAL SECURITY ACT OF 1935

Before the 1930s care of America's elderly, unemployed, and disabled citizens was left to families and private charities. But the widespread suffering caused by the Depression forced Franklin to send a message to Congress asking for social security legislation—a way for the federal government to help its citizens directly. His request caused an uproar. Many Americans considered social security "un-American," while others believed it would lead to the "ultimate socialist control of life and industry." Declared one Republican senator, "We are creating a welfare state."

Using her radio programs as well as her magazine articles and newspaper columns, Eleanor spoke out. "Now, it has come about when you talk about the welfare state as a rule people think it is a derogatory term—that a welfare state is not a good thing," she argued. "But if we could just change it around a little and say that we believed society included the government . . . working to increase the welfare of the individual then we could cease, I think, to have fear of the words 'welfare state.' We would have a true conception of what the words really mean—a mutual contribution toward security in old age, care for the blind and crippled—humanitarian gestures from a humanitarian state."

Eleanor originally hoped the bill creating a social security system would include health care for the aged as well as benefits for unemployed women and widows with children. But as opposition grew fiercer she declared she would take the law any way it was drafted.

Eventually Congress hammered out its differ-

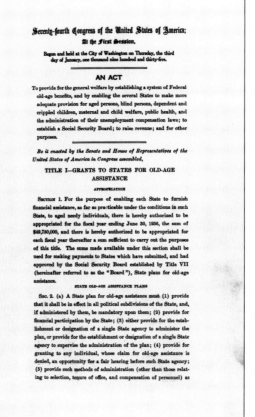

ences and created the Social Security Act, which provided two types of assistance for the aged. Those who were destitute could receive federal aid of up to fifteen dollars a person per month. Those who were working could receive payments when they retired. These payments—or insurance, as they were called—were supported by contributions in the form of taxes on workers' wages and on the employers' payroll. Additionally, the act provided aid to the blind and handicapped, and assistance for dependent mothers with children.

At a White House ceremony on August 14, 1935, Eleanor beamed as Franklin signed the act into law. Americans obviously understood how influential Eleanor had been in getting the bill passed. Over the next years she received thousands of notes like this one from grateful citizens:

Dear First Lady:
I am a widow, my husband died nine months ago, and since then I have received my social security each month, fifteen dollars.
I want to express my thankfulness to you and our president for being the means of this big help.

Both Social Security and Temporary Aid for Needy Families (formerly Aid to Families with Dependent Children) continue to be a big help to Americans. It is estimated that three million poor families receive help from TANF, while four out of five citizens receive some sort of Social Security benefit.

The Roosevelt Way

Franklin and Eleanor's vision of a government directly helping its citizens was known in Washington, D.C., as the Roosevelt Way, and it changed American thought forever. Almost overnight the concept of individualism—the belief that a man should make it on his own—was abandoned. With passage of the Social Security Act most Americans eagerly embraced the idea of government assistance and quickly built on the Roosevelts' ideas. As early as 1939 Congress amended the Social Security Act, extending federal aid to widows and orphaned children. Later changes made between 1950 and 1970 broadened coverage even more and increased the size of benefits. Medicare (health care for eligible retirees) was added in 1965, and a Supplemental Security Income (SSI) was instituted for income-needy elderly, blind, and disabled persons in 1972.

The Roosevelt Way has inspired hundreds of other federal programs as well. Later presidential administrations instituted public housing and rent supplements that help the needy pay for shelter. A food stamp program helps many poor people buy groceries. Medicaid subsidizes health care for those on welfare. And Temporary Aid for Needy Families (TANF) supports more than three million poor American families. Additionally, there is a federal unemployment insurance, which aids those out of work; federal student loan programs, which help needy Americans pay for college education; federally funded preschool programs; legal aid; medical clinics; family planning services; as well as hundreds of other public assistance programs.

Nowadays Americans truly believe what first lady Eleanor Roosevelt stated in 1936: "We should strive to give every individual a chance for a decent and secure existence; and in evolving our social patterns we are trying to give both hope for better things in the future, and freedom from want in the present."

Dear Mrs. Roosevelt

———— ❖ ————

Eleanor, because she was known as a first lady who cared about people's problems, was swamped with letters. Some of this mail, she admitted, was "purely advisory. . . . They tell me what they think of my traveling so much. They scold me for my policies." Most, however, were requests—requests for jobs, money, help. Aided by a secretary, Eleanor answered many herself or referred them to the appropriate agency, asking to be informed of the action taken. Occasionally she would send a letter to her husband with a penciled note, "How should I answer, or will you?" To friends who asked why she bothered with them all, she replied, "Whatever comes your way is yours to handle." Besides, she added, "I can sometimes relieve their sorrow a little." Below is just a sampling of the letters Eleanor received and how she responded.

One of the first letters to the first lady was from a young woman named Bertha Brodsky, who in wishing the Roosevelts well, added apologetically that she found it hard to write because her back was crooked and she had to walk bent sideways. Eleanor sent Bertha's letter to the doctor in charge of the New York Orthopaedic Hospital. "Might a free bed be found for the girl?" she asked. It was, and Bertha soon found herself undergoing the treatment her working-class family could never have afforded. While Bertha was hospitalized, Eleanor visited her faithfully and sent flowers and other gifts. When the girl was released, the first lady found her a job. And when she acquired a serious boyfriend, Bertha asked Eleanor to look him over. Eleanor went to Bertha's wedding, gave her marital advice, and became godmother to her child. A grateful Bertha called her "dear messenger of God."

In 1934 a high school boy asked for football shoes. "I thought one of your sons might have an old pair. . . . I'd be proud to wear them." Eleanor sent him a personal check for fifteen dollars—more than enough for a new pair.

In 1936 a teenager wrote to say she was graduating from high school as valedictorian of her class but had nothing but her brother's overalls to wear to the event. She begged the first lady for a "pretty outfit for my big day." Thoughtfully, the girl had included a page from a mail-order catalog with sizes, prices, and colors carefully written in. "I was suspicious," admitted Eleanor, "and asked someone to investigate and we found the whole story was untrue." She wasn't even graduating from high school, Eleanor recalled. "She simply wanted some new clothes."

A seventy-four-year-old man wrote to beg for the continuation of the adult education classes in his community. He had just learned to read and wanted the first lady to know what it meant suddenly to understand the printed word. "I am not the only one. My next door neighbor is 81, and he learned to read last winter, and it has just made life over for us!" Eleanor not only spoke with Franklin to ensure that funds for the program continued, but she also sent the man a set of books, "with many warm regards from Mrs. Roosevelt."

One day in 1939 a first grader from Lexington, Kentucky, wrote Eleanor a letter. In it he described how he lived in a tin shack without a foundation, and how every time it rained, his house slid farther down the hill. Could she help? Eleanor traveled to Kentucky, where she talked with the heads of realty associations and banks. Together they built new, affordable housing in Lexington. One of the first families to move into these homes was the first grader's. The next year he sent his second-grade picture to Eleanor. On the back he wrote, "Dear Mrs. Roosevelt. Thank you for my house. I know you did it."

In 1941 a six-page letter arrived detailing the sad life of the McClarrens. The father had lost his part-time job, the land was too sandy to produce decent crops, the cow had died, five children needed to be clothed and fed, and the youngest—a five-year-old—had been left crippled by polio. Could Mrs. Roosevelt send "our poor boy" to Warm Springs, Georgia, where Franklin had established a polio treatment center? Eager to help, Eleanor raised the necessary funds. While the boy underwent treatment, she aided the family by moving them into a government-built house and finding the father work. By the next Christmas, Mrs. McClarren was writing Mrs. Roosevelt again—"Our life has been changed because of you . . . !"

Civil Rights

Because she grew up among people who rarely questioned bigotry and prejudice, the only African Americans Eleanor had ever met were servants. Yes, she knew that in many parts of the country blacks were not allowed to vote. And she had heard about segregation, and how blacks were barred from restaurants, schools, and hotels. But it wasn't until she was forty-nine years old that she gave the issue of racial discrimination any serious thought.

As she traveled the nation and saw the suffering of black Americans, the first lady began to understand how deeply racial discrimination was embedded in American life. Almost overnight she became an outspoken champion of civil rights. She visited black communities and schools, made friends with black leaders, and learned firsthand about the indignities and humiliations endured by blacks.

Her views angered some Americans. "Dear madam," one citizen wrote after hearing Eleanor speak about the inequality of wages between blacks and whites. "You are about the most poorly informed person that I know of concerning the Negroes' relation to the white race, so I suggest you stop meddling."

But anger didn't stop Eleanor. Nor did Franklin try to stop her. He wholeheartedly supported his wife's racial views but allowed her to take the lead rather than speaking up himself. In this way he gained the political support of the black community without losing the support of powerful white segregationists who controlled so many important committees in Congress.

In 1938 Eleanor attended a meeting of the Southern Conference for Human Welfare in Birmingham, Alabama. At that time a state law prohibited blacks and whites from sitting together at public gatherings. When Eleanor arrived, the auditorium had been divided at the center aisle—one side for black participants, the other for whites. Wanting to sit with her dear friend the black educator Mary McLeod Bethune, the first lady plopped herself down on the black side. Only when police told her she was breaking the law did she leave her friend. But not for long. Placing a chair in the center aisle, she stubbornly sat there.

Just weeks later the Daughters of the American Revolution (DAR) refused to let Marian Anderson, a celebrated black opera singer, give a concert in their auditorium. The DAR declared that no black artist would be allowed to use Constitution Hall, the only hall big enough to accommodate all the singer's fans. When Eleanor heard about this, she promptly resigned

Eleanor was often photographed with African Americans, a practice unheard of among white Americans during the 1930s. When this picture of the first lady being escorted by members of the honor guard at Howard University (then a black college) hit the newspapers in 1936, segregationists were outraged. They used it to attack the "Negro-loving" policies of the Roosevelts. Indeed, replied Eleanor, "I am a Negro lover."

from the DAR, transforming the incident into one of national importance and debate. Folklore credits Eleanor with suggesting the Lincoln Memorial for the site of the concert, where more than 75,000 people eventually heard Ms. Anderson sing. More important, however, Eleanor convinced radio stations to broadcast the event live, then urged black leaders to use the broadcast as a fund-raising event for the National Association for the Advancement of Colored People (NAACP). "I am not surprised at Mrs. Roosevelt's action," Ms. Anderson said later, "because she seems to me the only one who really comprehends the true meaning of democracy."

By the time World War II began, Eleanor was declaring over and over again that there could be no real democracy in the United States that did not include African Americans. "Government," she insisted, "must provide protection against discrimination, and develop policies which create a level playing field." She found it especially galling that black

Eleanor with "the closest friend in my own age group," Mary McLeod Bethune

February 26, 1939.

Henry M.
My dear Mrs. Robert Jr.

I am afraid that I have never been a very useful member of the Daughters of the American Revolution, so I know it will make very little difference to you whether I resign, or whether I continue to be a member of your organization.

However, I am in complete disagreement with the attitude taken in refusing Constitution Hall to a great artist. You have set an example which seems to me unfortunate, and I feel obliged to send in to you my resignation. You had an opportunity to lead in an enlightened way and it seems to me that your organization has failed.

I realize that many people will not agree with me, but feeling as I do this seems to me the only proper procedure to follow.

Very sincerely yours,

Eleanor's letter of resignation from the DAR

soldiers, risking their lives for democracy, were treated unfairly. At the time even the United States Army practiced segregation. Unable to change this practice, Eleanor made a point of visiting both camps when touring army facilities. "One day," recalled Pvt. Calvin Thompson, "I was sitting in the negro canteen eating an ice cream cone. Suddenly there was some commotion at the door. Everyone looked and stared and when I turned around I saw a tall lady walking in. 'What do you know,' I said to myself, 'it's Mrs. Roosevelt.' She went behind the counter, shook hands with each of the men down the line, and asked them their names and where they were from. When she came to me I was still eating my ice cream cone . . . and she looked straight into my eyes and said, 'May I have some of that ice cream?'" Everyone in the room was shocked. Black and white people weren't allowed to eat in the same restaurant, much less off the same ice cream cone! "Very gently Mrs. Roosevelt took the cone out of my hand, took a big bite, and handed it back to me. 'You see,' she said and smiled real wide, 'that didn't hurt at all, did it?'"

LIBRARIES FOR EVERYONE

*E*leanor didn't worry just about the social and economic well-being of Americans. She worried about their intellectual development, too. Knowing the Depression had eliminated many educational opportunities, she turned to the nation's libraries.

"We have got to make our libraries the center of a new life in the mind, because people are hungry to use their minds. . . . It is the people who work in libraries who are going to lead the way, who are going to give other people the curiosity and the vision of useful things, and pleasant things, and amusing things. It is a very great responsibility because there is a great need . . . especially in rural America. There is a great need for imagination in the ways used to stir the interest of old and young . . . so we must insist on libraries for every community, and we must insist on paying for them, for what we get, in the end, is stimulation of intellectual thought, individual curiosity and the chance to make a democracy that will be a *real* democracy."

So Alone Inside

Beneath Eleanor's public face of courage, conviction, and good works there remained a heartbreaking vulnerability. One Christmas as she raced from one activity to the next, organizing charity parties, distributing gifts to the poor, attending the tree-lighting ceremony at the Salvation Army, she admitted this to her friend Joseph Lash:

"I have come to dread, not what I do for those I love, but the mass production side and the formal, impersonal things I have to do. I'm always with so many people, and always so alone inside."

FBI director J. Edgar Hoover disagreed with Eleanor's stances on most issues and ordered his agents to keep a close eye on her. From 1919—the year Eleanor's name first appeared in an FBI report—until her death in 1962, agents monitored her activities and taped her telephone conversations. In her file they assembled for the director's view reports on her many activities, newspaper editorials she'd written, gossip, and allegations. Hoover read every word. Often he was so disturbed by it, he wrote in the margin. "Nauseating," he once scrawled after reading Eleanor's speech to members of the National Association for the Advancement of Colored People. "Parlor pink," he wrote, using the slang term for *communist*, after learning about her support of labor unions. In 1943 Hoover had his agents install listening devices in Eleanor's Chicago hotel room. He was convinced he would uncover the link between the first lady and the Communist Party. All he uncovered, however, was a load of trouble. A hotel employee tipped off Eleanor about the surveillance. She, in turn, complained to Franklin, who lambasted the FBI director for investigating his wife. Hoover was contrite, but he wasn't stopped. He continued to tail Eleanor even as she publicly referred to his "Gestapo methods" and wrote outraged letters protesting investigations of her friends, business associates, and even her personal secretary. Despite her protestations, however, her file continued to grow, becoming one of the largest FBI files in American history—3,271 pages in all!

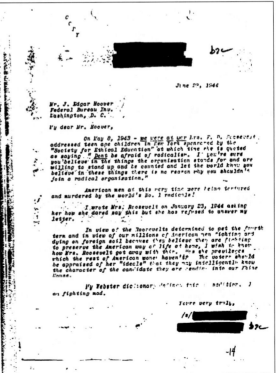

Eleanor's Enemies

Not everyone liked and admired Eleanor. Her hectic travel and honest talk may have earned her millions of admirers, but it also earned her millions of detractors. An opinion poll taken in 1944 showed that just 36 percent of Americans approved of her activities, while 45 percent disapproved and 19 percent had no opinion at all. Those critical of the first lady called her "The Busybody," "The Meddler," and "The Gab." Why couldn't she just stay home with her husband, she was frequently asked, "and tend to knitting as an example for other women to follow?" One woman, after visiting the White House on a tour, gave Eleanor this unwelcome advice: "Instead of tearing around the country, I think you should stay at home and personally see that the White House is clean. I soiled my white gloves yesterday morning on the stair-railing. It was disgraceful."

No one was more outspoken than newspaper columnist Westbrook Pegler. Pegler used his column, "Fair Enough" (which appeared in as many as 150 newspapers across the country with a total circulation of 4 to 5 million copies), to characterize Eleanor as a "traitor to her class," "an overreaching first lady with socialist leanings," and "a political naif." She was not, he wrote in 1939, a systematic thinker. She could not set priorities or focus on important problems. Instead she was a "victim of her own naive generosity and self-serving impulses, always rushing to help any person in trouble, whether their complaints were justified or not." Years later Pegler was asked about

his hatred for Eleanor Roosevelt. "I . . . do not hate [Mrs. Roosevelt]," he replied, "but I despise her pretense of humane motives."

Eleanor's critics, however, did not limit themselves to attacking her activities and interests. They made fun of her physical appearance as well, portraying her in political cartoons as big-toothed, weak-chinned, and loudmouthed. Photographers, too, looked for ways to portray Eleanor in an unattractive light. In 1938 *Life* magazine included a picture of the first lady asleep in an airplane with her mouth open. It was an ugly picture, making Eleanor the butt of many jokes. The incident, according to her friend Joe Lash, hurt her deeply. Still, she presented an unruffled appearance to the world. "Nobody looks very nice when he goes to sleep with his mouth open," she laughingly told reporters, "and this has served to remind me to carry a large heavy veil and swathe myself in it before I go to sleep on a plane again!"

A seasoned politician, Eleanor understood that a woman who insisted on her right to self-identity, a woman with power or the appearance of power, was bound to elicit people's rage and contempt. "If I . . . worried about mudslinging," she said, "I would have been dead long ago." Instead, she offered advice to other women with political aspirations. "You cannot take anything personally," she wrote in 1936. "You cannot bear grudges. . . . Women who are willing to be leaders must stand out and be shot at. . . ." And above all? Every political woman needs, she insisted, "to develop skin as tough as rhinoceros hide."

Just one of Westbrook Pegler's many newspaper columns criticizing Eleanor

A Lifelong Friend

On a rainy day in November 1939 fifty-five-year-old Eleanor Roosevelt quietly took a seat in the viewing area of the House of Representatives. She had come to watch the House Committee on Un-American Activities investigate possible communist activities within American youth groups. More important, she had come to show her support for the politically radical students she felt were being unfairly questioned.

On the floor a black-haired twenty-nine-year-old named Joseph Lash rose to testify. Formerly the head of the American Student Union, Lash had recently resigned his position within the group. In the months that followed he had tried unsuccessfully to find another job. "It was a confusing time for Joe," admitted one of Lash's friends. "He was lonely, depressed, and drifting aimlessly." He was also angry about being called before this committee. Still, he managed to express eloquently his feelings about the students and their political viewpoints. Eleanor was intrigued. When his testimony was over, she invited him back to the White House for dinner.

"It is funny how quickly one knows about people," Eleanor later wrote about that first meeting. "I knew we were going to be friends."

At first Lash couldn't understand why someone as famous and powerful as Eleanor would want him around so much. He knew they shared the same political goals—a government that took care of its people, a national policy that ensured equal rights for all citizens. But Lash also knew he often acted gloomy and depressed. He couldn't figure out why she was drawn to him.

Eleanor, however, opened her heart to him. She admitted to having her own insecurities and inadequacies. She talked freely about her bouts of depression. She described in detail the stories of her anguished childhood and the humiliation of Franklin's affair. In Lash she found a sympathetic soul who filled an emotional need in her life. "She had a compelling need to have people who were close, who in a sense were hers and upon whom she could lavish help, attention, tenderness," Lash later wrote. "Without such friends, she feared she would dry up and die."

Eleanor certainly lavished her help and attention on Lash. In 1944 she acted as matchmaker when he fell in love with Trude Pratt. The affair was especially complicated because Trude was already married. Still, Eleanor encouraged their relationship, offering advice, support, and the occasional safe cover for their meetings. "Of one thing I am sure," she wrote Lash, "don't accept a compromise. Trude must be yours, otherwise you will never be happy." When the couple finally married, Eleanor made a point of developing a close, personal friendship with Lash's bride. Trude Lash soon became Eleanor's "next best friend after Joe," daughter Anna once said.

Eleanor influenced Lash's life in other ways too. She joined with him to form Americans for Democratic Action, an anti-communist liberal group that lobbied for social programs such as national health care and affordable housing. Because of his close ties to Eleanor, Lash was appointed director of the New York office, a position he retained until 1948. In 1950 he joined the staff of the *New York Post* and covered the United Nations at the time Eleanor served on the U.S. delegation to that organization. And during the 1950s and 1960s he began his most famous pursuit—chronicling the Roosevelts' years in the White House. At first he edited Franklin's letters, but after Eleanor's death in 1962 he began writing about her life. By 1971 he had published *Eleanor and Franklin*, a biography that won him a Pulitzer Prize. Several other books about Eleanor followed, including a personal memoir of their friendship and two volumes based on her correspondence. For the rest of his life he was considered the leading authority on the Roosevelts. He was also considered Eleanor's dearest friend. "She personifies my belief and faith in the possibility of mankind," he wrote in his diary.

The War Years

❦

You don't want to go to war. I don't want to go to war.
But war may come to us.

—Eleanor Roosevelt, in a speech to the American Youth Congress, May 26, 1940

——— THREE REASONS FOR WORLD WAR II ———

Benito Mussolini,
premier of Italy

To promote his own rise to power, Benito Mussolini—nicknamed Il Duce ("the leader")—founded the Fascist Party in 1921. Believing military government should control all aspects of society, the Mussolini-led Fascists clashed with the existing Italian government in October 1922. The result? Mussolini proclaimed himself dictator. Immediately he limited freedom of speech, arrested political opponents, and resisted voting rights. He also sent Italian forces into the African nation of Ethiopia in an attempt to make Italy an imperial power. In Washington, D.C., Eleanor saw a newsreel of the slaughter in Africa. "I felt positively disgusted with human beings," she said. "How can we be such fools to go on senselessly taking human life in this way?"

Gen. Hideki Tōjō,
prime minister of Japan

Nicknamed the Razor for his swift decisions, Tōjō was the most influential adviser in wartime Japan. His goals were simple: He wanted to lessen Japan's reliance on foreign imports like rubber and oil, and he wanted to expand the empire of Japan throughout East Asia and the Pacific. Tōjō saw only one way to accomplish these goals— massive military buildup coupled with aggressive invasion. In 1931 his troops crossed the border and invaded Manchuria, seizing control of that region's iron, oil, and rubber production. In 1934—in violation of a treaty with the United States—he began building a formidable navy. And in 1937 he launched a full-scale invasion of China, brutally assaulting and occupying the Chinese city of Nanjing. Back in the U.S., Franklin condemned Tōjō's actions. But it was Eleanor who spoke most plainly. "Japan," she said, "was . . . the enemy in the Pacific."

Adolf Hitler,
dictator of Germany

In 1933 Adolf Hitler's National Socialist, or Nazi, Party won nearly 40 percent of the vote in the national election, making Hitler chancellor of the country. He determined that an ethnically pure Aryan race should rule the world, and his government—called the Third Reich ("empire")—prohibited Jews and non-Nazis from holding government jobs, outlawed strikes, and made serving in the military mandatory, while Nazi storm troopers called brownshirts crushed all political opposition. Some close to Hitler believed he was mentally unbalanced. A mesmerizing speaker who was unable to control himself once he got started, he often ranted on for hours at a time. These ravings moved many Germans, who supported his rearmament of the nation by pouring money and labor into planes, tanks, and submarines. In 1936 Hitler tested out his powerful new military by invading the Rhineland—the territory west of the Rhine River, which had formerly been part of Germany but was now occupied by France. Two years later he attacked the Sudetenland region of western Czechoslovakia. Watching from Washington, Eleanor declared, "Hitler is a sinister man with no scruples."

The front page of the *Chicago Daily News,*

September 1, 1939

"At five o'clock this morning our telephone rang," Eleanor wrote in her "My Day" column from Hyde Park, "and it was the President in Washington to tell me the sad news that Germany had invaded Poland and that her planes were bombing Polish cities."

But Germany didn't stop with Poland. In the spring of 1940 its army invaded Denmark, Norway, Holland, and Belgium, then turned its attention to France. Within days France fell, giving Hitler's Germany complete control of Europe's Atlantic coastline from Norway in the north to the Spanish border in the south. Only Great Britain was left to fight on against the Nazis.

In August 1940, Germany began an all-out air assault on England. Day after day Nazi bombers flew across the English Channel, dropping hundreds of bombs on London and other cities. The damage was catastrophic, but England stood tough. "We await undismayed the impending assault," Prime Minister Winston Churchill told the British people. "But be the ordeal sharp or long, we shall seek no terms, we shall tolerate no parley. We may show mercy—but we shall ask for none."

Britain did, however, ask for help. In December 1940, Churchill wrote to Franklin. He wanted the president to know that while Britain could endure the air attacks, she was facing an "equally deadly danger—lack of the crucial weapons of war." Britain needed guns, ships, planes, and ammunition. But she was "no longer able to pay for them . . . and it would be unfair to ask her to pay cash for these needed supplies while the victory is being won with our blood and civilization is being saved."

Franklin desperately wanted to help. But the national mood in the United States was isolationist—Americans did not want to involve themselves directly in the European conflict. They were, wrote Eleanor, "not yet ready to go along with any drastic steps toward war." So Franklin devised an ingenious plan. Called the Lend-Lease Act, it allowed the United States to loan war supplies to the British. Americans supported the plan. They saw it as an alternative to war. "Few," wrote Eleanor, "truly realized that war loomed on our horizons."

THE FATE OF EUROPE'S JEWS

"I'd rather be hung than seen at a gathering that was mostly Jews," thirty-six-year-old Eleanor wrote in 1920. Likewise, when first introduced to Harvard Law School professor Felix Frankfurter, she said he was "an interesting little man, but very Jew."

Eleanor came of age in the privileged world of the late nineteenth century—white Protestant America—where anti-Semitism was widespread. Thoughtlessly she often expressed an uneducated understanding of the Jewish people. But as her interests expanded, she came into contact with many Jewish men and women who shared her beliefs. Slowly Eleanor's anti-Semitic views began to change. Still, as late as 1939 she wrote a German friend that "there may be a need for curtailing the ascendancy of the Jewish people." But, she added, this should be done in a more humane and decent way than Hitler was doing it.

Americans were well aware that in Europe the Jews were being rounded up and deported to various labor camps. But they did not believe Jews were being killed by the thousands until a new and devastating report reached the United States in 1942. The report told how Hitler planned to deport all European Jews to concentration camps, where they would be "at one blow exterminated in order to resolve, once and for all, the Jewish question in Europe."

Not long after reading this report, Eleanor noticed a small item buried on the back page of the *New York Times*. According to the article, more than two thirds of the Jewish population in Poland had been murdered—nearly three million people.

Curiously, Eleanor remained vague about the plight of Europe's Jews. Just days later she declared a desire to "be of help in any way," but, she added, "I can not figure out what is to be done at the present time." If, however, a plan of action was formulated, she felt sure the American people, "who have been shocked and horrified by the attitude of the Axis powers toward the Jews," would help.

Franklin, too, was vague about helping the Jews. Even though some of his military strategists advised taking direct rescue action—destroying rail lines used to transport Jews east and bombing concentration camps—Franklin refused. Winning the war, he maintained, was the best way to rescue the Jews. "Our government," he said in a noncommittal speech to prominent Jewish leaders, "has made, and will continue to make, repeated efforts to crush Nazi power forever."

Americans, for the most part, did not disagree with the Roosevelts. American newspapers printed very little about the mass killings, and when they did, they presented the deaths as an unfortunate by-product of war. Most of Congress showed little concern. And most church leaders remained silent on the issue.

The ugly truth was that America in the 1940s was still largely anti-Semitic. American colleges and universities had limits on how many Jewish students could be enrolled. Jews were often denied membership in such organizations as country clubs. And many of the most desirable neighborhoods restricted Jewish home buyers. In his diary Joseph Goebbels—minister of propaganda in Hitler's Nazi regime—gloatingly wrote, "Deep down I believe . . . the Americans are happy that we are exterminating the Jewish riffraff."

Under heavy pressure from the American Jewish community, Franklin finally agreed to establish the War Refugee Board in January 1944. Its goal was "to develop positive, new American programs to aid the victims of Nazism while pressing the Allies and neutrals to take forceful diplomatic action in their behalf." In the spring of that year War Refugee Board director John Pehle got Franklin to agree to establish an emergency shelter for Jewish refugees in Oswego, New York. He also succeeded in getting the president to issue a strong statement accusing Germany of "the wholesale, systematic murder of the Jews" and promising the world that these crimes would not go unpunished. But it was too little too late. Said Director John Pehle wistfully, "If only it had been set up earlier things might have been different."

By the time the war in Europe ended in May 1945, more than six million Jews had been killed.

THE LUCKY FEW—ONE OF THE LAST BOATLOADS OF EUROPEAN REFUGEE CHILDREN TO ARRIVE IN THE UNITED STATES, JUST WEEKS BEFORE IMMIGRATION IS RESTRICTED

As thousands of Jewish and other anti-Nazi refugees clamored for asylum in America, Eleanor threw all her influence behind a campaign to rescue some of them. She lobbied Congress to ease the nation's strict immigration laws and provide a safe haven for people trying to escape Hitler. She backed legislation that provided for the admission of ten thousand additional children a year over and above the established immigration quota for Germany. Most of these children, she knew, would be Jewish. And though she often expressed little concern for Jewish adults trapped in Europe, her heart went out to their children, "the most persecuted of young souls." Assuming all the "horrid legal details" would soon be sorted out in Congress, Eleanor turned to the task of "finding homes in which to put the children when they arrived." But to her dismay, Congress refused to pass the Child Refugee Bill. Polls confirmed that while Americans disapproved of Hitler's brutal treatment of Jews in Europe, the majority were unwilling to help them, especially if it meant allowing more Jewish immigrants into the United States.

Franklin did not want to pit his presidency against the country's anti-Semitic mood. Instead he asked the State Department to tighten immigration restrictions. His purpose? To give Americans the impression that their government was preventing the infiltration of Nazi agents into the United States. The result? No Eastern Europeans were allowed to enter the country, not even the children.

His position resulted in a family argument. "[Franklin] was somewhat impatient and irritated," a friend recorded in his diary the day Eleanor huffed into his study. "He kept bringing up difficulties while Mrs. Roosevelt tenaciously kept pointing out the possibilities."

Eleanor couldn't help but voice her frustration. "What has happened to this country?" she railed. "If we study our history we find that we have always been ready to receive the unfortunates from other countries, and though this may seem a generous gesture on our part we have profited a thousand fold by what they have brought us." But her angry words did not change public opinion. Shamefully, only a handful of refugees found safety in the United States during the course of the war.

A *Third* Term

Until Franklin, no president had ever served more than two terms in office (and after him the Constitution was amended so no one ever could again). But in 1940, with war gripping Europe and Asia, Franklin's supporters urged him to run for a third term. Critics claimed he was trying to establish an "imperial presidency." Eleanor, however, knew the real reason he chose to run.

"I had every evidence to believe that he did not want to run again. However, as time went on, more and more people came to me saying that he must run, that the threat of war was just over the horizon and no one else had the prestige and the knowledge to carry on through a crisis. . . . In his mind, I think, there was a great seesaw; on one end the weariness that had already begun, and the desire to be home and his own master; on the other end, the overwhelming interest that was the culmination of a lifetime of preparation and work, and the desire to see and to have a hand in the affairs of the world in that critical period."

Eleanor to the rescue

Eleanor at the podium at the Democratic National Convention

On July 17, 1940, Eleanor sat in her living room at Val-Kill listening to the radio broadcast of the first night of the Democratic National Convention. Franklin, who had just been nominated for an unprecedented third term, sent word he wanted his secretary of agriculture, Henry Wallace, to be his running mate. But as Eleanor listened Wallace's name was met by jeers and catcalls. The delegates—remembering that Henry Wallace had once been a Republican—threatened not to nominate him. In response Franklin threatened not to run. The convention, recalled one delegate, was "spinning out of control." At Val-Kill the phone rang. "I got a call from the convention begging me to come out," Eleanor recalled. "I telephoned Franklin [in Washington, D.C.] and he said, 'Well, would you like to go?' and I said, 'No, I wouldn't *like* to go. I'm very busy and I wouldn't *like* to go at all.' He said, 'Well, they seem to think it might be well if you came out.' And I said, 'But do you really want me to go?' And he said, 'Well,

perhaps it would be a good idea.' So I went."

Twenty-four hours later, on the evening of July 18, she entered the raucous convention hall. "The noise in the room was deafening," she said. "You couldn't hear yourself, or speak to your next door neighbor." The delegates were in an ugly mood, surging up and down the aisles, screaming and yelling. "Oh, she can't go on now," wailed one of the convention's organizers. "It's a terrible thing to make her do." But Eleanor calmly stepped to the podium.

Eleanor speaks at the 1940 Democratic National Convention.

er brief, simple words brought silence to the convention hall. Pleading with the delegates, she asked them to remember that the world was on the brink of war. "This is no ordinary time," she said, "no time for weighing anything except what we can best do for the country as a whole. No man who is a candidate, who is president can carry this situation alone. This responsibility is only carried by a united people who love their country and who will live for it . . . to the fullest of their ability." When she finished, the convention's mood was transformed. Delegates applauded and hugged one another. Henry Wallace was nominated for vice president. And Eleanor Roosevelt made history. For the first time ever the wife of a presidential nominee had addressed a major political convention. It would be a precedent that other candidates' wives would continue to the present.

In the days that followed Eleanor was "swamped with wires and letters of approval." But the best accolade came from Franklin himself. He was not effusive, she later recalled, but several times he said to others, "Her speech was just right, wasn't it? It was grand."

The notes Eleanor wrote and used during her famous speech

A slogan pin from the 1940 presidential election shows just how controversial Eleanor had become.

In 1940 Franklin's Republican opponent was Wendell Willkie, a vocal adversary who chose to campaign not only against the president, but against the first lady as well. A vote for him, asserted Willkie, was a vote against meddlers like Mrs. Roosevelt, a vote against Negroes in the White House, and a vote against women working in factories. "We don't want Franklin," cried Willkie supporters. "And we don't want Eleanor, either!" Campaigning hard, Willkie soon saw his poll numbers soar while Franklin's victory margin began to shrink. Realizing her husband could lose the election, Eleanor pleaded with him to campaign harder. "Dearest Franklin," she wrote just weeks before election day, "I hope you will make a few more speeches. It seems pretty essential. . . . The people have a right to hear you oppose Willkie." Franklin took his wife's advice. He embarked on a strenuous speaking tour, which eventually won him an unprecedented third term as president of the United States.

As the president's mother, Sara assumed the role of grande dame, graciously receiving political friends at her Hyde Park home, posing regally for news reporters, and taking center stage at White House events. At one reception, noted a guest, Sara sat in the glare of the floodlights, enjoying "every bit of commotion she caused, and when I left at 12:30 she was still there, grand old war-horse that she was."

The "old war-horse" continued to be as domineering as ever. Once when Franklin and Eleanor were debating the issue of low-cost housing, Sara grew furious at her daughter-in-law for bickering with her dear boy. Motioning for the butler to bring Franklin's wheelchair, she rolled him away while Eleanor was in midsentence. Another time she picked up the telephone extension to eavesdrop on a conversation between Franklin and England's prime minister, Winston Churchill. "Please hang up the telephone, Mother," said Franklin. When there was no response, he said, "I know you're there, Mother. I can hear you breathing."

By June of 1941, however, Sara's strength was waning. She suffered a stroke and spent the rest of the summer in her bed. By September, Eleanor was so struck by her mother-in-law's pale face and labored breathing that she insisted Franklin leave his duties at the White House and travel to Hyde Park. He went, and remained at his mother's side until she died on September 7, just two weeks before her eighty-seventh birthday.

Eleanor saw to "the endless details," as she called them—"clothes to go through, checks, books, papers." Franklin tried to help sort through his mother's things, but one day he came across a box he'd never seen before. Inside were his first pair of shoes, his christening gown, a lock of his baby hair. Suddenly his broad shoulders shook and tears rolled down his cheeks. "No one," recalled White House staff member Geoffrey Ward, "had ever seen Franklin Roosevelt weep before. . . . It was a stunning occurrence."

Eleanor, on the other hand, was less emotional. Her mother-in-law's constant meddling had created a "blistering rage" in Eleanor's heart—an anger she never completely overcame. In a letter to friend Joseph Lash she confided, "It is dreadful to have lived so close to someone for 36 years & feel no deep affection or sense of loss."

Eleanor with an ailing Sara just weeks before the older woman died

Defense for the First Lady

꧁⚜꧂

With war clouds on the country's horizon Franklin created the Office of Civilian Defense (OCD) in May 1941 with the purpose of enlisting men and women as defense volunteers. When he named his friend and fellow liberal Mayor Fiorello La Guardia of New York City as its director, Eleanor was thrilled. She envisioned an OCD that would do more than practice air-raid drills. Instead she hoped this new government agency would be used to help people socially and economically. This was Eleanor's definition of defense: to give every person wishing to volunteer an opportunity to train for work; to provide meaningful jobs that would benefit the community, such as work in nursery schools, homes for the aged, and housing projects; and to prepare citizens to meet emergency calls. She believed liberal-minded La Guardia was just the man to turn her dream into reality. But in the months that followed, La Guardia and the OCD remained intent on recruiting volunteer air-raid wardens, buying firefighting equipment, and distributing blackout curtains. Other activities he dismissed as "sissy stuff."

Disappointed by his narrow vision, Eleanor commented that "no government as yet has given all civilian volunteers an . . . adequate opportunity to participate in the defense effort."

"There are 135,000,000 people in this country," La Guardia wrote to her. "The criticism of 134,999,999 wouldn't touch me. Yours did." He went on to suggest that if she really wanted to implement her ideas, she should come to work at the OCD.

His offer intrigued Eleanor. Ever since arriving in Washington, she had longed to hold an official government job—a job where she could focus her ideas and energy and see the results of her efforts. She took this one, becoming the first wife of a U.S. president to hold a government job. And she loved it! "I am ridiculously busy," she told a friend in a delighted tone of voice.

But her delight soon turned to dismay. When Eleanor—concerned about the morale of her staff—organized lunchtime dancing on the roof of the OCD headquarters, newspapers across the country ridiculed her. "Doesn't the first lady have anything better to do than the cancan on the capital's rooftops?" sneered the *New York Times*. Eleanor tried to laugh off the event, but it was just the beginning.

Anger swelled when Congress learned she had hired a friend, the dancer Mayris Chaney, to develop a recreational program for children in bomb shelters.

Eleanor with OCD director Fiorello La Guardia and Mrs. La Guardia

"The work of the OCD concerns the safety of this nation," wrote one newspaper columnist. "Yet it has become a personal parking lot for pets and protégés of Mrs. Roosevelt . . . some of them at salaries larger than a brigadier general."

For days one congressman after another rose to the floor of the House of Representatives to attack Eleanor and her friends publicly. The country, they declared, needed bombers not dancers. All "parasites and leeches should be struck from the payroll." They issued a ban on using civilian defense funds for "instruction in physical fitness by dancers."

It was a direct slap to Eleanor. Realizing she could not remain in her position without jeopardizing OCD programs, she resigned after only five months. "I still believe in all the things we started out to do," she told a friend, "but I know if I stayed I would bring more harm than good to the program." She remained proud of what she had accomplished—broadening the definition of defense to include nutrition, housing, recreation, and medical care.

THE JAPANESE BOMB PEARL HARBOR, HAWAII, ON THE MORNING OF DECEMBER 7, 1941.

At 7:30 A.M. while Americans across the country slept, ate breakfast, or read their morning newspapers, the first wave of 189 Japanese planes swooped down on the American naval base at Pearl Harbor. Within minutes half the American naval fleet—eight battleships, three destroyers, three light cruisers—had been hit. By the time the Japanese completed their third and final run, steel ship parts were scattered across the smoke-covered harbor, and 3,500 sailors and civilians were dead—the worst naval disaster in American history.

The horrifying news reached Franklin within the hour. He was on the telephone when Eleanor glanced into his study a few minutes later. She knew instantly that something was wrong. "All the secretaries were there, two telephones were in use, the senior military aides were on the way with messages," she recalled. "I said nothing because the words I heard were sufficient to tell me that finally the blow had fallen and we had been attacked."

Heartsick, knowing it was not the time to ask questions, Eleanor went to her room. There she rewrote the script for a radio broadcast she had promised to give that evening. "For months now," the new script began, "the knowledge that something of this kind might happen has been hanging over our heads. . . . That is all over now and there is no more uncertainty. We know what we have to face and we know we are ready to face it . . . we are the free and unconquerable people of the U.S.A."

ELEANOR'S SONS IN UNIFORM—ELLIOTT, IN THE AIR FORCE (TOP LEFT); JAMES, IN THE MARINES (TOP RIGHT); JOHN AND FRANKLIN JR., IN THE NAVY

In 1941 all four of the Roosevelt sons were called to active duty in the armed forces. "I imagine every mother felt as I did when I said goodbye to them," she said. "I had a feeling that I might be saying goodbye for the last time."

That year the Christmas holidays were especially distressing. Only one stocking hung from the mantel. Eleanor had put it there, labeled it for their dog Fala, and stuffed it with rubber bones and toys. When her close friend Joe Lash telephoned her, "her voice did not have the customary ring to it." Lash asked how she was. "There was a period of silence," he recalled. "Then we both mumbled something incoherent and hung up." But Lash, worried, rushed to the White House. "She started to scold me for having come," he said. "Then she confessed she had had a hard day and burst into tears." She told Lash how much she missed her boys and how much she worried about them. "She knew they had to do it, but it was hard. By the laws of chance, not all four boys would return. Again, she lost control and wept."

Japanese Americans

After the attack on Pearl Harbor a rising tide of prejudice toward citizens of Japanese descent swept across the nation. As fear and panic spread, government officials swooped down on Japanese banks, stores, and newspapers, locking their doors with giant padlocks. FBI agents searched Japanese-American homes, rummaging through closets and drawers for pictures or documents proving loyalty to the empire of Japan.

Eleanor tried to calm the situation. Traveling to California, she was photographed with a group of American-born Japanese. "Let's be honest," she said in the accompanying news story. "There is a chance now for great hysteria against minority groups—loyal Americans who have not suddenly ceased to be Americans." Her tolerant views, however, angered white Californians. Cried the *Los Angeles Times*, "When [Mrs. Roosevelt] starts bemoaning the plight of the treacherous snakes we call Japanese . . . she has reached the point where she should be forced to retire from public life."

West Coast politicians and military officials pressured the president to deal with the Japanese problem. It was, they claimed, a military necessity. Bowing to this pressure, Franklin signed Executive Order 9066, which required the forced removal of all people of Japanese descent from any area designated as a military zone, in February 1942. Since all of California, the western halves of Washington and Oregon, and the southern part of Arizona had all been named military zones, the order affected more than a hundred thousand citizens.

Told to bring only what they could carry, these evacuees were herded onto trains and buses. They were transported to makeshift centers hastily built by army engineers on racetracks and athletic fields along the West Coast. "Can this be the same America we left only a few days ago?" asked one evacuee after arriving at one of the detention centers. Appalled by the barracks' flimsy walls, overpowering smell of manure, and complete lack of privacy, he clung to his "bit of faith in . . . Mrs. Roosevelt's pledge of a future worthy of good American citizens."

Evacuees wait for the train that will take them from their lives and homes to makeshift camps on athletic fields and racetracks.

```
                    EXECUTIVE ORDER

                    - - - - - -

      AUTHORIZING THE SECRETARY OF WAR TO PRESCRIBE
                    MILITARY AREAS

        WHEREAS the successful prosecution of the war

   requires every possible protection against espionage

   and against sabotage to national-defense material,

   national-defense premises, and national-defense util-

   ities as defined in Section 4, Act of April 20, 1918,

   40 Stat. 533, as amended by the Act of November 30,

   1940, 54 Stat. 1220, and the Act of August 21, 1941,

   55 Stat. 655 (U. S. C., Title 50, Sec. 104):

        NOW, THEREFORE, by virtue of the authority

   vested in me as President of the United States, and

   Commander in Chief of the Army and Navy, I hereby
```

Executive Order 9066, signed by Franklin, authorized the forced relocation of Japanese Americans.

ELEANOR VISITS THE GILA RIVER INTERNMENT CAMP IN ARIZONA.

Eleanor was enraged by her husband's decision to displace Japanese Americans. "These people were not convicted of any crime," she argued. "We must adhere strictly to the American rule that a man is innocent until he is proved guilty." But no matter how hard she pressed, Franklin refused to change his mind. He firmly believed Japanese Americans presented a threat to national defense.

Then, in 1943, Franklin received a report in which the evacuees were described as "angry and becoming increasingly bitter. . . . They seem to be on the verge of a riot." Fearful of creating what he called "a hostile group right in our midst," Franklin asked Eleanor to visit the Gila River Internment Camp in Arizona and bring him back a clear picture of what was going on.

She arrived on April 23 in the midst of a dust storm. But regardless of the dust, Eleanor saw it all—the hospital, the school, the houses. "Everything is spotlessly clean," she marveled, "and you can see the results of their labors." Handmade screens created a sense of privacy between the tight rows of houses. "Sometimes there are little Japanese gardens, sometimes vegetables or flowers bloom. Makeshift porches have been improvised out of gunny sacks and bits of wood salvaged from packing cases."

Yes, everything looked decent on the surface. But Eleanor had been taught to look deeper. And what she saw was unbearable—barbed wire, and armed guards in sentry towers with orders to shoot anyone who came within twenty feet of the fence. No matter how hard authorities tried to make the camp look like an ordinary community, Eleanor concluded it was really a penitentiary, imprisoning people who had never done anything wrong.

Mrs. Jones, an elementary-school teacher hired by the government to teach at the camp, agreed. "To be frank with you," she admitted to the first lady, "it embarrasses me to teach them the flag salute. Is our nation indivisible? Does it stand for justice for all? Those questions come up to my mind constantly."

The only answer to the camps, Eleanor decided, was to allow Japanese Americans to return to their homes. This time Franklin listened. Even though his decision was met with criticism, he immediately relaxed Executive Order 9066 and by the end of 1943 began granting exits to Japanese Americans who had work and a place to live. But it was a slow process. Not until the middle of 1946—almost a year after the war ended—were the last of the camps' residents finally released.

Franklin and Winston Churchill plotting war strategy and enjoying each other's company

During the war Franklin and Great Britain's prime minister, Winston Churchill, became good friends. Franklin called Churchill "Winnie." And Churchill called Franklin "Chief." Together newspapers called them "the partnership that saved the west." But Eleanor called them "two little boys playing soldier." Eleanor didn't like Churchill, and she did little to hide the fact. She disliked the way he carried himself "like a big English bulldog taught to give his paw." She disliked his tendency to romanticize war—"Nobody enjoyed the war as much as Churchill. He loved the derring-do and rushing around. He got [Franklin] all steamed up in his boy's book of adventure." She disliked him for keeping Franklin up late at night, smoking cigars and drinking brandy. "Fuming, Mother went in and out making hints about bed, but the prime minister just sat there," recalled son Elliott. "It was as if Churchill was deliberately goading Mother." But above all else, Eleanor disliked Churchill's view of what the world should look like when the war was over. On a drive through the Virginia countryside on New Year's Day, 1942, Churchill said, "When peace comes, we must stress the control of English-speaking people." Eleanor, thinking "all people who believed in democracy" should be in control, gritted her teeth as Franklin kept nodding his head and saying, "Yes, yes, yes." Finally, unable to take it anymore, she blurted out, "You know, Winston, when Franklin says 'yes, yes, yes' it doesn't mean he agrees with you. It just means he's listening." Churchill shot her a "bulldog scowl." But Eleanor didn't bat an eye. Later she wrote her daughter, Anna, about the incident. "Mr. Churchill has thought a certain way for sixty years and doesn't want to change."

After Franklin's death Eleanor made no secret of her opinion about the prime minister. She told reporters he wasn't prepared for the social changes of the postwar world—civil rights, women's rights, labor unions. "The world that existed before the war has been a pleasant world as far as he was concerned," she critically observed. For his part, Churchill considered Eleanor a "meddler" and "a woman who does not know her place."

A WARTIME PRAYER

During the war Eleanor carried this prayer in her purse, perhaps as a reminder of the sacrifices being made all over the world:

> **Dear Lord,**
> **Lest I continue**
> **My complacent way,**
> **Help me to remember,**
> **Somewhere out there**
> **A man died for me today.**
> **As long as there be war,**
> **I then must**
> **Ask and answer**
> **Am I worth dying for?**

Eleanor, accompanied by the king and queen of England, tours bomb-ravaged London.

"I confide my missus to the care of you and Mrs. Churchill," Franklin wrote the prime minister just before Eleanor set off on October 21, 1942, for an inspection trip of England. "I know our better halves will hit it off beautifully." With only her secretary, Malvina Thompson, and one suitcase containing an evening dress, two day dresses, two pairs of shoes, and undergarments, Eleanor set off across the Atlantic. She looked forward to observing the work British women were doing in the war, as well as greeting the servicemen and bringing America's good will to the British people. Her first two days in London, however, were spent with the king and queen of England at Buckingham Palace. "My room," she wrote in her diary, "was magnificent but freezing." Only a tiny fire smoldered in the fireplace of the cavernous suite, proving that "royalty [was] rationed, too."

For three weeks she toured bomb-damaged London, then she spent a weekend with the Churchills, where she did indeed "hit it off" with Winston's better half, Clementine. She visited Red Cross canteens, factories, nurseries for wounded children, and a total of twenty-six military camps. By the final days of her trip the soles of her shoes were completely worn out, and the newspaper reporters who had been following her looked exhausted. Her remarkable ramblings gained lots of favorable press, and she became something of a celebrity abroad. Observed *Newsweek*, "Groups loiter about the American embassy all day in hopes of getting a glimpse of her. There are spontaneous outbursts of cheers and clapping . . . when . . . she appears." More important, she connected with the British people in a personal way. "Mrs. Roosevelt has done more to bring a real understanding of the spirit of the United States to the people of Britain than any other single American that has visited these islands," declared London's *Daily Mirror*.

"*Gosh!* There's Eleanor."

The minute her husband suggested she take a goodwill trip to the Pacific, Eleanor snatched the opportunity. She adored the idea of going to Australia and New Zealand but wanted to see more. "At once I put up a strong plea to be allowed to see our men at Guadalcanal and other islands," she wrote. Franklin had his doubts. Guadalcanal was considered a danger spot. Would Eleanor be safe? "I told [Franklin] that it would be an insult if I was not permitted to visit the places where these men had left their health or received their injuries." Franklin finally agreed, and in August 1943 fifty-eight-year-old Eleanor climbed into a cramped, unheated bomber bound for the Pacific. Twenty-three thousand miles later the plane, named *Our Eleanor* in her honor, arrived in Australia.

She was met at the airstrip by Adm. William Halsey, chief of all naval operation in Australia. He regarded the first lady as a nuisance and a meddlesome do-gooder. When Eleanor asked to go to Guadalcanal, he growled, "Guadalcanal is no place for you ma'am. If you go, I'll have to provide a fighter escort for you, and I haven't got one to spare."

His words shook Eleanor. Was her visit a bother? Was she a nuisance? She telegrammed Franklin. "In some ways I wish I had not come on this trip. I think the trouble I give far outweighs the momentary interest it may give the boys to see me."

As anxiety crowded in on her, Eleanor stepped up her schedule. On the go from dawn to dusk, she toured one hospital after another, drove hundreds of miles in an open jeep to talk with soldiers in their camps, gave dozens of speeches to huge crowds, and visited Red Cross canteens in every part of Australia and New Zealand. Everywhere she went, she assured the soldiers that they were not forgotten at home. "When I left," she told them, "my husband asked me to give you a message. . . . He said to tell you that you have done and are doing a wonderful job. He wants me to give you his deepest admiration and gratitude."

Once, while traveling in Queensland, she saw a convoy of army trucks ahead of her. Knowing these troops were headed for the battlefront, she insisted her driver catch up to them so she could say good-bye and good luck. She stopped at each truck and spoke to each soldier, "her shoes dusty and scarred by rocks,"

PICTURES FROM THE SOUTH PACIFIC

Eleanor meets Admiral Halsey (left) in Australia. She chose to wear a Red Cross uniform on her trip because it simplified the matter of luggage.

Eleanor, who made a point of meeting the people of New Zealand, rubs noses with a Maori woman.

reported the *New York Times*. "At one point her voice quavered but she quickly recovered and continued on down the line."

As her visit continued, Admiral Halsey's opinion began to change. Day after day he witnessed the magic she brought to the hospital wards. "When I say she inspected the hospitals," he reported, "I don't mean that she shook hands with the chief medical officer, glanced into a sun parlor, and left. I mean that she went into every ward, stopped at every bed, and spoke to every patient. What was his name? How did he feel? Was there anything he needed? Could she take a message home for him?"

Said one wounded soldier, "Over here she was something . . . none of us had seen in over a year, an American mother."

Halsey eventually admitted he was wrong. "I was ashamed of my original surliness," he later said. "She alone had accomplished more good than any other person, or group of civilians, who passed through my area." He granted Eleanor's request to visit Guadalcanal.

Guadalcanal had seen some of the bloodiest fighting of the war and was still being bombed by Japanese warplanes. As a security measure, no one had been told about the first lady's visit. "What a shock it was to suddenly see this gracious and magnificent lady emerge from a bomber," said one soldier. Exclaimed another, "Gosh! There's Eleanor."

It was a heartwarming beginning to what would become a heartbreaking trip. "One of the things I shall never forget," Eleanor later wrote, "is my visit to the cemetery. . . . It was very moving to walk among the graves and realize how united these boys had been in spite of differences in religion and background. The boy's mess kit or sometimes his helmet hung on the marker which some friend had carved with the appropriate symbol of the Jewish or Catholic or Protestant faith. Words that came from the heart were carved on the base, such as 'He was a grand guy'—'Best buddy ever.'"

She visited hospitals and barracks. In the evening an air-raid alert sent her scurrying to the hospital grounds for safety. "The atmosphere was tense, but somebody started to sing," she recalled, "and we all joined in."

All in all, it was an exhausting five-week trip. Eleanor covered seventeen islands, New Zealand, and Australia, visited approximately 400,000 men in camps and hospitals, lost thirty pounds, and wore out two pairs of shoes. She felt weary and depressed. Back home she wrote about her trip: "I wonder if I can transmit to you the feelings which I have so strongly. In a nation such as ours every man who fights for us in some way, is our man. His parents may be of any race or religion, but if that man dies, he dies side by side with all of his buddies, and if your heart is with any man, in some way it must be with all."

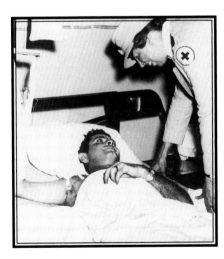

Eleanor visits with a wounded soldier in the South Pacific.

Eleanor peeks into a soldier's cooking pot on Christmas Island.

Eleanor greets American servicemen on Guadalcanal.

"You never know where Eleanor's going to turn up next," declared one soldier. And it was true. "Everywhere Eleanor" was dropping in on troops in Europe, Latin America, and the South Pacific. She suddenly appeared in hospitals, on ships, in camps, and in barracks. Once, she popped into a tent unannounced, only to be met by the sight of two soldiers without trousers. Did Eleanor shriek and run? "She cooly and graciously chatted with the boys," recalled one observer, as if it were perfectly natural to see them in their Skivvies. When she left, the boys collapsed into relief and laughter. At other times her sudden appearance evoked a range of responses, such as "Holy cow, there's Mrs. Roosevelt," "Howdy, Eleanor!" and "You came all this way to see *me*?" While some Americans thought she belonged at home, most admired her compassion and energy. They nicknamed her "Public Energy Number One" and kept an eye out for her.

Encouraged by Eleanor, many women—such as these working at the Douglas Aircraft plant in Los Angeles—found jobs in factories.

More and more women were entering the workforce, filling jobs left vacant by men in the service or taking new jobs created by wartime, such as working on ships and railroads, and in warehouses, factories, and plants. Some were reluctant to do so—working for a paycheck was a new concept to women of the 1940s—but Eleanor provided a powerful voice. "If I [were young enough] I would go into a factory where I could learn a skill and be useful," she declared. She saw this new role for women as more than a wartime necessity. "Women," she said, "will be given a chance to expand their horizons, grow independent, and earn their own money."

As the war drew to a close, women were sent home so that returning soldiers could take their jobs. By 1945 the layoff rate for women was 75 percent higher than for men. "Women ought to be delighted to give up any job and return to their proper sphere—the kitchen," became the prevailing idea. But Eleanor disagreed. She warned the nation not to return to an economy that denied women the right to work. What women needed, she argued, was the courage to ask for their rights with a loud voice, demanding equal pay for equal work, and a say in postwar planning. "Women," she said, "are as fully capable as men."

Eleanor took a great interest in the airmen of the Ninety-ninth Pursuit Squadron, the first unit of black combat pilots. The unit, trained at Tuskegee Army Air Field in Alabama, had been established in 1938 after a young black pilot who was denied admission to the all-white air corps sued. Throughout 1941 and 1942 the program had produced nearly one thousand combat pilots, but by the summer of 1942 not one had been sent overseas. "We are undoubtedly the most highly trained squadron in the U.S.," said one black pilot, "but the air brass can't decide what to do with us." Although the armed forces had been forced to create training programs for African Americans, they were under no obligation to use blacks in combat. So in all branches of the armed forces blacks were relegated to menial jobs like cooking, cleaning, and laundry.

Eleanor, who felt segregation in the military should be eliminated, began corresponding with some of the Tuskegee airmen as a way of showing her support of them. One young pilot, Cecil Peterson, became the first lady's pen pal for the next three years. "Write me and keep me informed about the flying school," she wrote in one of her first letters. Peterson did, asking her to remind the president that he was eager to "be of some service to Uncle Sam." Eleanor sent copies of Peterson's letters to Henry Stimson, secretary of war. "This seems to me a really crucial situation," she wrote in a cover note.

The first lady found other ways to show her support for the black airmen as well. She visited the airfield and asked to take a flight with one of the Ninety-ninth's pilots. With Secret Service agents pacing anxiously on the ground, she soared through the Alabama skies beside flight instructor Charles A. Anderson. After landing, she had her photograph taken with Anderson, then took the picture back to Franklin, successfully urging him to use the Ninety-ninth in combat missions. At last, on April 15, 1943, the airmen boarded a ship bound for North Africa. "It was a tremendous moment," remembered squadron leader Benjamin Davis Jr. "All the members of the 99th were beginning to understand the signifi-

cance of an assignment which went far beyond purely military considerations. If a black fighter squadron could get a good account of itself in combat, its success might lead the way to greater opportunities for black people throughout the armed services."

The airmen of the Ninety-ninth saw combat in more than fifteen hundred missions over Europe and North Africa. Credited with shooting down 111 airborne craft and destroying 150 on the ground, the group not only won one hundred Distinguished Flying Crosses, but never lost a bomber to enemy fire—the only U.S. squadron to hold that honor in World War II. In large part because of their tenacity, bravery, and success, President Harry S. Truman desegregated the military in 1948.

American forces invade German-occupied France at Normandy.

In the early hours of June 6, 1944, church bells across the U.S. tolled, school bells rang, and factory whistles sounded as people streamed into the street. "Outwardly [Americans] appeared to be celebrating a victory," wrote Winston Estes, "but underneath all that raucous uncontrolled excitement lay a cold fear and a grim anxiety which gnawed at their insides." It was D-day, the day the Allied forces landed on the beaches of Normandy, France, in their first step toward liberating Europe. "Give us Faith in Thee," Franklin said in a radio broadcast later that day, "faith in our sons; faith in each other; faith in our united crusade."

Eleanor now lived, she wrote, "suspended in space, waiting for news of the invasion, dreading the inevitable and horrible loss of life, yet wishing it success." Three weeks after D-day, when it appeared the invasion was indeed successful, Eleanor found it impossible to celebrate. "All emotion," she admitted, "is drained away."

Eleanor pictured with Franklin and their daughter, Anna Roosevelt Boettiger

By the end of his third term sixty-two-year-old Franklin found his health deteriorating. Thin and tired, he suffered from severe stomach and chest pains, frequent headaches, and a soft cough that accompanied him day and night. (Doctors later diagnosed his condition as congestive heart failure.) More than anything, he longed for loving, uncritical attention—something his relentless, strong-willed wife could never give him. So Franklin returned to Anna, who had recently remarried and moved to Seattle. Would she come back East, live in the White House, and help him?

Anna agreed and arrived in Washington, D.C., in the spring of 1944. Soon Sis, as her father called her, was Franklin's closest companion. She dined with him, read to him, brought his daily medication, phoned the doctor when he was ill, decided who could or could not visit, and fussed over him like a mother hen.

Eleanor observed this growing bond with mixed feelings. While Anna's presence freed her to travel, give speeches, and meet people, it was hard to accept that Anna now knew things she did not. More and more frequently Eleanor was heard to say, "Anna is the only one who would know about that," or "We'll have to ask Anna to ask the President."

Still, Eleanor never really felt replaced by her daughter until Franklin decided to travel to Yalta, a Russian port on the Black Sea, for an important diplomatic conference. Eleanor begged to go along. She believed the five-week trip would be history making, and

she desperately wanted to be part of it. But Franklin refused to take her. Instead he invited Anna because he needed someone to take care of him and help him preserve his strength. "If Anna goes it will be simpler," he said. Eleanor pretended to accept his decision good-naturedly, but her feelings were deeply hurt. After seeing her husband and daughter off, she returned to the White House, where she confessed to a friend, "I am tired and very depressed tonight."

Meanwhile, in Yalta father and daughter were growing even closer. "Life is assuming a definite pattern," Anna noted in her diary. In the mornings, while the president ate breakfast and dictated responses to America's domestic problems, she made the rounds of diplomats, picking up "information on the day's plans, meetings, gossip etc." Afterward, she went to her father's study "to . . . fill him in on any gossip" she had learned that might be "amusing or interesting or helpful" to him.

Did either of them miss Eleanor?

Probably not. Anna wrote to her mother daily to stay in her good graces. As for Franklin, wrote Anna, "the only times he mentioned [Mother] on this trip have been times when he griped about her." By the time they returned to Washington, Anna was the "new power behind the throne," wrote one reporter. "The rumor mongers have been busy whispering a new secret: control of access [to the president] has passed to Anna Roosevelt Boettiger, the long-legged, energetic and handsome eldest child . . . the free-speaking, free-cursing daughter of President Roosevelt." It was, Anna admitted later, "very hard for Mother to swallow."

A victorious Franklin appears with his family on the Springwood porch to greet well-wishers on election night, 1944.

In the summer of 1944 Franklin decided to run for an unprecedented fourth term as president of the United States. "All that is within me cries to go back to my home on the Hudson River," he explained to the chairman of the Democratic National Committee. But with America still fighting World War II, he believed, "the future existence of the nation, and the future existence of our chosen form of government are at stake. . . . I must finish the job I have begun."

Eleanor had mixed feelings about her husband's candidacy. While she, too, believed his victory was essential for the good of the country, the thought of four more years in the White House depressed her. "I am very conscious," she wrote to a friend, "of age, and the short time in which I have to live as I like."

She appeared to give little thought to Franklin's poor health, refusing to acknowledge that anything was seriously wrong with him. "She still believed," said their grandson John Boettiger, "that iron will and courage could conquer any illness. Though she was an unusually compassionate woman, she was never patient with illness—her own or anyone else's. This made it hard for her and hard for others."

At first neither Roosevelt campaigned. While the Republican candidate, Thomas E. Dewey, went about the country bashing the president, Franklin and Eleanor barely participated. Franklin was too sick and too busy trying to win the war. Eleanor was too busy traveling the world as his goodwill ambassador. Besides, no one thought FDR needed to get out the vote. Everyone on his campaign team felt confident he already had it. But just two months before the election Franklin's poll numbers took a drastic dip. Alarmed, Eleanor "had a long talk with [Franklin], sticking out my neck . . . trying to convince him to speak more often . . . and before crowds," she later reported. "I told him . . . if he did not really want to win he should not have run . . . and he told me I was right . . . then we talked about the kind of thing that should be done."

Franklin became a political whirlwind—shaking hands, giving speeches, riding in parades. How did the ailing president manage to find the strength? Said one campaign worker, "It was largely due to the determination of Mrs. Roosevelt."

On November 7, 1944, Franklin Delano Roosevelt became the first and only person to be elected president of the United States four times. "There was much excitement all through the evening," Eleanor wrote a few days later, "but I can't say that I felt half as much excitement as I will feel the day that I hear the war is over."

In the winter of 1944, as the war in Europe wound down, Franklin began looking forward to the day when he would no longer be president. How did he envision his life? Son Elliott recalled this conversation:

"You know," Franklin said, "I think Mother and I might be able to get together now and do some things together, take some trips maybe, learn to know each other again. . . . I only wish she wasn't so darned busy. I could have her with me more if she didn't have so many other engagements."

The next day Elliott told his mother what Franklin had said. "I hope this will come to pass," she said with a smile.

"THE PRESIDENT IS DEAD"

On April 12, 1945, sixty-year-old Eleanor was speaking at a fund-raiser in Washington, D.C., when she received a call telling her to go home immediately. "I got into the car and sat with my hands clenched all the way to the White House. In my heart of hearts I knew what had happened." When she arrived, she was told the news—Franklin had died from a brain hemorrhage that afternoon at the age of sixty-three while vacationing in Warm Springs, Georgia.

For a few moments Eleanor sat quietly. Then she turned to the sad duties before her. She sent a cable to her sons overseas that read: "Father slept away this afternoon. He would expect you to carry on and finish your jobs." She arranged to fly to Warm Springs. She changed into a simple black dress. And she summoned Vice President Harry Truman to the White House.

"Harry," she told him gently when he arrived, "the president is dead."

Stunned, Truman asked if there was anything he could do for her.

"Is there anything *we* can do for *you?*" Eleanor replied. "For you are the one in trouble now."

After watching Truman be sworn in as the new president, she left for Warm Springs. She arrived at midnight. There she was met by two cousins, Laura Delano and Margaret Suckley, who had accompanied Franklin on his trip. Hugging them, Eleanor asked what had happened.

Margaret told her. Franklin had been sitting for a portrait when he suddenly put his hand to the back of his head. "I have a terrific pain," he said. He collapsed, never to regain consciousness.

Then Laura Delano added a bitter truth. Lucy Mercer—the woman with whom Franklin had had an affair thirty years earlier—had been there too. As Eleanor paled, Laura continued. Lucy had been Franklin's guest for the past three days. Staying calm, Eleanor questioned Laura further. Had Franklin seen Lucy at other times in recent years? Yes, Laura replied, Lucy had dined at the White House whenever the first lady was away.

Eleanor gave no outward sign of the pain this news surely caused her. Instead, with heart and pride wounded, she went into the adjoining bedroom to view her husband's body. "At times like that," she later explained, "you don't really feel your own feelings. You recede as a person. You build a facade for everyone to see and live separately inside the facade."

The next morning she boarded the train that would take Franklin's body back to Washington, D.C.

The Nation's Last Tribute

In Washington, D.C., people line the streets as Franklin's flag-draped coffin moves down Constitution Avenue to the White House.

A "complete silence spread like a pall over the city," wrote one observer, "broken only by the sobs of the people."

Along the route thousands of weeping, mournful Americans gathered to watch the train pass. Alone with her memories, Eleanor "lay in [her] berth with the window shade up, looking out at the countryside [Franklin] had loved and watching the faces of the people at the stations, and even at the crossroads, who had come to pay their last tribute all through the night."

After a simple funeral service in Washington, D.C., the president's body headed to Hyde Park. There, in the rose garden of his beloved Springwood, he was buried. Only two of his children were there—John, Franklin Jr., and James were unable to get back from duty at sea. As the mourners moved away Eleanor remained. Silent and alone, she watched for a few moments as the workmen shoveled dirt into her husband's grave. Then, back straight, she walked away. "One cannot say goodbye to people whom they have loved . . . without deep emotion," she later said, "but at last even that was over. I was now on my own."

Eleanor sent this letter to President Harry Truman only four days after Franklin's death. Already, remarked a friend, she was doing what she always did— "turning her personal unhappiness into public good."

My dear Mr. President:

There have been many thousands of letters, telegrams and cards sent to me and my children which have brought great comfort and consolation to all of us. This outpouring of affectionate thought has touched us all deeply and we wish it were possible to thank each and everyone individually.

My children and I feel in view of the fact that we are faced with a paper shortage and are asked not to use paper when it can be avoided, that all we can do is to express our appreciation collectively. We would therefore consider it a great favor if you would be kind enough to express our gratitude for us.

Sincerely yours,

Eleanor Roosevelt

Eleanor follows her husband's body into the White House. Noted her friend Lorena Hickok, whenever the first lady was troubled, "she would usually walk erect with her head held high. She was walking very erect that day."

THE END

In May 1945, one month after Franklin's death, Germany surrendered to the Allies. In August, after the U.S. dropped atomic bombs on Hiroshima and Nagasaki, the Japanese surrendered and World War II ended. Eleanor felt relieved by the news, but she did not feel like celebrating. To her daughter, Anna, she wrote:

"I miss Pa's voice, and the words he would have spoken."

First Lady
of the World

❧

I had few definite plans, but I knew there were certain things I did not want to do. I did not want to run an elaborate household again. I did not want to cease being useful in some way. I did not want to feel old. —Eleanor Roosevelt, *On My Own*

A relaxed Eleanor at Val-Kill Cottage, 1948

Without Franklin, Eleanor divided her time between two homes—an apartment in New York City and her cottage at Val-Kill. In New York she bustled from interview to reception to speaking engagement. But at Val-Kill she became her true self. She did her shopping at roadside stands and made mock mincemeat from tomatoes grown in her garden. She attended her Hyde Park church on Sundays wearing cotton dresses and comfortable tennis shoes. And she filled her dining room with guests—foreign dignitaries, politicians, grandchildren, family friends. She often served scrambled eggs and Blueberry Delight, a dessert made of sugar, white bread, and blueberries all squashed together. At Val-Kill, claimed one friend, "lived the Eleanor Roosevelt few people ever saw."

FIRST PAGE OF THE INDENTURE BETWEEN FRANKLIN, ELEANOR, AND THE U.S. GOVERNMENT CONVEYING THE HYDE PARK ESTATE

After Franklin's death one of Eleanor's first concerns was what to do with the Hyde Park estate. Years earlier, in 1939, Franklin had deeded over the big house as well as some of the Roosevelt acreage to the government, then began construction of his presidential library—the first of its kind. His will, however, specified that Eleanor and the children be allowed to continue living in the house if they wished. Eleanor did not. "In the long night's trip from Warm Springs, Georgia, before my husband's funeral . . . I had made certain decisions," she wrote. "I did not want to live in the big house." She decided to turn it over to the government immediately. With only weeks to empty the place of anything she wanted, she went through the house top to bottom. She kept only, "a few things for sentiment—the Turner watercolors my husband had given me, some of the linens and other objects that we used for a long time. . . . Somehow," she added, "possessions seemed of little importance." Just two months after Franklin's death, on June 15, 1945, Eleanor locked the front door to the Hyde Park house for the last time. Having "disentangled" herself from Franklin's possessions, she now felt free to live as she wished at her beloved Val-Kill Cottage.

THIS INDENTURE made the - 24th - day of July , one thousand nine hundred and thirty-nine, between FRANKLIN D. ROOSEVELT and ANNA ELEANOR ROOSEVELT, his wife, both of the Town of Hyde Park, Dutchess County, State of New York, parties of the first part, and UNITED STATES OF AMERICA, party of the second part, WITNESSETH:

WHEREAS, Franklin D. Roosevelt, one of the parties of the first part, has agreed to convey unto the United States of America the land hereinafter described to be utilized as a site for the Franklin D. Roosevelt Library in accordance with the terms and conditions set forth in a Joint Resolution of Congress hereinafter mentioned, and subject also to certain conditions hereinafter set forth, and

WHEREAS, by virtue of the said Joint Resolution of Congress, approved July 18, 1939, (Pub. Res. No. 30, 76th Congress, 1st Session), which is hereby referred to and made a part hereof, The Archivist of the United States is authorized and empowered to accept for and in the name of the United States of America

Eleanor plays with Fala.

Fala, the most famous of the Roosevelts' dogs, was loved by both Franklin and Eleanor. The Scottish terrier, who arrived at the White House in 1940, quickly became the president's close companion. After Franklin's death Fala became a great source of comfort for Eleanor, and the two went everywhere together. He accompanied her on all her walks through Val-Kill's woods, and whenever he wandered off the path in pursuit of a good smell, her high-pitched "Fala!" called him back. He sat beside her chair in the living room and greeted her at the door when she came home. "He had a special way of meeting Mrs. Roosevelt," observed her secretary. "We call it his smile." When he covered himself in mud, Eleanor bathed him, getting as wet as Fala in the process. And when she fed him, she made him do all his tricks—stand on his hind legs, roll over, beg—just as Franklin had done. Once, on a trip to Campobello Island, Eleanor refused to stay in a luxurious hotel because Fala was with her. Instead she slept in a rather seedy cabin that welcomed pets. In 1952, just before his twelfth birthday, Fala died. As Franklin had requested, the terrier was buried in the rose garden near his master's feet. Eleanor, who had not shed a tear at her husband's funeral, sobbed openly at Fala's.

Eleanor takes a walk at Val-Kill with granddaughters Sally and Nina Roosevelt, and Fala.

Eleanor was blessed with an abundance of grandchildren. With them she experienced an easiness she had never had with her own children. And at Val-Kill she enjoyed their almost constant company. Said one granddaughter, "We were in [her] house as much as we were in [our own]." The children rode horses, swam in the pool, explored the countryside, or played in the playhouse. They also raced through their grandmother's cottage, shouting, roughhousing, and often bursting into her study while she was working. But Eleanor remained calm. She never scolded or grew angry. Instead she talked with her grandchildren and listened attentively as they told her about the things they were doing or what interested them. They affectionately called her Grandmère, the French word for "grandmother." She devotedly called them "the most important parts of my life."

Eleanor with her four sons (from left to right), John, James, Elliott, and Franklin Jr., in 1960

*E*ven in her later years much of Eleanor's time and money went to her grown-up sons. None of them, she sadly admitted, had been taught about duty and long-range purpose. "They were instantly gratified with positions, power, and prestige because of their last name." Blaming herself for their many problems, she desperately tried to help them.

In 1946 she financed Elliott's dream of running a farm on the remaining Roosevelt land at Hyde Park. But thirty-six-year-old Elliott knew little about farming and even less about business. The venture failed and he went bankrupt. So Eleanor gave him the rights to his father's presidential letters—a valuable asset. But instead of publishing the historic documents, as his mother had hoped, Elliott used them to write a controversial and inaccurate account of his father's administration called *As He Saw It*. Elliott hoped his book would become a best-seller. When it didn't, Eleanor helped him out again, this time letting him act as her agent. From 1949 to 1952 Elliott promised his mother's endorsement to any that would pay a fee—magazines, television shows, radio programs, even commercials. Why, asked Eleanor's friends, did she let him make money off her good name? Replied Eleanor, "I surmise Elliott has to be established and encouraged to become more secure." In 1952, without his mother's knowledge or permission, Elliott secretly sold some of the Roosevelts' Hyde Park land. Then he severed all business connections with Eleanor and moved away. "It was a terrible thing to do," recalled a neighbor, "like stealing money from your mother's purse." Still, Eleanor tried to forgive. "I've always loved you dearly and wanted you near," she wrote Elliott. "You have weaknesses and I know them, but I never loved you less because I understand you so well." This betrayal, however, was the last straw, straining their relationship for the rest of her life.

Eleanor's other sons had problems too. James married four times and made front-page news when his third wife stabbed him during a domestic dispute. In later life he admitted he had taken "a step forward, a step backward, some missteps along the way," but blamed these difficulties, as well as his premature baldness, on his mother's lack of attention. She was, he wrote, "more successful as a politician than a parent." John, meanwhile, stunned and disappointed his mother by becoming a Republican in 1947, while Franklin Jr. used his charm and skills at flattery to get himself elected to Congress in 1948. Said one New York State Democratic Committee member, "The boy has a golden future in politics." But for all his gifts, Franklin Jr. lacked self-discipline and spent more time playing than working. In 1954 voters did not reelect him, and his political career faded. One evening in 1961 Franklin Jr. burst into tears. "It's just too much . . . too much for one individual to bear," he sobbed to his mother, "to be the sons of Franklin D. Roosevelt, and Eleanor Roosevelt. It's so much to live up to, and I guess I've not done it."

Eleanor with her daughter, Anna, in 1959

───────────────── ❦ ─────────────────

*L*ike her brothers, Anna lived a life full of crisis—two divorces, a series of jobs, bankruptcy, and an ex-husband who committed suicide in 1949. Eleanor blamed herself for many of her daughter's difficulties, and in a moment of deep despair once admitted to her physician, "My children would be so much better off if I were not alive. I'm overshadowing them." In 1948 Eleanor helped Anna financially by agreeing to join her on a radio discussion program five days a week. But after only thirty-nine weeks the show was dropped for lack of advertisers. "We are disappointed, but not downhearted," wrote Eleanor. "The enterprise has connected our lives." The two remained connected until Anna married Dr. James Halstead in 1952. Dr. Halstead's job as a physician and teacher took him all over the world, frequently separating mother and daughter. Still, Eleanor was pleased. Anna, she believed, was "finally settled . . . independent and happy."

"It began with a telephone call [in early December 1945] from President Truman," remembered Eleanor's son Franklin Jr., "and he was asking [Mother] to be the United States representative to the United Nations."

The charter for the United Nations—an international organization created to settle problems between nations—had been drawn up in April 1945 by delegates from fifty countries. Soon afterward the Senate overwhelmingly approved U.S. membership in the UN, and on October 24, the UN officially came into existence. But who would be among America's first delegates to this organization? Harry Truman thought Eleanor should be. Would she be willing to serve?

Oh no, replied Eleanor. She could not possibly do it. "I don't know anything about parliamentary procedure," she told him. But Truman waved her argument away. Think about it, he insisted. Talk it over with the family. Eleanor debated her decision for days. A self-proclaimed pacifist who hated the ugly stupidity of war, she longed for the job but was terrified of failure. Finally, overcoming what she called her "fear and trembling," she accepted the position. After all, she wrote, there are "some things I can take to the meeting: A sincere desire to understand the problems of the rest of the world and our relationship to them; a real goodwill for people throughout the world; a hope that I shall be able to build a sense of personal trust and friendship with my coworkers." And so it was that just eight months after Franklin's death sixty-one-year-old Eleanor arrived in London to begin a new career—peacemaker.

"I knew that as the only woman I'd better be better than anybody else," she wrote. "So I read every paper. And they were very dull sometimes, because state papers can be very dull. And I used to almost go to sleep over them. . . . But I did read them all. I knew that if I in any way failed, it would not be just my failure, it would be the failure of all women. There'd never be another woman on the delegation."

As Eleanor had predicted, her all-male colleagues treated her with condescension. Theirs were some of the most prestigious names in American diplomacy—Secretary of State James F. Byrnes; Edward Stettinius Jr., a U.S. representative on the Security Council; Senator Tom Connally, chairman of the Senate Foreign Relations Committee; Senator Arthur Vandenberg, ranking member of the Senate Foreign Relations Committee. "Rattle-brained Mrs. Roosevelt," they called her. Believing she wasn't tough enough to stand up to the Russians, they assigned her to the UN's Committee on Humanitarian, Social, and Cultural Concerns (Committee III). "It was a committee of little consequence," one diplomat later admitted. "We figured Mrs. Roosevelt couldn't do much harm there."

But Committee III quickly became a hotbed of conflict—a political battleground between the United States and the Soviet Union. The problem? Refugees living in Europe. "A new type of political refugee is appearing," Eleanor wrote in her diary, "people who have been against the present governments and if they stay at home or go home will probably be killed." Approximately one million such refugees—men, women, children—were living in displaced-persons camps scattered across France, Germany, and England. Most were from Eastern Europe or Russia, where Communism now reigned. The Russian delegate, Andrey Vishinsky, demanded they be returned to their homelands. Eleanor, understanding their return would mean death or imprisonment, insisted they be given the freedom to choose their own homes.

The debate raged for weeks. Over and over the Russians repeated their points in long-winded speeches that added up to nothing and played for propaganda. At first Eleanor tried to get the Russians to see her point of view. But finally, she decided she could only fight their ideas, not change them. She began banging her gavel freely, shaming many of the Soviet speakers into shorter speeches. And she fought their fictitious arguments with eloquently presented facts. Her persistence paid off. When the General Assembly—a meeting of all the UN nations—voted on the issue, it sided with Eleanor. The refugees would be allowed to choose where they would live.

It was a political triumph for the United States. And a personal victory for Eleanor. "Rattle-brained Mrs. Roosevelt" had emerged as the world's foremost advocate of human rights. Said Senator Vandenberg, her most outspoken critic, "I want to take back everything I ever said about her, and believe me it's been plenty."

Eleanor visits Jewish children living in a European refugee camp.

After the UN agreed that refugees did not have to return to their homelands, a new question arose: Where should they go? Many immigrated to America, England, and Canada. Others chose to remain in France or Germany. But one group—nearly 100,000 homeless Holocaust survivors—still languished in refugee camps, largely because the United States and Western European countries refused to admit them. Many of these survivors longed to make a new life in an independent Jewish country. They petitioned the United Nations to divide Palestine, a small eastern Mediterranean country, into two states—one for Jews, one for Arabs.

Arabs living in the area protested vehemently. Angry that the UN might ask them to give up their homes and villages, they mobilized their armies and vowed to fight.

At first Eleanor didn't support the idea of a Jewish state either. She not only believed it would trigger an Arab uprising, but also felt it was illogical. "We will," she said, "simply be displacing Arabs to make room for displaced Jews. I do not see how this solves the problem." Then in 1946 she visited Jewish refugee camps in Germany. "In all the Jewish camps there were signs of the terrible events through which these people had passed and of the hardships they continued to suffer," she wrote. "In the mud of Zilcheim I remember an old woman whose family had been driven from home by war and madness and brutality. I had no idea who she was and we could not speak each other's language. But she knelt in the muddy road and threw her arms around my knees. 'Israel,' she murmured over and over. 'Israel! Israel!' As I looked at her weather-beaten face and heard her old voice, I knew for the first time what that small land meant to so many, many people." Eleanor changed her mind. Israel, she decided, "must become a reality."

◇◇◇◇◇◇◇◇◇◇◇◇◇◇◇◇ *Eleanor surveys the Israeli landscape.* ◇◇◇◇◇◇◇◇◇◇◇◇◇◇◇◇

Eleanor became one of Israel's most vigorous supporters. Writing to President Truman in 1946, she insisted on the creation of a Jewish state. In 1948, after Israel was founded, she argued strenuously that the United States recognize the new state as soon as possible. It did. And in 1953 she wrote to President Eisenhower, strongly suggesting that economic and military aid for Israel be increased because "a strong and democratic Israel can mean a strong and democratic Middle East." Even when the surrounding Arab countries resisted the creation of Israel by using military force, Eleanor refused to sympathize. She no longer saw Arabs as unfairly displaced, but considered them Israel's enemies. She adopted, said one UN diplomat, a "primitive view" of Arab people, going so far as to describe them as "desert-dwelling, tent-pitching sheiks interested neither in irrigation nor trees." When the Israeli army repulsed the Arabs, Eleanor rejoiced. She believed Israel was the best thing to happen to the region because the Jews were "the only people energetic enough" to turn the desert wasteland into fertile ground.

To show her support of Israel, she visited three times—in 1952, 1959, and 1962. Each trip increased her enthusiasm for it. "There is an atmosphere in Israel that one does not find in many other countries," she wrote in 1959. "The people are excited about the dream of building a country, and are willing to work with their full energy to achieve unbelievable results. They have imagination, they know how to handle people, and they have plenty of experience in adjusting themselves to people of different backgrounds, different religions and different customs." In short, Israel was "a breath of America."

A deeply satisfied Eleanor holds a Spanish translation of the Universal Declaration of Human Rights.

In 1947 Eleanor's fellow delegates were so impressed by her diplomatic skills that they unanimously elected her chairwoman of the eighteen-nation Human Rights Commission. The commission's first order of business? To write an international bill of rights defining the basic freedoms of people all over the world. These included freedom of speech and a fair trial, the right to education and a decent standard of living. It was, Eleanor believed, an important task. "There are many parts of the world that have not even an elementary understanding of what human rights mean," she wrote. She was especially eager to put these "high thoughts" into words the average person could understand. "I used to tell my husband that if he could make *me* understand something, it would be clear to all the other people in the country—and perhaps that will be my real value on this commission!"

Over the next two years Eleanor worked relentlessly to get nations with different customs, religions, and governments to agree on a set of basic rights. It was not an easy job. The first draft of the document, patterned after the United States' Declaration of Independence, began, "All men are created equal . . ."

This would never do, argued some delegates. In their countries the word "men" would be taken literally, and these rights would apply only to men.

So the committee changed the beginning to read, "All humans are created . . ."

Stop! cried delegates from the Communist countries. "Are created" implied a divine creator, something they did not believe in.

Again the wording was changed. Now it read, "All human beings are born . . ."

And so it went. Every comma in every language was scrutinized, debated, negotiated. But finally, at 3 A.M. on December 10, 1948, the Universal Declaration of Human Rights was overwhelmingly approved by the General Assembly of the United Nations. The document, written in the simple, eloquent style Eleanor had insisted on, expressed the rights of every single person on the planet.

It was a huge achievement, and the delegates knew it. In a rare display of emotion and tribute, the entire assembly rose to give Eleanor a standing ovation. Typically, Eleanor was more modest. After passage of the declaration she wrote in her diary simply, "Long job finished."

Always Diplomatic

Eleanor went out of her way to make people feel good about themselves, as this story, recalled by UN lawyer John Maktos, proves:

"I was coming out of the United Nations Headquarters in New York. I saw Mrs. Roosevelt standing near the curb. The delegate of a foreign country who was with me saw her, too. He declared that he would help her across the street. He ran up to her, took her arm, and carefully guided her to the other side. I saw her smile at him and shake hands with him when they got there. Then, as I kept watching her, I noticed Mrs. Roosevelt remaining standing there for another few moments. But just as soon as the foreign delegate had disappeared around a corner, she dashed back to my side of the street where, the next instant, her car drew up with her chauffeur."

Mrs. Franklin D. Roosevelt
The Park Sheraton Hotel
202 Fifty Sixth Street West
New York 19, N. Y.

Hyde Park, N.Y.
January 2, 1953

Dear Mr. President:

I had thought that because my work was finished as a delegate to the General Assembly of the United Nations, and as I was only appointed for this session, that you would not require a special resignation. I find that as there is to be an adjourned session we must all write you formal letters of resignation, so this is to resign as a delegate to the General Assembly which is still in session.

Very sincerely yours,

Eleanor Roosevelt

ELEANOR'S LETTER OF RESIGNATION FROM THE UN

In 1952, Americans elected a Republican, Dwight D. Eisenhower, as president. Knowing the president-elect intended to remove her from her position at the UN, Eleanor resigned before he took office. Now sixty-eight, she returned to private life. But her personal commitment to the UN continued. She traveled throughout the United States promoting the organization and educating citizens about it. "For it isn't enough to talk about peace," she once said. "One must believe in it. And it isn't enough to believe in it. One must work at it."

Having heard that President-elect Dwight D. Eisenhower intended to remove her from her position at the UN, Eleanor wrote this resignation letter to Harry Truman.

Mrs. Roosevelt on arrival at Idlewild Airport after her recent trip to the U.S.S.R.

Eleanor also decided to try her hand at writing another magazine column—a monthly feature for *McCall's* called "If You Ask Me." In it Eleanor answered questions selected by the magazine's editor from those sent in by readers, with topics ranging from the proper use of salad forks to civil rights legislation. Highly successful, the column ran from 1949 until Eleanor's death in 1962.

---

*E*leanor finally got around to writing more of her life story in 1949. It was not an easy task. "The book moves slowly," she told a friend, "but it moves." When she finally finished, she sent it to Bruce Gould, owner of *Ladies' Home Journal* and the publisher of the first installment of her autobiography. Did he like it? No! "You have written this too hastily, as though composing it on a bicycle while pedaling to a fire," he sneered. "Except for a few good passages, it stinks!" He demanded Eleanor work with a professional writer. She refused. "I wouldn't have felt the book was mine," she later explained. In response Gould told her to take her book elsewhere. She did—to *McCall's*. And what happened when they began publishing chapters of it in their magazine? It sold, recalled one of Eleanor's friends, "like hot cakes."

Still the whole of Eleanor's life had not been told. *This I Remember* ended with Franklin's death in 1945. So in 1958 she published *On My Own*, an account of her independent activity and widowhood. Again her words were met with delight and acclaim. But Eleanor wasn't done yet. In 1961 she collected the three books into one, made a few minor changes to the text, added a preface, and included a section called "The Search for Understanding," which expressed her political and moral philosophy. She called this new volume *The Autobiography of Eleanor Roosevelt*.

Cover from the second installment of Eleanor's autobiography, *This I Remember*

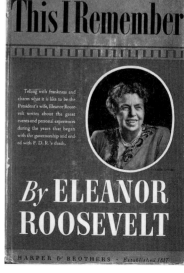

A Friend to Garbage Men

Eleanor at the "Bond Between Us" luncheon for the Women's Division of the State of Israel Bond in 1959— just one of the many fund-raisers she attended in her later years. Pictured with her are (from left to right) the luncheon's chairwoman, Mrs. Louis E. Levinthal; radio and television star Gertrude Berg; actress Susan Strasberg; and opera singer Marian Anderson.

Eleanor was a tireless fund-raiser, appearing at hundreds of luncheons, dinners, conventions, and receptions each year. "One must support the causes one believes in," she said. Among her favorites were the Eleanor Roosevelt Cancer Foundation, dedicated to building new cancer facilities and setting up an international research program; the Tractors for Freedom Committee, organized to raise money for the release of political prisoners in Cuba; and UNICEF, a United Nations campaign to feed hungry children around the world. She also helped raise hundreds of thousands of dollars for the reestablishment of a Jewish nation in Palestine, and close to a million dollars for the Democratic National Committee.

When she was in New York City, Eleanor was frequently spotted in cabs and on subways, buses, and sidewalks. Proof she touched people's lives was reflected in the fact that everywhere she went, she was greeted like an old friend. She responded in kind, as this incident, remembered by a business associate, shows:

When we finished the work, I took Mrs. Roosevelt to the elevator. . . . Two garbage men were . . . there with their reeking containers overflowing with trash. . . . When the garbage men saw Mrs. Roosevelt, one of them said casually, as though he had seen her just the day before, "Oh, hi, Eleanor! Do you think we're going to have a war over this Suez business?"

She said, "Well, the situation is a serious one, but—I don't think it will develop into anything large." She then plunged into a long-drawn-out political discussion with the two garbage men. It was noisy in the elevator. The lids of the garbage cans made a hard metallic noise, something like bang-bang-bang. And then there was Eleanor Roosevelt's high-pitched voice . . . and the deep, resonant voices of the . . . men. And of course there was the awful stench. But she did not seem to notice any of it. When the elevator finally got to the ground floor, Mrs. Roosevelt remained . . . until she had completed her discussion. . . . Only when there was nothing more to ask her did she shake hands with them and step out of the elevator. It was all really quite incredible.

Eleanor reads to the boys of the Wiltwyck School.

The Wiltwyck School was a place for boys aged eight to fourteen who had been abused, abandoned, or in trouble with the law. Because of the school's care many of its students overcame their problems. Some even became famous, such as Floyd Patterson, onetime heavyweight boxing champion of the world, and Claude Brown, who dedicated his best-selling book, *Manchild in the Promised Land,* to Eleanor. She served on Wiltwyck's board of directors for twenty years, from 1942 to her death, and often visited the school, which was just across the Hudson River from the Roosevelt estate at Hyde Park. Every summer after Franklin died, she hosted a big picnic there. "We feed the boys plenty and then we usually lie on the grass a while and I read a story such as Kipling's 'Rikki-tikki-tavi,' or 'How the Elephant Got His Trunk,'" she said. At one picnic Eleanor, wearing a plain white dress, her gray hair drooping and her face perspiring, was broiling hot dogs and buttering hundreds of rolls before placing them on the grill. One of the school's officials begged her not to work so hard. "The boys don't need their rolls buttered," he assured her. But Eleanor shot him an indignant look. "When the King and Queen of England had hot dogs here we buttered the rolls. Why should we do less for the boys of Wiltwyck?"

Far Distant Places

As a child, Eleanor had dreamed of going to "far distant places" with her father. Now, in her late sixties, she embarked on her longest, most exotic voyages ever.

Eleanor visits with women in Pakistan.

In 1952 Eleanor visited Pakistan. During her stay she saw women wearing burkas—long robes covering them from head to toe, with slits at the eyes—who were too timid to vote. Worried about the status of women in that country, she told the story of American women's struggle for a political voice. At one reception women sang and danced native songs for her. In response Eleanor taught them the Virginia reel.

Eleanor samples the curries at a restaurant in Bombay, India.

Eleanor traveled from Pakistan to India. "I have come here to learn," she said when she stepped off the airplane. For the next thirty days she sat with beggars as they spoke of their need for job skills instead of charity; crawled into native mud huts; made her way through dusty village roads; learned how to weave a rug. She attended a formal reception in a linen dress and tennis shoes because she had not bothered to pack formal evening clothes, and addressed the Indian Parliament. She even saw the Taj Mahal by moonlight.

Eleanor talks with Arab sheik
Suleiman Ali en Sayid and
Israeli colonel Michael Haneghi,
1952.

When Eleanor briefly visited
the Middle East—Syria,
Jordan, and Israel—she made
a favorable impression on
Sheik Suleiman of Egypt.
Although he was seventy
years old and the husband of
thirty-nine wives, the sheik
presented Eleanor with a silver
dagger—his way of asking her
to become wife number forty!
Since joining a harem had
never been one of her goals,
Eleanor politely declined.

Visiting a Japanese temple

Since the end of World War II, Japan had
been struggling to become democratic
but felt it needed further enlightenment.
At the request of Japanese officials
Eleanor traveled there in the spring of
1953. Enthusiastically she went across
the country explaining how democracy
worked. She spoke to women's groups
about the importance of voting. She
discussed the need for political education
with Empress Nagako. And she visited
universities, teahouses, and factories.
Before leaving, she made a pilgrimage
to Hiroshima, the first city to know the
terrible devastation of the atomic bomb.
"God grant to men greater wisdom in the
future," she said sadly.

In 1957 seventy-three-year-old Eleanor spent a month in the Soviet Russia. It had not been an easy trip to plan. After World War II, hostilities erupted between the United States and the Soviet Union. Known as the Cold War, these hostilities stemmed from disagreements over how war-torn Eastern Europe should be rebuilt. The United States had wanted a capitalistic system put in place, but the Soviet government insisted on spreading its system of Communism. Soon a bitter and intense rivalry sprang up as each nation vied for world control. In this atmosphere of anger and mistrust the Soviet Union sealed itself off from travelers, especially those from the United States. Very few outsiders were allowed into the country. One of the lucky few was Eleanor. "The wife of Franklin D. Roosevelt is always welcome," said one Soviet official. In Russia, Eleanor was especially interested in how Communism affected the citizens. She visited farms and factories, shops and homes, and came away admiring the country's health care system and efficient division of labor. Still, she found herself deeply concerned about the lack of personal freedoms. The soviet people, she discovered, were not "free to discuss, challenge, or think whatever they pleased"—a frightening prospect for a woman "weaned on the Bill of Rights." The highlight of her trip came when Nikita Khrushchev, leader of the Communist Party, agreed to meet with Eleanor. The two discussed the problems developing between the United States and the Soviet Union—the increasing distrust, the Soviet Union's refusal to disarm, its belief that Communism must be extended worldwide. At the end of their two-and-a-half-hour talk Khrushchev asked, "Can I tell the newspapers we had a friendly conversation?" "You can say," replied Eleanor, "that we had a friendly conversation *but that we differ*." Khrushchev grinned. "At least," he said, "we did not shoot each other."

Eleanor, carrying her own suitcase, boards yet another airplane.

There were other trips to "far distant places" both long and short. She visited Morocco in North Africa; the World's Fair in Brussels, Belgium. She made a second trip to the Soviet Union, visited Poland and Yugoslavia, Hong Kong and Greece. And everywhere she went, crowds thronged to catch a glimpse of her. "She has walked with kings," wrote one English reporter, "but has never lost the common touch."

Eleanor cuts her seventieth birthday cake.

"Of course I know—it's Mrs. Roosevelt!"

A cartoon by Herblock (Herbert Block), auctioned at Eleanor's fund-raiser birthday party

By the 1950s Eleanor Roosevelt, more than anyone else, represented America's conscience. "She has," said a close friend, "a heart that never hardens, a touch that never hurts, and a smile that never tires." No wonder the *Chicago Daily News* noted that Mrs. Roosevelt was "as much a symbol of Democracy as the Statue of Liberty."

Eleanor believed birthdays—hers, at least—should go unnoticed. Her friends, however, felt otherwise, and on October 11, 1954, one thousand of them crowded into the ballroom of New York's Waldorf-Astoria Hotel to celebrate her seventieth birthday with a festive fund-raising dinner for the American Association for the United Nations. "Here's to Eleanor," declared Clare Boothe Luce, ambassador to Rome. "No woman has ever so comforted the distressed, or so distressed the comfortable." The assembly laughed, then Eleanor rose to say a few words. "Life has got to be lived—that's all there is to it. At seventy, I would say the advantage is that you take life more calmly. You know that 'this too shall pass.'" White-haired and deaf in the left ear, she still possessed boundless energy.

❦ Awards ❧

Numerous organizations, both in America and abroad, bestowed awards on Eleanor during her lifetime. She received honors for advancing human rights and humanitarian causes, peace, international understanding, and civil rights, as well as for her work on behalf of education, refugees, labor unions, and those with disabilities. Below is just a sampling of the many awards she received:

1938   Life membership key from the National Education Association

1940   *The Nation* magazine's first annual award for distinguished service in the cause of American social progress

1948   M. Carey Thomas Award from Bryn Mawr College for her UN work

1949   Henrietta Szold Award from Hadassah, the Women's Zionist Organization of America, for her efforts on behalf of Israel

1950   Distinguished Service Medal from the National Society for Crippled Children and Adults

1950   Prince Carl Medal from Sweden for humanitarianism

1954   Nansen Medal from the United Nations General Assembly in recognition of distinguished service on behalf of refugees

1956   Benjamin Franklin Medal, given on the 250th anniversary of Franklin's birth by the city of Philadelphia, for her work in promoting world understanding

1960   Mary McLeod Bethune Human Rights Award from the National Council of Negro Women for her civil rights work

1961   Constance Lindsay Skinner Award from the Women's National Book Association for her contribution to the world of books

1968   United Nations Prize in the field of Human Rights, awarded posthumously by the United Nations

1973   Posthumous induction into the National Women's Hall of Fame for her efforts to end discrimination against minorities

Eleanor also received thirty-five honorary degrees from such colleges as Amherst, Smith, the University of Delhi (India), the University of Lyon (France), and Yeshiva University.

Additionally, she was nominated for the Nobel Peace Prize four times as "a world symbol of the unity of mankind and the hope of peace."

While she admitted that she did not have "much time to watch television," Eleanor understood its potential to reach millions of Americans. And she exploited this potential skillfully. During the last thirteen years of her life she regularly appeared on a variety of public-affairs programs where she voiced her controversial opinions on everything from civil rights to public education. When Eleanor first appeared on *Meet the Press*, a delegation of angry women armed with a list of suspected communists visited the show's producer. At the top of this list, they informed the producer, was Eleanor Roosevelt. It was a dangerous accusation to make. This was the height of the Cold War, when many Americans feared and hated communists. Suspected communists could be subjected to public hearings, FBI investigations, and criminal prosecutions.

Many lost their jobs. Now the women demanded Eleanor be pulled from the show. But *Meet the Press* did no such thing. Not only did they allow her on the air, but they had "a wonderful reaction" from the viewing public. She was frequently invited back, appearing on the program fifteen times in ten years. During her 1956 appearance she challenged the qualifications of President Dwight D. Eisenhower and Vice President Richard Nixon to lead the nation for a second term. And her 1957 appearance drew national attention when she discussed her trip to the Soviet Union. On these programs, observed her friend Joe Lash, "she showed her deadly capacity for setting off dynamite charges while looking and sounding her most grandmotherly."

ELEANOR SITS WITH THE FAMOUS SINGER FRANK SINATRA.

For someone who skillfully used television to give voice to her opinions, Eleanor knew little about the popular programs most people watched. "I went down [to Eleanor's apartment] for lunch one day," recalled her friend Edna Gurewitsch, "and while I was there her secretary said, 'Mrs. Roosevelt, it's a telephone call from California! It's Frank Sinatra!'" At the time Sinatra was not only the best-selling recording artist in America, he was also a popular radio personality and movie actor. Everyone knew his name—everyone, that is, except Eleanor. "Find out who he is, dear," she told her secretary, "and what he wants."

What he wanted was for Mrs. Roosevelt to appear on his television show. She agreed, and on February 15, 1960, she stepped out onto the stage. Sinatra introduced her. "There is a Gallup poll every year to select the ten most admired women in the world. This year for the eleventh time, the name at the top of the list is that of a lady whose friendship I treasure very much—Mrs. Eleanor Roosevelt." Sinatra turned to face her. "Now then, if you had one minute to leave one word with

say 25 million people, what would that word be?" Eleanor looked deep into the camera and delivered the lines she had carefully rehearsed. "That one word would be hope, Frank. Next time you are found with your chin on the ground there's a lot to be learned, so look around." Then she and Sinatra burst into a duet: "Once there was a silly old ant, thought he could move a rubber tree plant, everyone knows an ant can't move a rubber tree plant, but he had high hopes." She was a smash success! Soon she appeared as a celebrity guest on other entertainment shows.

Eleanor's venture into popular entertainment resulted in a flood of criticism. "The mail was pretty evenly divided," she said. "One half was sad because I had damaged my reputation. The other half was happy because I had damaged my reputation." But Eleanor didn't care. She used the earnings from these appearances on CARE packages for the relief of hungry children. "For that amount of money," she told her booking agent, "I can save 6,000 lives."

Album jacket of *Hello, World!*
a children's record Eleanor made for RCA Victor in 1959

When RCA Victor decided to produce a children's record—a musical trip around the world that would teach children how to say hello in various languages—the producers immediately thought of Eleanor for the narrator's part. "She was, after all, so wonderful with children," they explained. But would Eleanor do it? After hearing *Hello, World*'s message of brotherhood, friendship, and understanding, seventy-four-year-old Eleanor agreed. Weeks later she arrived at the New York recording studio to begin work. All went smoothly at first as Eleanor read the opening lines: "Wherever in the world you go, to Maine, or Spain, or Mexico, it's most important that you know how to say hello. So let's take a trip, a musical trip in rhythms from all around the world." She had no difficulty saying *bonjour* or *buenos días* or *guten Tag*. But when the "musical trip" arrived in the Congo, she couldn't pronounce *m'bote* correctly. It took eight takes to get it right.

"You know," said Eleanor when the recording was finally done, "I think I'll send a copy of this . . . to an acquaintance of mine."

On September 27, 1959, the following paragraph appeared in the *New York Times*: "Mrs. Franklin D. Roosevelt has sent a special gift to Premier and Mme Khrushchev and to their grandchildren, an advance copy of her new long-playing record, *Hello, World!* It has a message close to the hearts of all peace-loving people everywhere, old and young alike."

A Body of Work

Besides the two volumes of her autobiography, Eleanor published thirteen books after Franklin's death. Meant to teach, advise, or advocate, these books are:

If You Ask Me (1946) is a collection of practical advice culled from her monthly magazine column.

Partners: The United Nations and Youth (1950) discusses the need for young people's participation in the UN.

India and the Awakening East (1953) shares insights from her trip to India.

UN: Today and Tomorrow (1953), coauthored by William De Witt, explains how the United Nations works and what role it should serve in the future.

Ladies of Courage (1954), coauthored by Lorena Hickok, profiles courageous women in American history.

It Seems to Me (1954) is another collection of advice pulled from her magazine columns.

United Nations: What You Should Know About It (1955) lists questions and answers about the UN.

You Learn by Living (1960) presents the everyday wisdom Eleanor acquired over the years. The book's dominant theme is Be useful to others.

Growing Toward Peace (1960) is a treatise on world peace.

Your Teens and Mine (1961) is an advice book on parenting teenagers.

Eleanor Roosevelt's Book of Common Sense Etiquette (1962) appeared on bookshelves just months after her death. Edited by Robert O. Ballou, it contains advice on handling social situations.

Tomorrow Is Now (1963), published after Eleanor's death, addresses the dangers and challenges of world conditions during the 1960s.

Eleanor Roosevelt's Christmas Book (1963), published after her death, details memories of her family holidays.

Bad News

In October 1958 Eleanor visited her physician, Dr. David Gurewitsch, complaining of chills, fevers, body aches, and fatigue. Assuming she had the flu, he ordered some tests. Their results? Eleanor was very sick with a blood disease called aplastic anemia. The disease left her "utterly exhausted," and Dr. Gurewitsch advised her to give up her activities. But Eleanor refused and swore him to secrecy. "Why?" he asked. Replied Eleanor:

"When you cease to make a contribution, you die."

Seventy-five-year-old Eleanor gives a lecture at Brandeis University and begins a new career.

When the president of Brandeis University appointed Eleanor as a member of the college faculty in 1959, he said, "Well, now you are in a new role, Professor Roosevelt."

"Oh, don't you call me professor," protested Eleanor. "I never went to college. I'd be embarrassed if you put me down in that role." "What role then?" asked the university president. "Can I be put down as lecturer?" she suggested modestly. And so it was that at the bottom of the faculty roster, after the professors, associate professors, and assistant professors, came "Eleanor Roosevelt, Lecturer." Her class was on international organization and law. "I was a little staggered by this assignment," she later wrote in her autobiography. "I felt sure that many of these young people were better versed in questions of international organization than I was. But at least I could discuss with them the tangled problems of foreign policy." Her students were eager to hear her. Said one professor, "She would sprinkle the lecture with anecdotes and wonderful portraits of people who were famous and with sparkling insights into problems in international affairs." Eleanor wanted to hear from the young people too. "She had an unusual trust in them," noted another professor, "and endless patience in listening to their opinions and judgments. . . . She was able to bring out the best in them." Eleanor taught at Brandeis until her death.

Eleanor campaigns in Michigan with Adlai Stevenson (in the striped tie), the man she desperately wanted for president.

Eleanor was anxious for Democrats to regain control of the White House. With this goal in mind, she strongly endorsed Adlai Stevenson, governor of Illinois, for both the 1952 and the 1956 presidential elections. She admired his humility and oratory skills, and the two shared similar views on domestic issues and foreign affairs. Stevenson did, however, have one drawback. "He has difficulty communicating with the man in the street," she said, and she urged him to "don an old suit, get into a jalopy and travel about the country talking to farmers, gas station attendants, housewives and not leave an area until you can feel what they're feeling." Unfortunately, Stevenson did not take her advice. To Eleanor's disappointment, he lost both elections to Dwight D. Eisenhower.

Eleanor with John F. Kennedy

When Kennedy won the Democratic nomination for president in 1960, Eleanor was keenly disappointed. Kennedy, she thought, was too young, too inexperienced, too conservative. Kennedy, on the other hand, needed Eleanor's support. In the late 1950s she commanded power and respect within the Democratic Party, and without her endorsement, Kennedy believed, he might not win the election. So he went to Val-Kill Cottage. There in her cozy, cluttered living room the two talked. To her surprise, she discovered he "was a man who could learn," a man with a "mind that [was] open to new ideas." She liked his eloquence and vision. And although she was just months shy of her seventy-sixth birthday, she agreed to actively campaign for him. She appeared in his radio and television commercials and traveled to a number of states on his behalf. When Kennedy became president in 1961, she accepted several assignments from him. She again became a delegate to the United Nations. She took a position on the Advisory Council of the Peace Corps, and she chaired his Commission on the Status of Women. "There is so much to do," she said. "So many engrossing challenges, so many heartbreaking and pressing needs, so much in every day that is profoundly interesting."

Eleanor at a meeting of the National Association for the Advancement of Colored People (NAACP), 1956

Eleanor's most active efforts against racial discrimination came after Franklin's death. No longer worried about hurting him politically, she joined the NAACP's board of directors and the board of the Congress of Racial Equality (CORE). When a race riot nearly destroyed the town of Columbia, Tennessee, in 1946, NAACP officials asked her to chair the committee investigating the riot's cause. Working with future Supreme Court justice Thurgood Marshall, she forced the Justice Department to look beyond the story told by the town's white officials. Next she pressured President Truman into speaking at the NAACP's national convention. He agreed, becoming the first president to do so. Using her newspaper and magazine columns, her radio programs and lecture tours, she debated segregated schools, employment discrimination, literacy testing, and poll taxes. In 1957, impatient with the country's slow commitment to civil rights, she publicly criticized any politician—Republican or Democrat—who evaded the issue. She advocated civil disobedience and even wrote the introduction to a pamphlet called "Cracking the Color Code," which gave tips on how to stage sit-ins. When some people called her an anarchist, she impatiently responded that "advocating civil rights does not constitute anarchy." Over and over she urged Americans to take a stand against racial discrimination. "Staying aloof," she declared, "is not a solution; it is a cowardly evasion."

Civil rights leader and Eleanor's friend, the Reverend Dr. Martin Luther King Jr.

Both Martin Luther King Jr. and Eleanor worked hard to bring civil rights to African Americans, so it's not surprising the two formed a respectful friendship. Eleanor used her considerable clout to raise money for the Southern Christian Leadership Council (SCLC), of which Dr. King was president, and both attended a civil rights rally in Madison Square Garden. But most important, Eleanor served as an intermediary between President John F. Kennedy and Dr. King. In 1961, worried about alienating white voters in the Democratic Party, Kennedy distanced himself from the civil rights leader. Communication broke down between the men. What to do? Turn to Eleanor, of course. She made sure the White House understood Dr. King's views on civil rights by writing endless letters—letters President Kennedy felt obligated to read. But Eleanor didn't always make demands. When the president took actions supporting civil rights, she praised him. "You are doing very well," she wrote in one note, "and the results are gratifying."

Eleanor expressed her admiration for Dr. King, too. In her "My Day" column of February 6, 1961, she wrote, "Dr. King is a very moving speaker. . . . He is simple and direct, and the spiritual quality which has made him the leader of nonviolence in this country touches all of us."

Dr. King was equally glowing about Eleanor. On November 24, 1962, he described her as a "humanitarian . . . friend of the fallen . . . and a foe of injustice. . . . The courage she displayed in taking sides on matters considered controversial gave strength . . . and commitment to the great issues of our times."

By mid 1962 Eleanor could no longer shake off her poor health. Now in constant pain, she entered the hospital for extensive tests and discovered the true nature of her illness—bone marrow tuberculosis, a rare bacterial disease inhibiting bone marrow's ability to make red blood cells. As her friend Trude Lash recalled, "There was only suffering for Mrs. Roosevelt from the first day she was taken to the hospital. . . . There was no moment of serenity. There was only anger, helpless anger at the doctors and nurses and the world who tried to keep her alive. . . . She was not afraid of death at all. She welcomed it."

And so Eleanor was moved back to her apartment, where she was surrounded by friends, family, and around-the-clock nursing care. One night she told her nurse she wanted to die. The nurse replied that the Lord would take her when she finished the job she'd been put on Earth to do. "Utter nonsense," replied Eleanor. And she grew more determined. She refused pills, clenched her teeth to keep the nurse from administering them, spit them out if the nurse managed to get them past her bared teeth, and even managed to hide them under the edge of her mattress. As the weeks passed, she grew confused, incoherent. "It seemed as though she had to suffer every indignity, every weakness, every failure that she had resisted and conquered so daringly during her whole life," Trude Lash added. Finally, on November 7, 1962, her heart simply stopped beating.

"Our dear Mrs. Roosevelt died last evening," wrote her friend Edna Gurewitsch. "Around a quarter of nine, I saw from my bedroom window, the simple casket leaving the house, it being placed on the hearse and Mrs. Roosevelt . . . driving away from 74th Street for the last time. I called out many goodbyes from the window." Eleanor Roosevelt was seventy-eight years old.

The White House flag flies at half-mast.

News of Eleanor's death resulted in tributes from all over the world. Queen Elizabeth of England noted, "The British people held her in deep respect and affection." Indian prime minister Jawaharlal Nehru wrote, "No woman of this generation and few in the annals of history have so well understood and articulated the yearnings of men and women for social justice." Even Soviet leader Nikita Khrushchev telegrammed his condolences. In the United States flags everywhere flew at half-mast, the first time such an honor had been accorded a woman. President John F. Kennedy called her "one of the great ladies in the history of this country." And at the United Nations headquarters in New York delegates from 110 countries stood for a one-minute silent tribute. But it was these tributes from ordinary people that probably would have pleased Eleanor most:

"The folks will miss her. She was always on their side."
—a truck driver from the Bronx

"Eleanor Roosevelt was like a mother to the world and we are like orphans because of her death."
—a fifth grader from Public School 233, New York

"But she couldn't have died at 6:15. We were eating dinner then, and we were happy!"
—a Brooklyn housewife

On November 10, a gray and gloomy day, one thousand people crowded onto the Roosevelt estate at Hyde Park to pay their last respects to Eleanor. Among those attending were presidents and vice presidents, foreign dignitaries, politicians, family friends, and relatives.

Her son James was among them. "I stood there remembering how Mother never stopped being a mother. Once, seated next to her on the dais at a dinner, she noticed I wasn't eating very much. Even though I was in my early fifties, she leaned over and whispered, 'James, eat your peas.' The memory made me smile."

Elliott was there too. "There was much to regret. She and I had spent too long apart of late, and too much had been left unsaid. She had been told too seldom of my love. . . . I wondered now if she remembered."

Looking pale and exhausted, Anna leaned against her husband. She, along with her brother John, had made all the funeral arrangements. Now she worried about the luncheon that was to follow at Val-Kill Cottage. Would everyone be shoehorned in? She looked toward John. He winked and placed a hand on Franklin Jr.'s shoulder.

Standing on wooden planks laid across the muddy ground, the guests shivered. "The gray and cold of the outside matched the gray and cold of my inside," recalled one longtime family friend. "Then, just as they brought [Eleanor's] casket in, the sun came out and stayed out the entire service. It gave me an eerie feeling." After the funeral, guests lingered at the grave site, unwilling to leave their dear friend so soon. That's when Eleanor's personal physician, Dr. David Gurewitsch, approached former president Dwight D. Eisenhower. "How could it happen that you did not make use of this lady?" he asked, referring to Eleanor's resignation from the UN following Eisenhower's election to the presidency. "We had no better ambassador." In reply Eisenhower simply shrugged and moved away. "I made use of her," said former president Harry S. Truman, who had overheard. "I told her she was the first lady of the world."

These crowded hours have been interesting and stimulating. They have,
I hope, been useful. They have, at least, been lived to the hilt.

—Eleanor Roosevelt, December 1960

More About Eleanor

Books About Eleanor for Young Readers

Adler, David A. *A Picture Book of Eleanor Roosevelt.* New York: Holiday House, 1995.

Freedman, Russell. *Eleanor Roosevelt: A Life of Discovery.* New York: Clarion, 1993.

Hoffman, Nancy. *Eleanor Roosevelt and the Arthurdale Experiment.* New York: Linnet Books, 2001.

Kulling, Monica. *Eleanor Everywhere: The Life of Eleanor Roosevelt.* New York: Random House, 1999.

Parks, Deborah A. *Eleanor Roosevelt: Freedom's Champion* New York: Time-Life, 2000.

Thompson, Gare. *Who Was Eleanor Roosevelt?* New York: Grosset & Dunlap, 2004.

Weil, Ann. *Eleanor Roosevelt: a Fighter for Social Justice.* New York: Aladdin Paperbacks, 1989.

Videos About Eleanor Roosevelt

The American Experience: Eleanor Roosevelt. Boston: WGBH and America Productions, 1998. Videocassette.

Eleanor and Franklin. New York: HBO Video, 1975, 1993. Videocassette.

Eleanor Roosevelt: A Restless Spirit. New York: A&E Home Video, 1994. Videocassette.

The Eleanor Roosevelt Story. New York: Kino on Video, 1965, 1997. Videocassette.

Eleanor Roosevelt Web Sites

www.fdrlibrary.marist.edu

This site features thousands of online photographs, as well as original documents. It also provides links to other online information about Eleanor.

http://foia.fbi.gov/

The FBI's official Web site allows you to read Eleanor's file for yourself. From its home page, click on "Reading Room Index" in the righthand corner, then click on R, and then choose "Roosevelt, Eleanor."

www.gwu.edu/~erpapers/abouteleanor

Part of the Eleanor Roosevelt Papers project at George Washington University, this site is dedicated to educating the public about Eleanor's writings (and radio and TV appearances) on democracy and human rights. It includes a brief biographical essay about Eleanor, as well as a complete bibliography of her works, a time line of her life, and frequently asked questions and answers about Eleanor.

http://newdeal.feri.org

Award-winning site containing photographs, speeches, articles, poems, Web projects, and more related to the Great Depression and the New Deal.

www.nps.gov/elro

National Parks Service site for Eleanor's home at Val-Kill, this site includes photographs, facts, and activities for kids. Best of all, it includes an extensive glossary which defines the many people and events important in Eleanor's life.

www.pbs.org/wgbh/amex/eleanor

Includes biographical material, time lines, interviews with people who knew Eleanor, a family tree, and audio and video clips.

Picture Credits

All photographs and illustrations not specifically credited below were provided by the Franklin D. Roosevelt Library in Hyde Park, New York. All contributors are herewith gratefully acknowledged:

AP/ Wide World: 26 (top), 65, 66 (bottom), 72 (top), 79, 87, 89 (top), 145 (bottom), 154 (top)

Bettmann/CORBIS: 69 (top), 88, 133

Brandeis University Library: 151 (top)

Brown Brothers: 22

Federal Bureau of Investigation: 103, 104

Candace Fleming: 27 (bottom), 72 (bottom), 74 (top), 76 (top), 83, 108, 112 (bottom), 140, 149, 150

The Herb Block Foundation: 146 (right)

Library of Congress: 6, 18 (top), 38 (bottom), 39 (bottom), 40, 41, 44, 50, 51, 54, 61 (bottom), 64, 80, 81, 84, 85, 91, 93, 94, 95, 100, 106, 107 (right), 110, 120 (right), 128 (top), 153, 154 (bottom)

National Archives: 39 (top), 96, 107 (left), 115 (right)

New York Public Library: 56, 63

Holly Pribble: family tree, 8

Anne Schwartz: 141

Harry S. Truman Presidential Library: 139

White House Photo Office: 85 (far right)

Source Notes

In writing this book, I went straight to the source—Eleanor herself. Lucky for me, so many of her personal papers still exist. Housed at the Franklin D. Roosevelt Library in Hyde Park, New York, the Anna Eleanor Roosevelt Manuscript Collection includes two million pages of private letters, diaries, office files, memoranda, invitations, scrapbooks, pamphlets, magazine articles, newspaper clippings, and much more. I pored over Eleanor's childhood diaries and sifted through her White House scrapbooks. And to my delight, I uncovered many telling, enlightening details in that time: A diary entry revealed the poetic side of fifteen-year-old Eleanor; a newspaper clipping detailed the first lady's menu for nutritious, inexpensive meals; a letter described Eleanor's "My Day" column as "nonsensical and demented."

Especially wonderful were the Eleanor Roosevelt Oral History Transcripts also found at the FDR Library. These engaging personal reminiscences of Eleanor's family and friends, associates and employees, provided some of my favorite anecdotes: the sun coming out just before Eleanor's casket was carried into the Hyde Park rose garden; the wonderful description of Winston Churchill "all steamed up in his boy's book of adventure." I used oral transcripts from the following people:

John Boettiger—Eleanor's grandson
Maureen Corr—Eleanor's secretary
Martha Gellhorn—Eleanor's friend
Nina Roosevelt Gibson—Eleanor's granddaughter
Anne Ward Gilbert—Eleanor's student at the Todhunter School
James Frederick Green—adviser to Eleanor in the United Nations
Edna Gurewitsch—Eleanor's close friend and wife of Eleanor's physician
Trude Lash—Eleanor's close friend and wife of Eleanor's biographer Joseph Lash
Pauli Murray—civil rights pioneer
Justine Polier—children's rights advocate, friend and coworker of Eleanor
Elliott Roosevelt—Eleanor's son
Franklin D. Roosevelt III—Eleanor's grandson
James Roosevelt—Eleanor's son
Abram L. Sachar—president of Brandeis University, 1948–68

Additionally, Eleanor's own books and recollections added immensely to my understanding of her life and thoughts. The ones I relied on most were:

Roosevelt, Eleanor. *The Autobiography of Eleanor Roosevelt*. New York: Da Capo Press, 1992.
——. *On My Own*. New York: Harper and Brothers, 1958.
——. *This I Remember*. New York: Harper and Brothers, 1949.
——. *This Is My Story*. New York: Harper and Brothers, 1937.
——. *What I Hope to Leave Behind: The Essential Essays of Eleanor Roosevelt*. Brooklyn: Carlson Publications, 1995.
Roosevelt, Eleanor, and William De Witt. *UN: Today and Tomorrow*. New York: Harper and Brothers, 1953.

A remarkable amount of information also came from my own search for Eleanor Roosevelt detritus. I began prowling Internet search engines, memorabilia auctions, and obscure bookstores, and was quickly amazed by how much history is tucked away in people's attics and basements, dresser drawers and closet shelves. At a local flea market I unearthed dozens of faded, yellowed magazines—*Life, Literary Digest, Family Circle, Saturday Evening Post*. Between their mildewed covers I discovered articles about Eleanor, long interviews with her, and several eyewitness accounts of her speeches and public appearances. At an antiquarian book fair I stumbled across an envelope of rare photographs taken at the 1952 Democratic National Convention. A 1942 biography of Fala found at a local garage sale provided details on the Roosevelts' relationship with their pets. I also searched out several notes handwritten by Eleanor, handfuls of original newspaper clippings, a 1940 slogan button, and the 1962 congressional tribute to Eleanor. I was the only bidder in an auction for what turned out to be a rare recording of a 1958 interview with Eleanor Roosevelt. How incredible it was to sit and listen as Eleanor herself told me her life story. All of these finds added something of value to this book—a forgotten anecdote, an explanation of an event—small but telling details that added texture and resonance to Eleanor's personality.

Source Citations
For clarity's sake I have sourced quotations by individual entry, rather than by page number. Additionally, at the request of the archivists at the Franklin D. Roosevelt Library in Hyde Park, I did not include box numbers in my citations. Over time collections can be moved into different containers, but because the original order of the documents never changes, the information included in my citations will provide the exact location of the document regardless of the box number.

SAD LITTLE NELL
Eleanor's Mother in 1881
"She is [the] loveliest . . .": Ward McAllister, *Society As I Have Found It* (New York: Cassell, 1890), 380.

"simply gaze upon . . .": Letter from Anna H. Roosevelt to Anna Roosevelt Cowles, 5 August 1897, Papers of Anna Roosevelt Cowles, Houghton Library, Harvard Library, Harvard University.

"the most brilliant . . .": *New York Herald,* 2 December 1893, 10.

"appeared every bit . . .": Ibid.

"was worthy of her": Ibid.

Eleanor's Father in 1881

"the Swells": Joseph P. Lash, *Eleanor and Franklin: The Story of Their Relationship Based on Eleanor Roosevelt's Private Papers* (New York: Norton, 1971), 21.

Record of Eleanor's Birth

"more wrinkled . . .": Lash, *Eleanor and Franklin,* 24.

"precious boy": Ibid., 25.

"She is a miracle . . .": Ibid., 24.

Bouncing Baby Eleanor

"She seemed helpless . . .": Anna Bulloch Gracie to Corinne Roosevelt, 9 August 1886, Theodore Roosevelt Collection, Houghton Library, Harvard University.

"Baby Eleanor is . . .": Lash, *Eleanor and Franklin,* 31.

Four-Year-Old Eleanor

"I always had . . .": *A Recorded Portrait: Eleanor Roosevelt in Conversation with Arnold Michaelis,* Recorded Communications RCI-102, sound recording.

"as a child senses . . .": Russell Freedman, *Eleanor Roosevelt* (New York: Clarion, 1993), 5.

"I can remember . . .": Eleanor Roosevelt *The Autobiography of Eleanor Roosevelt* (New York: Da Capo Press, 1992), 9.

"The feeling that . . .": Blanche Wiesen Cook, *Eleanor Roosevelt,* vol. 1, 1884–1933 (New York: Viking, 1992), 69.

Eleanor with Her Brothers

"heart's desire": Lash, *Eleanor and Franklin,* 32.

"first in his heart": Eleanor Roosevelt, *Autobiography,* 6.

"My mother made . . .": Ibid., 8–9.

"[Elliott Jr.] is a . . .": Lash, *Eleanor and Franklin,* 42.

"a problem" and "so grave": Ibid., 42.

"felt a curious . . .": Eleanor Roosevelt, *Autobiography,* 8.

Eleanor with Her Father

"With my father . . .": Eleanor Roosevelt, *Autobiography,* 5.

Newsboys' Lodge

"Very early I . . .": Eleanor Roosevelt, *Autobiography,* 12.

"life blessed with plenty . . .": *Recorded Portrait.*

Theodore Roosevelt

"He was horrified . . .": *Recorded Portrait.*

"fight for the less . . ." and "lasting changes . . .": Ibid.

So Many Fears

"I was afraid . . .": Eleanor Roosevelt, "Conquer Fear and You Will Enjoy Living," n.d., Lorena Hickok Papers, Franklin D. Roosevelt Library, Hyde Park, N.Y. (Later published in *Look,* May 1939.)

Father's Weakness

"Dearest, throw your . . .": Cook, *Eleanor Roosevelt,* 54.

"weakness": Eleanor Roosevelt, *Autobiography,* 5.

"regain command of . . .": Teddy Roosevelt to Anna Roosevelt Cowles, 22 February 1892, Theodore Roosevelt Collection, Houghton Library, Harvard University.

"wicked and foolish" and "it [was] Anna's wish": Cook, *Eleanor Roosevelt,* 21.

"I will do . . .": Lash, *Eleanor and Franklin,* 39.

"I so long . . .": Ibid., 38.

"I acquired a . . .": Eleanor Roosevelt, *Autobiography,* 8.

The Habit of Lying

"I longed to . . .": Eleanor Roosevelt, *Autobiography,* 8.

Eleanor Is Taught

"a Prince Albert coat": Lash, *Eleanor and Franklin,* 62.

"make intellects . . .": Ibid., 42.

"frozen by shyness" and "could not imagine . . .": Ibid., 42.

"Now I want . . .": Eleanor Roosevelt to Edward Hall, 2 March 1894, Unnumbered Family and Personal Correspondence, 1884–1957, Eleanor Roosevelt Papers.

"Suddenly, Life Changed!"

"I can remember . . .": Eleanor Roosevelt, *Autobiography,* 9–10.

Grandmother Mary Hall

"As sorely as . . .": Eleanor Roosevelt to Anna Roosevelt Cowles, 10 December 1892, Papers of Anna Roosevelt Cowles.

"grim and ill-kept . . .": Lash, *Eleanor and Franklin,* 61.

"I never wanted . . .": Ibid.

"I was brought up . . .": *Recorded Portrait.*

Eleanor and Hall

"Dear little Ellie . . .": Lash, *Eleanor and Franklin,* 49.

"Now there was . . .": Eleanor Roosevelt, *Autobiography,* 13.

"A half dozen . . .": *Recorded Portrait.*

Letter from Eleanor to Her Father

"When he failed . . .": Lash, *Eleanor and Franklin,* 51.

"He is charming . . .": Ibid.

"I thought of you . . .": Eleanor Roosevelt to Elliott Roosevelt, 30 July 1894, Unnumbered Family and Personal Correspondence, 1894–1957, Eleanor Roosevelt Papers.

"I wish you were . . .": Lash, *Eleanor and Franklin,* 53.

"There are a lot . . .": Elliott Roosevelt to Eleanor Roosevelt, 20 January 1893, Unnumbered Early Family Papers, 1860–1910, Eleanor Roosevelt Papers.

"Devote yourself . . .": Lash, *Eleanor and Franklin,* 48.

"I knew a child . . .": Eleanor Roosevelt, "Ethics of Parents," Speech and Article File, 1927, Eleanor Roosevelt Papers.

"Darling Little Nell . . .": Elliott Roosevelt to Eleanor Roosevelt, 13 August 1894, Unnumbered Family and Personal Correspondence, 1894–1957, Eleanor Roosevelt Papers.

"There were no . . .": *Recorded Portrait.*

Heartbreak

"While I wept . . .": Eleanor Roosevelt, *Autobiography,* 13.

Eleanor at Tivoli

"When I expressed . . .": Eleanor Roosevelt, "Ethics of Parents," Speech and Article File, 1927, Eleanor Roosevelt Papers.

"out into the fields . . .": Eleanor Roosevelt, *Autobiography,* 16.

"Sometimes I even managed . . .": Lash, *Eleanor and Franklin,* 67–68.

Eleanor's Fifth Cousin

"I was different . . .": Eleanor Roosevelt, *Autobiography,* 19.

"more pain than pleasure": *Recorded Portrait*.

"Cousin Eleanor has . . .": Richard Harrity and Ralph G. Martin, *Eleanor Roosevelt: Her Life in Pictures* (New York: Duell, Sloan, and Pearce, 1958), 17.

Eleanor at Fifteen

"Poor little soul . . .": Lash, *Eleanor and Franklin*, 72.

Sent Away

"Your mother wanted . . .": Lash, *Eleanor and Franklin*, 73.

"Thus, the second . . .": Eleanor Roosevelt, *Autobiography*, 20.

Eleanor with Allenswood Classmates

"lost and very lonely": Eleanor Roosevelt, *Autobiography*, 20.

"first meal when . . .": Joseph P. Lash, *Love, Eleanor: Eleanor Roosevelt and Her Friends* (Garden City, N.Y.: Doubleday, 1982), 27.

"She was 'everything' . . .": Lash, *Eleanor and Franklin*, 84.

"supreme favorite": Ibid.

Rules

"former sins" and "There was nothing . . .": Eleanor Roosevelt, *Autobiography*, 24.

"On the outside . . .": Ibid., 21–23.

An Entry in Eleanor's Diary

"To be the thing . . .": Eleanor Roosevelt diary, 13 November 1899, Unnumbered School Exercise Books, ca. 1892–1902, Eleanor Roosevelt Papers.

Mlle Marie Souvestre

"She exerted perhaps . . .": Eleanor Roosevelt, *Autobiography*, 35.

"Why was your mind . . .": Lash, *Eleanor and Franklin*, 81.

"[She] shocked me . . .": *Recorded Portrait*.

"could give a great . . .": Lash, *Eleanor and Franklin*, 83.

"I still remember . . .": Eleanor Roosevelt, *Autobiography*, 29.

"Never again would . . .": Ibid., 31.

"the thought of . . .": Ibid., 35.

"I miss you . . .": Eleanor Roosevelt to Marie Souvestre, 5 October 1902, typed translation in Unnumbered Family and Personal Correspondence, 1894–1957, Eleanor Roosevelt Papers.

Eleanor's Report Card

"a tall, slim . . .": Lash, *Eleanor and Franklin*, 76.

"could not draw . . .": Ibid.

"I struggled over . . .": Ibid.

"envied every good . . .": Ibid.

"I had never seen . . .": Eleanor Roosevelt, *Autobiography*, 23.

"It was one . . .": Ibid.

"very advanced"; "very industrious"; and "excellent": Lash, *Eleanor and Franklin*, 79.

"Eleanor has had . . .": Eleanor Roosevelt report card, 1902, Unnumbered Early Family Papers, 1860–1910, Eleanor Roosevelt Papers.

Nineteen-Year-Old Franklin

"Gibson-girl figure . . .": Lash, *Eleanor and Franklin*, 102.

"smitten to the core . . .": Margaret Logan Marquez, interview with author, 31 January 2003.

A Few Words About Franklin

"You couldn't find . . .": Doris Kearns Goodwin, *No Ordinary Time: Franklin and Eleanor Roosevelt, the Home Front in World War II* (New York: Touchstone Books, 1994), 373.

"He was the kind . . .": Lash, *Eleanor and Franklin*, 103.

Eleanor's Coming-Out Portrait

"state of nervous collapse": Eleanor Roosevelt, *Autobiography*, 37.

The Assembly Ball

"the social event . . .": *New York Times*, 13 December 1902, 17.

"utter agony": Eleanor Roosevelt, *Autobiography*, 37.

Eleanor with Society Friends

"[Eleanor] wasn't a . . .": Lash, *Eleanor and Franklin*, 95.

"softened the hearts . . .": Ibid.

Rivington Street

"The dirty streets . . .": Eleanor Roosevelt, *Autobiography*, 40.

"[Susie] says . . .": Lash, *Eleanor and Franklin*, 98.

"I still remember . . .": Eleanor Roosevelt, *Autobiography*, 48.

"worried [she] would . . .": *Recorded Portrait*.

"an occupation . . .": Ibid.

Dating in Eleanor's Day

"It was understood . . .": Eleanor Roosevelt, *Autobiography*, 41.

Eleanor with a Playful Franklin

"walked to the river . . .": Lash, *Eleanor and Franklin*, 102.

"That first summer . . .": Ibid., 103.

Childhood's Last Summer

"As I try . . .": Eleanor Roosevelt, *Autobiography*, 40.

A DEVOTED WIFE AND MOTHER

Franklin and Eleanor

"With your help . . .": Harrity and Martin, *Eleanor Roosevelt*, 19.

"Why me? . . .": Lash, *Eleanor and Franklin*, 107.

"the most remarkable . . .": Goodwin, *No Ordinary Time*, 371.

"You are never . . .": Lash, *Eleanor and Franklin*, 110.

"I am the happiest . . .": Franklin D. Roosevelt, *FDR: His Personal Letters*, vol. 1, *The Early Years*, ed. Elliott Roosevelt (New York: Duell, Sloan, and Pearce, 1947), 518.

Sara Delano Roosevelt

"darling Franklin": Lash, *Eleanor and Franklin*, 116.

"I think he . . .": Ibid., 133.

"The world . . .": Ibid., 125.

"Hurrah! Hurrah! . . .": Ibid., 137.

"I am feeling . . .": Ibid., 128.

Why Franklin?

"[Franklin] was very . . .": Martha Gellhorn, Oral History Project, Eleanor Roosevelt Papers.

Why Eleanor?

"[Franklin] harbored large . . .": Lash, *Eleanor and Franklin*, 105.

Eleanor's Uncle, President Theodore Roosevelt

"on that day . . .": Edith Carow Roosevelt to Eleanor Roosevelt, 19 December 1904, Unnumbered Family and Personal Correspondence, 1894–1957, Eleanor Roosevelt Papers.

"Well, Franklin . . .": Cook, *Eleanor Roosevelt*, 167.

"were more concerned . . .": Sara Delano Roosevelt diary, 17 March 1905, Roosevelt Family Papers Donated by the Children, Franklin D. Roosevelt Library, Hyde Park, N.Y.

"We simply followed . . .": Eleanor Roosevelt, *Autobiography*, 50.

A (Very) Few Words About Sex

"Well, you know . . .": Franklin D.

Roosevelt Jr., Oral History Project, Eleanor Roosevelt Papers.

Honeymooning in Italy

"never realized . . ." and "I vowed that . . .": Eleanor Roosevelt, *Autobiography*, 55.

Mother-in-Law Problems

"determined to bend . . .": Eleanor Roosevelt, "I Remember Hyde Park: A Final Reminiscence," *McCall's*, February 1963, 21.

"I was beginning . . .": Eleanor Roosevelt, *Autobiography*, 55.

"If you'd just . . .": Geoffrey C. Ward, *A First-Class Temperament: The Emergence of Franklin Roosevelt* (New York: Harper and Row, 1989), 175.

"Oh, yes, Eleanor . . .": Gellhorn, Oral History Project, Eleanor Roosevelt Papers.

"Granny's ace in . . .": Lash, *Eleanor and Franklin*, 162.

"Your mother only . . .": James Roosevelt, *My Parents: A Differing View* (Chicago: Playboy Press, 1976), 25.

"If something was . . .": *Recorded Portrait*.

Franklin and Eleanor Five Years After

"I was horribly . . .": Lash, *Eleanor and Franklin*, 158.

"Anything left undone . . .": Ibid.

Griselda Mood

"I developed a . . .": Eleanor Roosevelt, *Autobiography*, 59–60.

A Sketch Drawn by Sara

"You were never . . .": Eleanor Roosevelt, "I Remember Hyde Park," 21.

"Being an eminently . . .": Eleanor Roosevelt, *Autobiography*, 61.

The Roosevelt Cottage

"rearrange all the . . .": Lash, *Eleanor and Franklin*, 163.

"that bunch of . . .": David B. Roosevelt, *Grandmère: A Personal History of Eleanor Roosevelt* (New York: Warner Books, 2002), 227.

"There [were] good . . .": Ibid., 219.

Springwood

"All that is in . . .": Lash, *Eleanor and Franklin*, 116.

"For over forty years . . .": Eleanor Roosevelt, "I Remember Hyde Park," 72.

"[It] is now to be . . .": Lillian Rogers Parks, *The Roosevelts: A Family in Turmoil* (Englewood, N.J.: Fleet, 1981), 241.

It's a Girl!

"a beautiful girl . . .": Lash, *Eleanor and Franklin*, 154.

"just a helpless . . .": Ibid.

"What she [really] . . .": Eleanor Roosevelt, "I Remember Hyde Park," 22.

"Anna is upset . . .": Lash, *Eleanor and Franklin*, 160.

"I am to take . . ." and "I never knew . . .": Ibid.

"She was very . . .": Lash, *Love, Eleanor*, 232.

It's a Boy!

"He is lovely . . .": Lash, *Eleanor and Franklin*, 159.

"heart sang . . .": Ibid.

"James won't sit . . .": Ibid., 164.

"He is very naughty . . .": Ibid.

"enforced a discipline . . .": Eleanor Roosevelt, "My Children," Speech and Article File, 1934, Eleanor Roosevelt Papers.

"the chicks run wild": Lash, *Eleanor and Franklin*, 197.

"often unreasonable" and "I can remember . . .": Eleanor Roosevelt, "My Children."

"on a hunt for . . ."; "poor, unadventurous darlings"; and "primly parade on . . .": Frances Theodora Parsons, *Perchance Some Day* (New York. n.p., 1951), 249.

"We fished off . . .": Lash, *Eleanor and Franklin*, 198.

"A good exercise . . .": Ibid.

"could hardly drag . . .": Ibid.

Little Angel

"really lovely and . . .": Sara Delano Roosevelt diary, 18 March 1909, Roosevelt Family Papers Donated by the Children.

"little heart had . . .": Sara Delano Roosevelt diary, 29 October 1909.

"the little angel . . .": Sara Delano Roosevelt diary, 1 November 1909.

"How cruel it . . .": Eleanor Roosevelt, *Autobiography*, 62.

"having done so . . .": Ibid.

The Middle Child

"a loud, active, excitable . . .": Eleanor Roosevelt, "My Children," Speech and Article File, 1934, Eleanor Roosevelt Papers.

"He made a long . . .": Lash, *Eleanor and Franklin*, 196.

"he went for me . . .": Ibid.

"Oh, let them . . .": Ibid., 197.

"Elliott goes to . . .": Ibid., 195.

"Relax your muscles . . .": James Roosevelt and Sidney Shalett, *Affectionately, FDR: A Son's Story of a Courageous Man* (New York: Harcourt, Brace, 1959), 38.

The Team

"I went out . . .": Lash, *Eleanor and Franklin*, 240.

"I love you . . .": Ibid.

"I asked Franklin Jr. . . .": Ibid., 241.

"Granny, I intend . . .": Ibid.

"I am *not* . . .": Ibid.

"I feel sure . . .": Ibid.

"procession of English . . .": James Roosevelt and Shalett, *Affectionately, FDR*, 39.

"more confidence in . . .": Eleanor Roosevelt, "My Children," Speech and Article File, 1934, Eleanor Roosevelt Papers.

Sparing the Rod

"Father was known . . .": Elliott Roosevelt, Oral History Project, Eleanor Roosevelt Papers.

Memories of Mother

"very unpredictable and . . .": Bernard Asbell ed., *Mother and Daughter: The Letters of Eleanor and Anna Roosevelt* (New York: Fromm, 1988), 9.

"I don't think . . .": Lash, *Eleanor and Franklin*, 241.

"My earliest memories . . .": Elliott Roosevelt, Oral History Project, Eleanor Roosevelt Papers.

"She did her . . .": Lash, *Eleanor and Franklin*, 241.

"She felt tremendous . . .": John R. Boettiger, *A Love in Shadow* (New York: Norton, 1978), 45.

"It did not come . . .": Lash, *Love, Eleanor*, 57.

Franklin and Eleanor After Eleven Years

"Isn't it grand? . . ." Ellen Feldman, *Lucy* (New York: W.W. Norton, 2003), 73.

"She sometimes acted . . .": Lash, *Love, Eleanor*, 70.

"She bothered him . . .": Goodwin, *No Ordinary Time*, 373.

"I think you . . .": Ibid., 376.

Lucy Mercer

"gay . . . smiling and . . .": Elliott Roosevelt

and James Brough, *An Untold Story: The Roosevelts of Hyde Park* (New York: Putnam, 1973), 73.

"I saw you . . .": Lash, *Eleanor and Franklin*, 225–26.

"Isn't she perfectly . . .": Ibid.

"You were being . . .": Ibid., 223.

"I do miss . . .": Ibid., 224.

"The bottom dropped . . .": Ibid., 220.

"I cannot forget": Kenneth S. Davis, *Invincible Summer: An Intimate Portrait of the Roosevelts, Based on the Recollections of Marion Dickerman* (New York: Atheneum, 1974), 93.

"1918": Goodwin, *No Ordinary Time*, 378.

Franklin and Eleanor After the Affair

"myself, my surroundings . . .": *Recorded Portrait.*

"There is no . . .": Joseph P. Lash, *A World of Love: Eleanor Roosevelt and Her Friends, 1943–1962* (Garden City, N.Y.: Doubleday, 1984), 150.

"1/2 a Loaf of Love"

"Of one thing . . .": Lash, *Love, Eleanor*, 383–84.

SELF-DISCOVERY

A Quick Peek at Franklin's Career

"He needs a . . .": Earle Looker, *This Man Roosevelt* (New York: Brewer, Warren and Putnam, 1932), 48.

"I willingly made . . .": Lash, *Eleanor and Franklin*, 167.

"Many of the . . .": *Recorded Portrait.*

"It hardly mattered . . .": Ibid.

State Senator FDR

"I listened to . . .": Eleanor Roosevelt, *Autobiography*, 63.

"We held a . . .": Ibid., 65.

"My shyness was . . .": *Recorded Portrait.*

Wife of the Assistant Secretary

"I've paid 60 . . .": Lash, *Eleanor and Franklin*, 185.

"nerve-wracking and . . .": Eleanor Roosevelt, *Autobiography*, 76.

"political game for . . .": Lash, *Eleanor and Franklin*, 192.

Washington Home

"Dined at 1733 N. Street . . .": Lash, *Eleanor and Franklin*, 187.

Zimmerman Telegram

"I listened breathlessly . . .": Eleanor Roosevelt, *Autobiography*, 87.

Emotionally Charged Poster

"meatless Mondays" and "wheatless Wednesdays": Eric Foner and John A. Garraty, eds., *The Reader's Companion to American History* (Boston: Houghton Mifflin, 1991), 1171.

"It doesn't seem . . .": James Roosevelt, Oral History Project, Eleanor Roosevelt Papers.

"Mrs. Roosevelt does . . .": Elliott Roosevelt, ed., *FDR: His Personal Letters*, 1: 349–50.

"I am proud to be . . .": Ibid.

"I'd like to . . .": Margaret Logan Marquez, interview by author, 31 January 2003.

Red Cross Canteen

"The shop was . . .": Lash, *Eleanor and Franklin*, 213.

"Mrs. Roosevelt! Your hand!": Ibid., 215.

"There was no time . . .": Freedman, 58.

"It was not . . .": Eleanor Roosevelt, *Autobiography*, 95.

"I was learning . . .": Ibid., 91.

"It is a fearful . . .": Lash, *Eleanor and Franklin*, 215.

"my heart of . . .": Ibid.

Wounded Soldiers Relax

"There was a woman . . .": Eleanor Roosevelt, *Autobiography*, 93.

"Eleanor had a . . .": Lash, *Eleanor and Franklin*, 216.

"I was beginning . . .": *Recorded Portrait.*

St. Elizabeth's Hospital

"I drove through . . .": Eleanor Roosevelt, *Autobiography*, 92.

"into a model . . .": Ibid.

"Out of these . . .": Ibid., 95.

A Defining Moment

"If she had . . ." and "Life was meant . . .": Eleanor Roosevelt, *Autobiography*, 104.

Letter from Former First Lady

"yanking [Franklin's] coat tails": Lash, *Eleanor and Franklin*, 256.

"volumes about national . . .": *Recorded Portrait.*

"They tried, and . . .": Eleanor Roosevelt, *Autobiography*, 110.

"Eleanor is your . . .": Marquez, interview.

Eleanor Exercising Her Right to Vote

"took it for granted . . ." and "While I realized . . .": Eleanor Roosevelt, *Autobiography*, 68.

"I had learned . . .": Lash, *Eleanor and Franklin*, 289.

The "Intensive Education of Eleanor Roosevelt"

"I did not look . . .": Eleanor Roosevelt, *Autobiography*, 112.

National League of Women Voters Poster

"I doubted my . . .": Eleanor Roosevelt, *Autobiography*, 112.

"I recognized in . . .": Mary Gray Peck, *Carrie Chapman Catt* (New York: H. W. Wilson, 1944), 214.

"It was a fine . . .": *Recorded Portrait.*

Photograph and Article Chronicling Car Mishap

"Your running into . . .": Goodwin, *No Ordinary Time*, 378.

"Mother's driving was . . .": James Roosevelt, *My Parents*, 48.

Polio

"It was getting near . . .": *Recorded Portrait.*

"without discouragement . . .": Eleanor Roosevelt, *Autobiography*, 117.

"She had made . . ." and "he retire to . . .": *Recorded Portrait.*

"In many ways . . .": Eleanor Roosevelt, *Autobiography*, 117.

"I could not . . .": Ibid., 119.

"Dr. Draper, I'm . . .": Harrity and Martin, *Eleanor Roosevelt*, 89.

"I know my husband . . .": Ibid.

"I ought to know . . .": Ibid.

"We must do . . .": Ibid.

"You are right . . .": Ibid.

"She dominated me . . ."; "made me stand"; and "a completely colorless . . .": Ibid., 88.

(In caption) "I dread the time . . .": Ibid., 86.

Eleanor on the Dock

"They had to learn . . .": Eleanor Roosevelt, *Autobiography*, 121.

"You will never . . ." and "holding him head down . . .": Goodwin, *No Ordinary Time*, 333–34.

Wrestling with Anna

"Granny [Sara Roosevelt] . . .": Anna Roosevelt Halstead, "My Life with FDR," *Woman*, July 1949, 20.

"got on my nerves . . ." and "poured out some . . .": Eleanor Roosevelt and Helen Ferris, *Your Teens and Mine* (Garden City, N.Y.: Doubleday, 1961), 71.

"I got married . . .": Elliott Roosevelt,

Oral History Project, Eleanor Roosevelt Papers.

Louis Howe

"one of the . . .": Lash, *Eleanor and Franklin*, 178.

"odd, disheveled . . .": Ibid.

"extraordinary eyes and . . .": Eleanor Roosevelt, *Autobiography*, 109.

"Louis was . . . convinced . . .": Ibid., 120.

"Why do you . . .": *Recorded Portrait*.

"create [her own] persona": Ibid.

"Eleanor, if you . . ." and "One politician . . .": Lash, *Eleanor and Franklin*, 390.

"[Louis] gave Mother . . .": Elliott Roosevelt, Oral History Project, Eleanor Roosevelt Papers.

"most influenced . . .": Eleanor Roosevelt, "The Seven People Who Shaped My Life," *Look*, 19 June 1951, 56.

Out of the Kitchen and into Politics

"women have the . . .": Eleanor Roosevelt, "Women Must Play the Game As Men Do," *Redbook*, April 1928, 27.

"to checkmate her . . .": Ibid.

"We want to gain . . .": Eleanor Roosevelt, "Women Are in Revolt," *New York Times*, 15 April 1924.

"the ladies have . . .": Ibid.

Esther Lape and Elizabeth Read

"felt humble and . . ." and "I liked [them] . . .": Eleanor Roosevelt, *Autobiography*, 112.

"I don't care . . .": Ralph G. Martin, *Cissy: The Extraordinary Life of Eleanor Medill Patterson* (New York: Simon and Schuster, 1979), 360.

"They played a . . .": *Recorded Portrait*.

"squaws" and "she-men": Cook, *Eleanor Roosevelt*, 302.

Marion Dickerman and Nancy Cook

"a warm, wonderful relationship": Joseph Lash, *Love, Eleanor: Eleanor Roosevelt and Her Friends* (Garden City, N.Y.: Doubleday, 1982), 96.

"They are the sort . . .": Lash, *Eleanor and Franklin*, 304.

"Why don't you girls . . .": Ibid.

"The peace of it . . .": Ward, *First-Class Temperament*, 740.

"Can't you tell . . .": Ibid.

"honeymoon cottage" and "the love nest": Rodger Streitmatter, ed., *Empty Without You: The Intimate Letters of Eleanor Roosevelt and Lorena Hickok* (New York: Free Press, 1998), xiv.

"ENM": Ibid.

"things that should . . .": Lash, *Eleanor and Franklin*, 477.

Seal of the WTUL

"roses as well . . .": Maurine H. Beasley, Holly C. Shulman, and Henry R. Beasley, eds., *The Eleanor Roosevelt Encyclopedia* (Westport, Conn.: Greenwood Press), 580.

"Never before had . . .": *New York Times*, 9 June 1929, 3.

"fairy godmember" and "the regular gals": Maurine H. Beasley, Shulman, and Henry R. Beasley, eds., *Eleanor Roosevelt Encyclopedia*, 580.

"symbolic, even . . .": Ibid., 581.

FDR on a Deep-Sea Fishing Trip

"a somewhat negligee . . .": Franklin D. Roosevelt to Sara Delano Roosevelt, 5 March 1923, *FDR: His Personal Letters*, vol. 2, *1905–1928*, 535–36.

"It all seemed eerie . . .": Eleanor Roosevelt, *This Is My Story* (New York: Harper and Brothers, 1937), 345–46.

"Florida's mosquitoes . . .": Ibid.

Soothing a Husband's Ego

"Eleanor has been leading . . .": Lash, *Eleanor and Franklin*, 287.

"I'm only active . . .": Ibid.

Women's Democratic News

"because I promised . . .": Cook, *Eleanor Roosevelt*, 383.

FDR Sworn In

"No, I am not . . .": Cook, *Eleanor Roosevelt*, 320.

"really wanted Franklin . . .": Ibid., 379.

"savored of politics": Lash, *Eleanor and Franklin*, 327.

"Sending Eleanor is . . .": Ibid.

"Arrived at 12:30 . . .": Eleanor Roosevelt to Franklin D. Roosevelt, 1 May 1929, Unnumbered Family and Personal Correspondence, 1894–1957, Eleanor Roosevelt Papers.

First Draft of a Test

"I teach because . . .": Cook, *Eleanor Roosevelt*, 399.

"the connection between . . .": Eleanor Roosevelt, "Todhunter: Its History and Philosophy," n.d., Speech and Article File, Eleanor Roosevelt Papers.

"Read any life . . .": Lash, *Eleanor and Franklin*, 307.

"It was an exciting class . . .": Ibid.

"better than anything . . .": Eunice Fuller Barnard, "Mrs. Roosevelt in the Classroom," *New York Times Magazine*, 4 December 1932.

"One cannot be both . . .": Eleanor Roosevelt to Marion Dickerman, 9 November 1933, Unnumbered Family and Personal Correspondence, 1894–1957, Eleanor Roosevelt Papers.

A Real Romance?

"Imagine being assigned . . .": James Roosevelt, *My Parents*, 111.

"was never one . . .": Lash, *Love, Eleanor*, 120.

"Oh, I was expecting . . .": Cook, *Eleanor Roosevelt*, 434.

"into a real lather . . .": Maureen Corr, Oral History Project, Eleanor Roosevelt Papers.

"one real romance": James Roosevelt, *My Parents*, 110.

Restlessness . . . Hopelessness . . . Despair

"Everybody in America . . .": Annenberg/ CPB Learner.org, "A Biography of America: FDR and the Depression," transcript of video program, http://www.learner.org/biographyofamerica/prog21/transcript/page03.html

"If, with the advantages . . .": Ibid.

"The country needs . . .": Samuel I. Rosenman, comp., *The Public Papers and Addresses of Franklin D. Roosevelt*, vol. 1, *The Genesis of the New Deal, 1928–1932* (New York: Russell and Russell, 1938–1950), 646.

"Our desire was . . .": *Recorded Portrait*.

"Almost overnight . . .": Robert S. McElvaine, *The Great Depression: America, 1929–1941* (New York: Three Rivers Press, 1993), 115.

"I do not see . . .": Ibid., 112.

Policy Maker

"I hope you . . .": Lash, *Eleanor and Franklin*, 323.

The Importance of Eleanor

"had it all" and "He was handsome . . .": James A. Farley, *Behind the Ballots: The Personal History of a Politician* (New York: McGraw-Hill, 1938), 83.

"She was prepared . . .": Ibid.

On the Campaign Trail

"Franklin did not . . .": Eleanor Roosevelt, *Autobiography*, 158.

"to help make life . . .": Ibid., 159.

"I did not want . . ."; "deeply troubled"; and "As I saw it . . .": Ibid., 160.

Front Page of the *New York Times*

"I never wanted . . .": Lash, *Eleanor and Franklin*, 355.

"quizzically": Eleanor Roosevelt, *This I Remember* (New York: Harper and Brothers, 1949), 76.

"I knew he was . . .": Ibid.

"have to work . . .": Lash, *Eleanor and Franklin*, 355.

A First Lady Like No Other

It Happened on the Way to the Capitol

"I silently vowed . . .": Eleanor Roosevelt, *This I Remember*, 68.

"Eleanor blue": Lash, *Eleanor and Franklin*, 360.

Franklin Takes the Oath of Office

"It was a little . . .": Lorena A. Hickok, *Reluctant First Lady* (New York: Dodd, Mead, 1962), 104–5.

"Let me assert . . .": Rosenman, comp., *Public Papers and Addresses*, vol. 5, *The People Approve*, 1936, 61.

"passed along some . . .": Marquez, interview.

"We are in a . . ." and "willingness to accept . . .": Hickok, *Reluctant First Lady*, 104–5.

White House Chief Usher

"went poking around . . .": Eleanor Roosevelt, *Autobiography*, 164.

"That is not . . .": Robin McKown, *Eleanor Roosevelt's World* (New York: Grossett and Dunlap, 1964), 40.

"Oh, but it . . .": Ibid.

"Washington has never . . .": Harrity and Martin, *Eleanor Roosevelt*, 92.

The White House As It Looked

"a chair was . . .": White House Historical Association, *The White House: An Historic Guide* (Washington, D.C.: White House Historical Association, 2001), 144.

"old fashioned and . . .": Marquez, interview.

"The White House . . .": David Mc-Cullough, *Truman* (New York: Simon and Schuster, 1992), 373.

"has the appearance . . .": J. B. West, *Upstairs at the White House: My Life with the First Ladies* (New York: Coward, McCann, and Geoghegan, 1973), 58.

"Mrs. Roosevelt was . . .": Goodwin, *No Ordinary Time*, 617.

Lorena Hickok

"like one of the boys" and "they took me seriously": Streitmatter, *Empty Without You*, 4.

"bedazzled" and "The candidate's wife . . .": Hickok, *Reluctant First Lady*, 26.

"Hick darling . . .": Streitmatter, *Empty Without You*, 19.

"Franklin used to tease . . .": Doris Faber, *The Life of Lorena Hickok: ER's Friend* (New York: Morrow, 1980), 94.

"The nicest time . . .": Streitmatter, *Empty Without You*, 25.

"Remember one thing . . .": Goodwin, *No Ordinary Time*, 222.

"Funny how even . . .": Streitmatter, *Empty Without You*, 52.

"You taught me . . .": Lash, *Love, Eleanor*, 211.

"Once Eleanor began . . .": Goodwin, *No Ordinary Time*, 223.

"I know you . . .": Lash, *Love, Eleanor*, 223.

"Of course you . . .": Faber, *Life of Lorena Hickok*, 283.

Was She or Wasn't She?

"No form of . . .": Cook, *Eleanor Roosevelt*, 318.

First-Ever Press Conference

"newspaper girls": Maurine H. Beasley, Shulman, and Henry R. Beasley, eds., *Eleanor Roosevelt Encyclopedia*, 413.

"Women only . . .": "Interview with Members of Eleanor Roosevelt's Press Conference Association" (Washington, D.C.: Washington Press Club Foundation, 1989), 4.

"although she would . . .": Harrity and Martin, *Eleanor Roosevelt*, 137.

"God's gift to . . .": Lash, *Eleanor and Franklin*, 364.

From an Airplane Window

"I'd give a lot . . .": *New York Times*, 21 April 1933, 3.

"I know how . . .": James Roosevelt, Oral History Project, Eleanor Roosevelt Papers.

"our flying First Lady": Irene Juno, "In the Air with Our Flying First Lady," *Good Housekeeping*, June 1933, 26.

"I have no regrets": *New York Times*, 20 July 1937, 2.

Eleanor in Receiving Line

"useless burden . . .": Eleanor Roosevelt, *Autobiography*, 167.

"While shaking hands . . .": Ibid., 168.

"Don't let the . . .": Harrity and Martin, *Eleanor Roosevelt*, 142.

Fashionable Eleanor Models Gown

"I haven't the . . .": Harrity and Martin, *Eleanor Roosevelt*, 146.

"marvelous things for . . .": Maurine H. Beasley, *Eleanor Roosevelt and the Media: A Public Quest for Self-Fulfillment* (Chicago: University of Illinois Press, 1987), 27.

"off with a vague . . .": Maurine Beasley, ed., *The White House Press Conferences of Eleanor Roosevelt* (New York: Garland Press, 1983), 27.

"that title" and "grandest": Eleanor Roosevelt, "My Day," United Feature Syndicate, 3 December 1954.

Eleanor Christens a Ship

"a twist of . . .": Harrity and Martin, *Eleanor Roosevelt*, 147.

Eleanor Packs a Pistol

"Don't you dare . . .": Lash, *Eleanor and Franklin*, 367.

"Mr. President, if . . .": James Roosevelt, *My Parents*, 216.

Eleanor Poses at Egg Roll

"The average attendance . . .": Eleanor Roosevelt, *Autobiography*, 170.

The First Lady Travels Again

"Just for one day . . .": Harrity and Martin, *Eleanor Roosevelt*, 157.

"She was working away . . .": Goodwin, *No Ordinary Time*, 36.

"outwalk, outwork, outwit . . .": Elliott Roosevelt, Oral History Project, Eleanor Roosevelt Papers.

Busy, Busy Eleanor

"that a president's . . .": Eleanor Roosevelt, *Autobiography*, 169.

"Monday 1:00 P.M. . . .": Ibid.

A Typical Day at the White House

"The First Lady . . ." and "gaze at a . . .": Stella K. Hershan, *A Woman of Quality: Eleanor Roosevelt* (Hyde Park, N.Y.: Eleanor Roosevelt Center at Val-Kill, 1970), 56.

"There is sometimes . . ." and "I warned you . . .": Ibid.

"first showing of . . .": Ibid.

"deciding for once . . ." and "Come in": Ibid., 57.

"What do you . . .": Ibid.

"Remember when I . . ." and "stood on her . . .": Ibid.

Debut of "Mrs. Roosevelt's Page"

"I want you . . .": Eleanor Roosevelt, "Mrs. Roosevelt's Page," *Woman's Home Companion*, August 1933.

The First "My Day" Column

"When do I . . .": Lash, *Eleanor and Franklin*, 424.

"So I said . . .": Eleanor Roosevelt, "My Day," 30 December 1935.

"I simply tell . . .": Lash, *Eleanor and Franklin*, 426.

"Of all the nonsensical . . .": Martha Gellhorn, Oral History Project, Eleanor Roosevelt Papers.

"artless"; "rambling"; and "a puffed up . . .": Ibid.

"She talked to . . .": Rochelle Chadakoff, ed., *Eleanor Roosevelt's "My Day,"* vol. 1, *Her Acclaimed Columns, 1936–1945* (New York: Pharos Books, 1989), xi.

"if it once . . .": *Eleanor Roosevelt, "My Day,"* 21 September 1936.

Cover of *This Is My Story*

"We are thrilled . . ." and "I can't tell you . . .": Bruce Gould and Beatrice Blackmar Gould, *An American Story: Memories and Reflections of Bruce Gould and Beatrice Blackmar Gould* (New York: Harper and Row, 1968), 188.

"startling honesty . . ." and "the story of . . .": Ibid., 272.

"But this chapter . . ." and "I did not waste . . .": Lash, *Eleanor and Franklin*, 431.

"This is . . . unfair . . .": Ibid., 432.

"picked up the . . ." and "illuminating": Bruce Gould to Eleanor Roosevelt, 7 May 1937, Personal Letters, 1933–1945, Eleanor Roosevelt Papers.

"required reading" and "the greatest human . . .": Lash, *Eleanor and Franklin*, 433.

Speaking to the American People

"She tried consciously . . .": Lash, *Eleanor and Franklin*, 419.

"It does not seem . . .": Ibid., 418.

"take both the . . .": Maurine H. Beasley and Paul Belgrade, "Eleanor Roosevelt: First Lady As Radio Pioneer," *Journalism History* 11 (Autumn/winter 1984): 42.

"Her microphone manners . . .": "First Lady of the Land Is First Lady of Radio," *Radio Guide*, November 1933.

Eleanor Takes a Stand

"You go right . . ."; "If some idea . . ."; and "was a political reality": *Recorded Portrait.*

"One of the main . . .": Allida M. Black, *Casting Her Own Shadow: Eleanor Roosevelt and the Shaping of Postwar Liberalism* (New York: Columbia University Press, 1996), 89.

"Wherever the standard . . .": Eleanor Roosevelt, "Address to the National Conference on the Education of Negroes," *Journal of Negro Education* 3 (October 1934): 574.

"Decent housing is . . .": Eleanor Roosevelt, *The Moral Basis of Democracy* (New York: Harper and Brothers, 1940), 48.

"A woman can . . .": Eleanor Roosevelt, "My Day," 7 September 1945.

"An economic policy . . .": *World of Quotes*, s.v. "Eleanor Roosevelt," http://www.worldofquotes.com/author/Eleanor-Roosevelt/1/index.html

"The function of . . .": Eleanor Roosevelt, *Tomorrow Is Now* (New York: Harper and Row, 1963), 59.

"How can a few . . .": Ibid., 46.

The Secret Politician

"satisfied her own . . .": Cook, *Eleanor Roosevelt*, 371.

"She was as much . . .": Martha Gellhorn, Oral History Project, Eleanor Roosevelt Papers.

"dim bulb" and "That's grand . . .": Cook, *Eleanor Roosevelt*, 342.

"I am merely . . .": *Recorded Portrait.*

"wider experience and . . ." and "interfere with her . . .": S. J. Woolf, "A Woman Speaks Her Political Mind," *New York Times Magazine*, 8 April 1928.

President Roosevelt Kisses His First Lady

"an extraordinary team": Elliott Roosevelt, Oral History Project, Eleanor Roosevelt Papers.

"Men and women who . . .": Eleanor Roosevelt, *This I Remember*, 349.

"He also served . . .": Lois Scharf, *Eleanor Roosevelt: First Lady of American Liberalism* (Boston: Twayne Publishers, 1987), 140–41.

"You know, I've . . ." and "light in his eyes . . .": Goodwin, *No Ordinary Time*, 629.

"constantly talking about . . .": Maureen Corr, Oral History Project, Eleanor Roosevelt Papers.

Nagging Eleanor

"It was the only . . .": Robert E. Sherwood, *Roosevelt and Hopkins: An Intimate History* (New York: Harper, 1948), 609.

"I remember one day . . .": Asbell, ed., *Mother and Daughter*, 177.

Christmas Morning, 1939

"a rambunctious place . . .": Lash, *Eleanor and Franklin*, 485.

"her three sons . . .": Harold L. Ickes, The *Secret Diary of Harold L. Ickes*, vol. 3, *The Lowering Clouds, 1939–1941* (New York: Simon and Schuster, 1953), 184.

"unofficial Harvard . . .": Lash, *Eleanor and Franklin*, 492.

"One of the worst . . .": James Roosevelt and Shalett, *Affectionately, FDR*, 218.

"There is a bond . . .": Lash, *Eleanor and Franklin*, 497.

Eleanor's Grandchildren on the White House Lawn

"I have lived . . .": Harrity and Martin, Eleanor Roosevelt, 150.

"the constant feeling . . .": David B. Roosevelt, *Grandmère*, 3.

Missy LeHand

"Marguerite 'Missy' LeHand . . .": *Newsweek*, 12 August 1933, 15.

"tangled relationship": Lash, *Eleanor and Franklin*, 509.

"Missy alleviated . . .": Goodwin, *No Ordinary Time*, 120.

"While Mother was . . .": Lash, *Eleanor and Franklin*, 507.

"must learn to allow . . .": Eleanor Roosevelt, *You Learn by Living* (New York: Harper, 1960), 67.

Eleanor Converts the Furniture Factory

"some old fashioned . . .": Eleanor Roosevelt to Matthew Hasbrouck, 18 May 1937, Personal Letters, 1933–1945, Eleanor Roosevelt Papers.

"In the morning . . .": Lash, *Eleanor and Franklin*, 479.

The Eleanor Effect

"I couldn't possibly . . .": Carl Sferrazza Anthony, *First Ladies: The Saga of the Presidents' Wives and Their Power*, vol. 1, *1789–1961* (New York: Quill-William Morrow, 1990), 517.

"It sounds a . . .": Ibid., 569.

"I am not . . .": Anthony, *First Ladies*, vol. 2, *1961–1990* (New York: William Morrow, 1991), 39.

"A woman is like . . .": Alex Ayres, ed., *The Wit and Wisdom of Eleanor Roosevelt* (New York: Meridian, 1996), 199.

FRIEND OF THE PEOPLE

Children at Colored Orphan Asylum

"You know, one of . . .": Harrity and Martin, *Eleanor Roosevelt*, 138.

Bonus Marchers

"Hesitatingly, I got . . .": Eleanor Roosevelt, *Autobiography*, 175.

"Then, I got into . . .": Ibid., 176.

"remarkably clean" and "grand looking boys": Alfred B. Rollins, *Roosevelt and Howe* (New York: Knopf, 1962), 389.

"Hoover sent the . . .": Lash, *Eleanor and Franklin*, 367.

Everywhere Eleanor

"At first, my . . .": Eleanor Roosevelt, *Autobiography*, 154.

"taught me how . . .": Ibid., 161.

"Everywhere Eleanor": David B. Roosevelt, *Grandmère*, 156.

"dark, dank and . . .": Harrity and Martin, *Eleanor Roosevelt*, 141.

"a painful chore because . . .": McKown, *Eleanor Roosevelt's World*, 48.

"In prison" and "I'm not surprised . . .": Eleanor Roosevelt, *Autobiography*, 193.

"pitiful situation": Ibid., 184.

"often managing to . . .": Lash, *Eleanor and Franklin*, 331.

Poking Fun at the First Lady

"Hi diddle diddle . . .": Harrity and Martin, *Eleanor Roosevelt*, 160.

A New Deal for All Americans

"I'm the agitator . . .": *Recorded Portrait*.

"the keeper and . . .": Roger Biles, *A New Deal for the American People* (De Kalb, Ill.: Northern Illinois University Press 1991), 182.

America's First Liberal

"Liberalism is plain . . .": Freedman, *Eleanor Roosevelt*, 106.

"The biggest achievement . . .": Ann Cottrell Free, "Eleanor Roosevelt and the Female White House Press Corp," *Modern Maturity*, October-November, 1984, 98.

First Lady of Influence

"No one who ever . . .": Maurine H. Beasley, Shulman, and Henry R. Beasley, eds., *Eleanor Roosevelt Encyclopedia*, 529.

NYA Poster

"real moments of terror" and "We have to bring . . .": *New York Times*, 7 May 1934, 6.

"the missus' organization": *Recorded Portrait*.

"In short, the NYA . . .": Betty Lindley and Ernest K. Lindley, *A New Deal for Youth: The Story of the National Youth Administration* (New York: Viking, 1938), 14.

"What would we . . .": Lindley, *A New Deal for Youth*, 16.

Eleanor's Baby

"The two women . . .": Hershan, *Woman of Quality*, 169.

"the kind most . . ." and "He thinks we're . . .": Ibid., 170.

"That little boy . . .": Ibid.

"I hope this . . .": Lash, *Eleanor and Franklin*, 394.

"baby": Ibid., 398.

"design for permanent . . .": Harold M. Ware, "Planning for Permanent Poverty," *Harper's*, April 1935.

"We are spending . . .": Ickes, *Secret Diary*, 207.

"Well, in a matter . . .": Ibid.

"That day changed . . .": *The American Experience: Eleanor Roosevelt*, PBS Home Video, 1997.

"They seemed to feel . . .": Lash, *Eleanor and Franklin*, 416.

"Much money was . . .": Eleanor Roosevelt, *This I Remember*, 149.

The Social Security Act

"un-American"; "ultimate socialist control . . ."; and "We are creating . . .": Bill Hunst, *FDR and the Origins of Social Security* (Washington, D.C.: Social Security Administration, 2002).

"Now, it has come . . .": Eleanor Roosevelt, "Social Responsibility for Individual Welfare," *National Policies for Educational, Health, and Social Services*, ed. James Earl Russell (Garden City, N.Y.: Doubleday, 1955), 35.

"Dear First Lady . . .": Letter on display, 7 August 1941, Franklin D. Roosevelt Museum, Hyde Park, N.Y.

The Roosevelt Way

"We should strive . . .": James Earl Russell, ed., National Policies for Educational Health and Social Services, 38.

Dear Mrs. Roosevelt

"purely advisory . . .": Eleanor Roosevelt, "My Mail," Speech and Article File, 1933, Eleanor Roosevelt Papers.

"How should I . . .": Ibid.

"Whatever comes your . . ." and "I can sometimes relieve . . .": Lash, *Eleanor and Franklin*, 392.

"Might a free bed . . ." and "dear messenger . . .": Ibid., 392.

"I thought one of your . . .": misc. letter to Eleanor Roosevelt, n.d., General Correspondence, 1934, Eleanor Roosevelt Papers.

"pretty outfit for . . ."; "I was suspicious . . ."; and "She simply wanted . . .": Eleanor Roosevelt, "Mail of a President's Wife," Speech and Article File, 1939, Eleanor Roosevelt Papers.

"I am not the only . . .": misc. letter to Eleanor Roosevelt, n.d., General Correspondence, 1938, Eleanor Roosevelt Papers.

"Dear Mrs. Roosevelt . . .": Hillary Rodham Clinton, "The Eleanor Roosevelt Lectures" (lecture series sponsored by the Eleanor Roosevelt Center at Val-Kill, Georgetown University, Washington, D.C., 4 December 1998) www.ervk.org/HRClecture.html.

"poor boy" and "Our life has been . . .": General Correspondence, 1941, Eleanor Roosevelt Papers.

Civil Rights

"Dear madam . . .": misc. letters to Eleanor Roosevelt n.d. Criticism Regarding Negro Question, 1942, Eleanor Roosevelt Papers.

"I am not surprised . . .": *New York Times*, 28 February 1939, 16.

"Government must provide . . .": Eleanor Roosevelt, *Moral Basis of Democracy*, 50.

"One day I was . . ." and "Very gently . . .": Hershan, *Woman of Quality*, 163.

(In caption, *top*) "the closest friend . . .": Eleanor Roosevelt, "Some of My Best Friends Are Negro," *Ebony* (February 1953): 17.

(In caption, *bottom*) "Negro-loving" and "I am a Negro lover": Ibid.

Libraries for Everyone

"We have got . . .": Eleanor Roosevelt, "What Libraries Mean to the Nation," Speech and Article File, 1936, Eleanor Roosevelt Papers.

So Alone Inside

"I have come to . . .": Joseph Lash diary, 26 December 1941, Lash Papers, Franklin D. Roosevelt Library, Hyde Park, N.Y.

FBI File

"Nauseating" and "Parlor pink": Eleanor Roosevelt FBI File, Department of Justice, Washington, D.C.

"Gestapo methods": Eleanor Roosevelt to J. Edgar Hoover, 26 January 1941, Eleanor Roosevelt FBI File, Department of Justice, Washington, D.C.

Eleanor's Enemies

"The Busybody"; "The Meddler"; and "The Gab": Goodwin, *No Ordinary Time*, 628.

"and tend to knitting . . .": J. William T. Young, *Eleanor Roosevelt: A Personal and Private Life* (Boston: Little, Brown, 1985), 198.

"Instead of tearing . . .": Tamara Hareven, *Eleanor Roosevelt: An American Conscience* (Chicago: Quadrangle, 1968), 271.

"traitor to her class"; "an overreaching first lady . . ."; and "a political naïf": *American Experience.*

"victim of her own naïve . . .": Hareven, *Eleanor Roosevelt*, 198.

"I . . . do not hate . . .": Westbrook Pegler, "Westbrook Pegler: Self-Portrait," *Esquire*, January 1962, 58.

"Nobody looks very nice . . .": Lash, *Eleanor and Franklin*, 500.

"If I worried about . . .": Goodwin, *No Ordinary Time*, 205.

"You cannot take anything . . .": Eleanor Roosevelt, "Good Advice From Mrs. Roosevelt," *Democratic Digest*, July 1936, 3.

"to develop skin as . . .": Cook, *Eleanor Roosevelt*, 6.

A Lifelong Friend

"It was a confusing time . . .": Goodwin, *No Ordinary Time*, 122.

"It is funny how . . .": Ibid.

"She had a compelling . . .": Joseph P. Lash, *Eleanor Roosevelt: A Friend's Memoir* (Garden City, N.Y.: Doubleday, 1964), 140–41.

"Of one thing I am . . ." and "next best friend . . .": Goodwin, *No Ordinary Time*, 338.

"She personifies my . . .": Ibid., 124.

THE WAR YEARS

Three Reasons for World War II

"I felt positively . . .": Martha Gellhorn, Oral History Project, Eleanor Roosevelt Papers.

"Japan was . . .": Lash, *Eleanor and Franklin*, 556.

"Hitler is a sinister . . .": Eleanor Roosevelt to Helen Gifford, 14 October 1938, Personal Letters, 1933–1945, Eleanor Roosevelt Papers.

Front Page of the *Chicago Daily News*

"At five o'clock . . .": Lash, *Eleanor and Franklin*, 583.

"We await undismayed . . .": James Cross Giblin, *The Life and Death of Adolf Hitler* (New York: Clarion, 2002), 146.

"equally deadly danger . . ." and "no longer able . . .": Goodwin, *No Ordinary Time*, 192.

"not yet ready . . .": *Recorded Portrait.*

"Few truly realized . . .": Ibid.

The Fate of Europe's Jews

"I'd rather be hung . . .": Maurine H. Beasley, Shulman, and Henry R. Beasley, eds., *Eleanor Roosevelt Encyclopedia*, 281.

"an interesting little . . .": Lash, *Eleanor and Franklin*, 214.

"there may be . . .": Maurine H. Beasley, Shulman, and Henry R. Beasley, eds., *Eleanor Roosevelt Encyclopedia*, 275.

"at one blow . . .": Goodwin, *No Ordinary Time*, 396.

"be of help . . ."; "I can not figure . . ."; and "who have been . . .": David S. Wyman, *The Abandonment of the Jews: America and the Holocaust, 1941–1945* (New York: Pantheon, 1984), 115.

"our government has . . .": *New York Times*, 26 July 1943, 19.

"Deep down I believe . . .": Goodwin, *No Ordinary Time*, 397.

"to develop positive . . ."; "the wholesale . . ."; and "If only it had . . .": Ibid., 515.

The Lucky Few

"the most persecuted . . ."; "horrid legal details"; and "finding homes in . . .": Eleanor Roosevelt, "My Day," 13 July 1940.

"[Franklin] was somewhat . . .": Joseph Lash diary, 25 June 1940, Lash Papers.

"What has happened . . .": Eleanor Roosevelt, "My Day," 28 July 1940.

A Third Term

"imperial presidency": *U.S. News*, 12 July 1940, 24.

"I had every evidence . . .": Eleanor Roosevelt, *Autobiography*, 214.

Eleanor to the Rescue

"spinning out of control . . .": *Recorded Portrait.*

"I got a call . . .": Goodwin, *No Ordinary Time*, 127.

"The noise in . . .": Ibid., 130.

"Oh, she can't . . .": Ibid., 132.

Eleanor Speaks at the 1940 Democratic National Convention

"This is no ordinary time" and "no time for weighing . . .": *New York Times*, 19 July 1940, 1, 5.

"swamped with wires . . .": Goodwin, *No Ordinary Time*, 135.

"Her speech was . . .": Eleanor Roosevelt, *Autobiography*, 218.

Slogan Pin, 1940

"We don't want . . .": Harrity and Martin, *Eleanor Roosevelt*, 184.

"Dearest Franklin, I . . .": Eleanor Roosevelt to Franklin D. Roosevelt, 11 October 1940, Roosevelt Family Papers Donated by the Children.

Eleanor with an Ailing Sara

"every bit of . . .": Lash, *Eleanor and Franklin*, 500.

"Please hang up . . ." and "I know you're . . .": Goodwin, *No Ordinary Time*, 273.

"the endless details" and "clothes to go . . .": Lash, *Love, Eleanor*, 355.

"No one had . . .": Ward, *First-Class Temperament*, 9.

"blistering rage" and "It is dreadful . . .": Goodwin, *No Ordinary Time*, 275.

Defense for the First Lady

"sissy stuff": Lash, *Eleanor and Franklin*, 642.

"no government as . . .": *New York Times*, 26 August 1941, 5.

"There are 135,000,000 . . .": Lash, *Eleanor and Franklin*, 642.

"I am ridiculously busy . . .": Goodwin, *No Ordinary Time*, 281.

"Doesn't the first . . .": *New York Times*, 7 February 1942, Unnumbered Scrapbooks Presented to Eleanor Roosevelt 1933–1945, Eleanor Roosevelt Papers.

"The work of . . .": *Liberty*, 7 April 1942, Unnumbered Scrapbooks Presented to Eleanor Roosevelt 1933–1945, Eleanor Roosevelt Papers.

"parasites and leeches . . ." and "instruction in physical . . .": Goodwin, *No Ordinary Time*, 325.

"I still believe . . .": Ibid.

Japanese Bomb Pearl Harbor

"All the secretaries . . .": Eleanor Roosevelt, "My Day," 7 December 1941.

"For months now . . .": Lash, *Eleanor and Franklin*, 646.

Sons in Uniform

"I imagine every . . .": *Recorded Portrait*.

"her voice did not . . ."; "There was a period . . ."; "She started to scold . . ."; and "She knew they had . . .": Joseph Lash diary, 26 December 1941, Lash Papers.

Japanese Americans

"Let's be honest . . .": *New York Times*, 15 December 1941, 9.

"When [Mrs. Roosevelt] . . .": Tamara K. Hareven, *Eleanor Roosevelt: An American Conscience* (Chicago: Quadrangle, 1968), 167.

"Can this be . . ." and "bit of faith . . .": *New Republic*, 15 June 1942, 822.

"These people were . . .": Goodwin, *No Ordinary Time*, 321.

"angry and becoming . . ." and "a hostile group . . .": Ibid., 427.

"Everything is spotlessly . . ." and "Sometimes there are . . .": Eleanor Roosevelt, "My Day," 23 April 1943.

"To be frank with . . .": Carey McWilliams, *Prejudice: Japanese-Americans, Symbols of Racial Intolerance* (Boston: Little, Brown, 1944), 212.

Franklin and Winston Churchill

"Winnie"; "Chief"; and "the partnership that . . .": Elliott Roosevelt, Oral History Project, Eleanor Roosevelt Papers.

"two little boys . . .": Goodwin, *No Ordinary Time*, 311.

"like a big English . . .": Martha Gellhorn, Oral History Project.

"Nobody enjoyed the . . .": Ibid.

"Fuming, Mother went . . .": Elliott Roosevelt, Oral History Project.

"When peace comes . . ."; "all people who . . ."; "Yes, yes, yes"; "You know, Winston . . ."; and "bulldog scowl": Justine Polier, Oral History Project.

"Mr. Churchill has . . .": Asbell, ed., *Mother and Daughter*, 141.

"The world that . . .": Goodwin, *No Ordinary Time*, 543.

"meddler" and "a woman who does . . .": Ibid.

Wartime Prayer

"Dear Lord . . .": David B. Roosevelt, *Grandmère*, 175.

Eleanor Tours London

"I confide my missus . . .": Franklin D. Roosevelt to Winston Churchill, 19 October 1942, Roosevelt Family Papers Donated by the Children.

"My room was magnificent . . ." and "royalty [was] rationed, too": McKown, *Eleanor Roosevelt's World*, 58.

"Groups loiter about . . .": Goodwin, *No Ordinary Time*, 383.

"Mrs. Roosevelt has done . . .": *Daily Mirror* article, Trip File, England, 1942, Eleanor Roosevelt Papers.

Gosh! There's Eleanor

"At once I . . ." and "I told [Franklin] . . .": Eleanor Roosevelt, *Autobiography*, 253.

"Guadalcanal is no . . .": Lash, *Eleanor and Franklin*, 684.

"In some ways . . .": Lash, *World of Love*, 60.

"When I left . . .": *New York Times*, 28 August 1943, 13.

"her shoes dusty . . ." and "At one point . . .": *New York Times*, 13 September 1943, 21.

"When I say . . .": Lash, *Eleanor and Franklin*, 685.

"Over here she . . .": *New York Times*, 6 September 1943, 19.

"I was ashamed . . .": Lash, *Eleanor and Franklin*, 691.

"What a shock . . .": Misc. newspaper clipping, Trip File, Pacific Theater, 1943, Eleanor Roosevelt Papers.

"Gosh! There's Eleanor . . .": Eleanor Roosevelt, *Autobiography*, 258.

"One of the things . . .": Ibid., 259.

"The atmosphere was . . .": Ibid.

"I wonder if I . . .": Eleanor Roosevelt's radio broadcast for war bonds, 27 September 1943, Speech and Article File, Eleanor Roosevelt Papers.

Cartoon Pokes Fun

"You never know . . .": Misc. newspaper clipping, Unnumbered Scrapbooks Presented to Eleanor Roosevelt, 1933–1945, Eleanor Roosevelt Papers.

"She coolly and . . .": Goodwin, *No Ordinary Time*, 463.

"Holy cow . . ."; "Howdy, Eleanor!"; and "You came all . . .": misc. newspaper clipping, Unnumbered Scrapbooks Presented to Eleanor Roosevelt, 1933–1945, Eleanor Roosevelt Papers.

"Public Energy Number One": Ibid.

Women Working in Factories

"If I [were] . . .": Goodwin, *No Ordinary Time*, 365.

"Women will be . . .": Ibid.

"Women ought to . . .": Frieda Miller, "Women's Conference on War and Postwar Adjustments of Women Workers," 1–5 December 1944, Record Group 86, National Archives, Washington, D.C.

"Women are as . . .": Eleanor Roosevelt, "My Day," 7 September 1945.

Cecil Peterson Letter

"We are undoubtedly . . .": *Air and Space*, October–November 1989, 35.

"Write me and keep . . .": Eleanor Roosevelt to Cecil Peterson, 28 May 1942, Personal Letters, 1933–1945, Eleanor Roosevelt Papers.

"be of some . . .": Peterson to Eleanor Roosevelt, 7 July 1942, Personal Letters, 1933–1945.

"This seems to me . . .": Eleanor Roosevelt to Henry Stimson, 10 April 1943, Correspondence with Government Departments, 1934–1945, Eleanor Roosevelt Papers.

"It was a tremendous . . .": Benjamin O. Davis Jr., *Benjamin O. Davis Jr., American: An Autobiography* (New York: Plume, 1992), 90.

American Forces Invade

"Outwardly [Americans] appeared . . .": Winston M. Estes, *Homefront: A Novel* (New York: Avon, 1976), 257.

"Give us Faith . . .": Rosenman, comp., *Public Papers and Addresses*, vol. 13, Victory and the Threshold of Peace, 1944–1945, 159.

"suspended in space . . .": Eleanor Roosevelt to Franklin D. Roosevelt, 2 May 1944, Roosevelt Family Papers Donated by the Children.

"All emotion is . . .": Eleanor Roosevelt, "My Day," 6 June 1944.

Eleanor with Franklin and Anna

"Anna is the . . ." and "We'll have to . . .": Lash, *Eleanor and Franklin*, 700.

"If Anna goes . . .": Eleanor Roosevelt, *This I Remember*, 339.

"I am tired . . .": Lash, *World of Love*, 164.

"Life is assuming . . ."; "information on the . . ."; and "to . . . fill him in . . .": Anna Boettiger notes on Yalta, February 1945, Anna Roosevelt Halstead Papers, Franklin D. Roosevelt Library, Hyde Park, N.Y.

"the only times . . .": Goodwin, *No Ordinary Time*, 575.

"new power behind . . .": John Chamberlain, "Close up: FDR's Daughter," Life, 5 March 1945, 96.

"very hard for . . .": Marquez, interview.

Victorious Franklin, 1944

"All that is . . ." and "the future existence . . .": *U.S. News*, 21 July 1944, 27.

"I am very conscious . . .": Lash, *World of Love*, 130.

"She still believed . . .": Goodwin, *No Ordinary Time*, 492.

"had a long talk . . .": *Recorded Portrait*.

"It was largely . . .": Marquez, interview.

"There was much . . .": Eleanor Roosevelt, "My Day," 10 November 1944.

After the White House

"You know . . .": Elliott Roosevelt and James Brough, *Mother R.: Eleanor Roosevelt's Untold Story* (New York: Putnam, 1977), 308.

"The President Is Dead"

"I got into . . .": Eleanor Roosevelt, *Autobiography*, 276.

"Father slept away . . .": Ibid.

"Harry, the president . . .": McCullough, *Truman*, 342.

"Is there anything . . .": Ibid.

"I have a terrific . . .": Goodwin, *No Ordinary Time*, 602.

"At times like . . .": Ibid., 611–12.

The Nation's Last Tribute

"complete silence . . .": Goodwin, *No Ordinary Time*, 613.

"lay in [her] berth . . .": Eleanor Roosevelt, *This I Remember*, 345.

"One cannot say . . .": Eleanor Roosevelt, *Autobiography*, 280.

(In caption, *bottom left*) "turning her personal . . .": Harrity and Martin, *Eleanor Roosevelt*, 206.

(In caption, *top right*) "she would usually . . .": Ibid.

The End

"I miss Pa's . . .": Goodwin, *No Ordinary Time*, 622.

FIRST LADY OF THE WORLD

The End?

"The story is over . . .": *Newsweek*, 30 April 1945, 44.

Without Franklin

"lived the Eleanor . . .": Marquez, interview.

First Page of the Indenture

"In the long night's . . .": Eleanor Roosevelt, *Autobiography*, 284.

"a few things . . .": Ibid., 285.

"disentangled": Lash, *Eleanor: The Years Alone*, 14.

Eleanor and Fala

"He had a special . . .": Maureen Corr, Oral History Project, Eleanor Roosevelt Papers.

Eleanor Walks with Her Granddaughters

"We were in . . .": Nina Roosevelt Gibson, Oral History Project, Eleanor Roosevelt Papers.

"the most important . . .": Lash, *World of Love*, 68.

Eleanor with Her Sons

"They were instantly . . .": Eleanor Roosevelt, *This I Remember*, 135.

"I surmise Elliott . . .": Lash, *World of Love*, 232.

"It was a terrible . . .": Marquez, interview.

"I've always loved . . .": Elliott Roosevelt and Brough, *Mother R.*, 202.

"a step forward . . ." and "more successful as . . .": James Roosevelt, *My Parents*, 303.

"The boy has . . .": Ibid., 326.

"It's just too . . .": *American Experience*.

Eleanor with Anna

"My children would . . .": Joseph P. Lash, *Eleanor: The Years Alone* (New York: Signet, 1973), 176.

"We are disappointed . . .": Ibid., 178–79.

"finally settled . . .": Ibid., 233.

Eleanor at the UN

"It began with . . .": James F. Byrnes, *All in One Lifetime* (New York: Harper, 1958), 373.

"I don't know . . .": Ibid.

"fear and trembling": Eleanor Roosevelt, *On My Own* (New York: Harper, 1958), 299.

"some things I . . .": Eleanor Roosevelt, "My Day," 21 December 1945.

"I knew that . . .": *Recorded Portrait*.

"Rattle-brained Mrs. Roosevelt": Lash, *Eleanor*, 44.

"It was a committee . . .": James Frederick Green, Oral History Project, Eleanor Roosevelt Papers.

"A new type . . .": Lash, *Eleanor*, 42.

"I want to take . . .": Ibid., 47.

Eleanor Visits Jewish Children

"We will simply . . .": James Frederick Green, Oral History Project, Eleanor Roosevelt Papers.

"In all the Jewish . . ." and "must become a reality": Eleanor Roosevelt, *On My Own*, 310.

Eleanor Surveys Israel

"a strong and . . .": Eleanor Roosevelt, "My Day," 17 April 1959.

"primitive view" and "desert dwelling . . .": Lash, *Eleanor*, 130.

"the only people . . .": Ibid., 129.

"There is an atmosphere . . ." and "breath of America": Ibid.

Universal Declaration of Human Rights

"There are many . . ."; "high thoughts"; and "I used to tell . . .": Eleanor Roosevelt, "My Day," 12 February 1947.

"Long job finished": David B. Roosevelt, *Grandmère*, 207.

Always Diplomatic

"I was coming . . .": Hershan, *Woman of Quality*, 236.

Eleanor's Letter of Resignation

"For it isn't enough . . .": Transcript of Voice of America broadcast, 11 November 1951, Speech and Article File, Eleanor Roosevelt Papers.

Cover of *This I Remember*

"The book moves . . .": Lash, *Eleanor*, 181.

"You have written . . .": Bruce Gould and Beatrice Blackmar Gould, *American Story*, 285.

"I wouldn't have . . .": Lash, *Eleanor*, 182.

"like hot cakes": Marquez, interview.

"Bond Between Us" Luncheon

"One must support . . .": *Recorded Portrait*.

A Friend to Garbage Men

"When we finished . . .": Hershan, *Woman of Quality*, 110.

Wiltwyck School

"We feed the boys . . .": Eleanor Roosevelt, *On My Own*, 293.

"The boys don't need . . ." and "When the King . . .": Hershan, *Woman of Quality*, 27.

"Far Distant Places"

"far distant places": McKown, *Eleanor Roosevelt's World*, 71.

"I have come . . .": Lash, *Eleanor*, 193.

"God grant to . . .": McKown, *Eleanor Roosevelt's World*, 76.

"The wife of Franklin . . .": *Recorded Portrait*.

"free to discuss . . ." and "weaned on the . . .": Eleanor Roosevelt, *On My Own*, 397–98.

"Can I tell . . .": McKown, *Eleanor Roosevelt's World*, 77.

"She has walked . . .": Ibid.

Eleanor Cuts Her Cake

"Here's to Eleanor . . .": McKown, *Eleanor Roosevelt's World*, 79.

"Life has got . . .": Lash, *Eleanor*, 233.

Cartoon by Herblock

"She has a heart . . .": Trude Lash, Oral History Project, Eleanor Roosevelt Papers.

"as much a symbol . . .": *Chicago Daily News*, 13 October 1954, 18.

Awards

"a world symbol . . .": Lash, *Eleanor*, 331.

Meet the Press

"much time to . . .": Maurine H. Beasley, Shulman, and Henry R. Beasley, eds., *Eleanor Roosevelt Encyclopedia*, 509.

"a wonderful reaction": Lash, *Eleanor*, 180.

"she showed her . . .": Ibid., 257.

Eleanor and Frank Sinatra

"I went down . . ." and "Find out who . . .": *American Experience*.

"There is a Gallup . . ."; "Now then, if . . ."; "That one word . . ."; and "Once there was . . .": Ibid.

"The mail was . . .": Lash, *Eleanor*, 309.

"For that amount . . .": Ibid.

Album Jacket of *Hello, World!*

"She was, after all . . .": Hershan, *Woman of Quality*, 109.

"Wherever in the world . . .": *Hello, World!* RCA Victor LM-2332, sound recording.

"You know, I . . .": Hershan, *Woman of Quality*, 111.

"Mrs. Franklin D. Roosevelt . . .": *New York Times*, 27 September 1959, 8.

Bad News

"utterly exhausted"; "Why?"; and "When you cease . . .": Edna P. Gurewitsch, Oral History Project, Eleanor Roosevelt Papers.

Eleanor at Brandeis University

"Well, now you . . ."; "Oh, don't you . . ."; "What role then?"; and "Can I be put . . .": Abram L. Sachar, Oral History Project, Eleanor Roosevelt Papers.

"I was a little . . .": Eleanor Roosevelt, *On My Own*, 405.

"She would sprinkle . . ." and "She had an unusual . . .": Hershan, *Woman of Quality*, 117.

Eleanor with Adlai Stevenson

"He has difficulty . . ." and "don an old suit . . .": Lash, *Eleanor*, 237.

Eleanor with JFK

"was a man . . ." and "mind that [was] . . .": Eleanor Roosevelt to Adlai Stevenson supporters, 15 August 1960, General Correspondence, Eleanor Roosevelt Papers.

"There is so much . . .": Eleanor Roosevelt, *Autobiography*, 439.

NAACP

"advocating civil rights . . .": Black, *Casting Her Own Shadow*, 127.

"Staying aloof is not . . .": Eleanor Roosevelt, *Tomorrow Is Now* (New York: Harper Collins, 1963), 19.

Rev. Martin Luther King Jr.

"You are doing . . .": Lash, *Eleanor*, 315.

"Dr. King is . . .": Eleanor Roosevelt, "My Day," 6 February 1961.

"humanitarian . . . friend of . . .": Martin Luther King Jr., "Epitaph for Mrs. FDR," *New York Amsterdam News*, 24 November 1962, 2.

An Ailing Eleanor

"There was only . . .": Lash, *Eleanor*, 324.

"Utter nonsense": Ibid., 327.

"It seemed as . . .": Ibid., 324.

"Our dear Mrs. Roosevelt . . .": *American Experience*.

Flag at Half-Mast

"The British people . . .": *New York Times*, 9 November 1962, 2.

"No woman of . . .": Maurine H. Beasley, Shulman, and Henry R. Beasley, eds., *Eleanor Roosevelt Encyclopedia*, 122.

"one of the great . . .": *New York Times*, 8 November 1962, 1.

"The folks will . . .": McKown, *Eleanor Roosevelt's World*, 93.

"Eleanor Roosevelt was . . .": Ibid.

"But she couldn't . . .": Newspaper clipping, *New York Times*, November 1962, Greetings, Condolences, and Tributes, Eleanor Roosevelt Papers.

Eleanor Laid to Rest

"I stood there . . .": James Roosevelt, Oral History Project, Eleanor Roosevelt Papers.

"There was much . . .": Elliott Roosevelt and Brough, *Mother R.*, 274.

"The gray and cold . . .": Marquez, interview.

"How could it . . ." and "I made use . . .": Elliott Roosevelt, Oral History Project, Eleanor Roosevelt Papers.

Index

Peace Corps Advisory Council, 152
Pearl Harbor, 115
Pegler, Westbrook, 104
Pehle, John, 109
Periscope magazine, 75
Perkins, Frances, 62, 79
Peterson, Cecil, 123
Poland, 108, 109, 145
polio, 27, 46–47, 48
Pratt, Trude, 105
preschool programs, 97
presidential library, 131
press conferences, all-female, 68
"Psyche" (Moore), 34
public assistance programs, 97
"Public Energy Number One," 122
public housing, 94–95, 97

racism, 77, 100–101
radio career, Eleanor's, 76, 134
Radio Guide, 76
rationing plan, 39
RCA Victor, 149
Read, Elizabeth, 52
Reagan, Nancy, 84
receiving lines, 69
record *Hello World*, 149
Redbook, 75
Red Cross, 40
refugees, political, 135, 136
rent supplements, 97
Republicans, 36
Rivington Street, 18
Robbins, Muriel, 22
Roosevelt, Alice, 22, 34
Roosevelt, Anna, 28, 32, 48, 79, 80, 125, 134, 155
Roosevelt, Anna Eleanor, 80, 81
Roosevelt, Anna Hall, 2, 5, 9, 49
Roosevelt Campobello International Park, 27
Roosevelt, Corrine, 21, 22
Roosevelt, Eleanor. *See also* Roosevelt, Eleanor and Franklin
 appearance of, 12, 16, 17, 70, 104
 as author, 73, 74–76, 150
 awards won by, 147
 birth of, 2–3
 changes in, 53
 childhood of, 4–15
 as "copresident," 92
 criticism of, 104, 112, 114
 debut of, 17, 18
 defense and, 114
 as Democratic National Convention speaker, 111–112

depression of, 105
driving mishaps of, 45
energy level of, 72, 73, 79, 122
fashion and, 70
father and, 3, 5, 7, 49
female friends of, 52–53, 67, 68
as feminist, 42, 43, 50, 52, 62, 77, 122
FBI and, 71, 103
Franklin's influence on, 49
as Franklin's manager, 25, 112
as fund-raiser, 141, 146
funeral of, 155
grandmother and, 9
as grandmother, 80, 81, 132
health of, 154
independence of, 44, 52, 64, 66, 71
insecurities of, 4, 32, 33, 105
leadership abilities of, 44
letters to, 92, 98–99
as martyr, 33
moodiness of, 25
mother and, 5, 9, 49, 80
as mother, 32, 80, 133, 134
New Deal and, 90, 91, 92
organizational skills, 42, 45
personality of, 4, 5, 6, 8, 13, 17, 21, 102, 105
politics and, 36, 49, 50, 54–57, 62, 77, 78, 96–97
Sara and, 21, 24, 26, 27, 28, 46–47, 49, 53, 113
schooling of, 8, 13–15
self-confidence of, 31, 43–44, 49
self-consciousness and shyness of, 4, 12, 37, 59
sexuality of, 68
successive first ladies and, 84–85
as suffragist, 43, 44
as teacher, 18, 58
Theodore and, 6, 22
travels of. *See* travels, Eleanor's
United Nations and, 135–139, 141, 152
voice of, 49, 76, 141
Roosevelt, Eleanor and Franklin
 assistant secretary of navy position and, 38, 41
 conflicts between, 31, 33
 death of, 127–128, 154–155
 discipline of children and, 31
 engagement of, 20, 21
 first inauguration and, 65
 first meetings between, 12, 18, 19
 governorship and, 57, 60–61, 62
 grandchildren of, 80, 81, 132
 honeymoon of, 23

LeHand and, 82–83
Mercer and, 35, 127
New York City homes of, 26, 131
political activities of, 55, 57, 62, 77
presidential campaign and, 62
presidential term of, first, 63–66, 73
presidential term of, fourth, 126
presidential term of, third, 111, 112
relationship between, 23, 35, 79
Sara's death and, 113
sexual relationship between, 23, 35
vice presidential candidacy and, 42
Washington, D.C., home of, 38
wedding of, 22
in White House, 66–67, 80, 81
World War II and, 109, 110, 126
Roosevelt, Elliott (Eleanor's son), 30, 32, 79, 80, 115, 127, 133, 155
Roosevelt, Elliott Jr. (Eleanor's brother), 5, 10
Roosevelt, Elliott Sr., (Eleanor's father), 2, 3, 5, 7, 10, 49
Roosevelt, Franklin Delano. *See also* Roosevelt, Eleanor and Franklin
 ambitions of, 21
 Anna and, 125
 as assistant secretary of navy, 38, 41
 childhood of, 16
 death of, 127–129
 Eleanor's autobiography and, 76
 Eleanor's outspokenness and, 77
 as father, 80
 first inauguration of, 65
 in Florida, 55
 funeral of, 129
 as governor of New York, 57, 60–61, 62
 as grandfather, 80
 health of, 27, 46–47, 48, 126, 127
 LeHand and, 82–83
 as liberal, 91
 Mercer and, 35, 127
 mother's death and, 113
 personality of, 16, 21
 polio and, 27, 46–47, 48
 political career of, 36–37
 post-presidential plans of, 127
 presidential election of, 63
 as senator, 37
 third term of, 111, 112
Roosevelt, Franklin Jr. (first), 30
Roosevelt, Franklin Jr. (second), 31, 32, 48, 80, 115, 133, 155
Roosevelt, Hall, 5
Roosevelt, James, 29, 32, 80, 115, 133, 155